35.00

The Bitter Fruit of American Justice

The

INTERNATIONAL AND

Bitter Fruit

DOMESTIC RESISTANCE

# of American

TO THE DEATH PENALTY

Justice

ALAN W. CLARKE & LAURELYN WHITT

NORTHEASTERN UNIVERSITY PRESS Boston

Published by UNIVERSITY PRESS OF NEW ENGLAND

Hanover and London

NORTHEASTERN UNIVERSITY PRESS
Published by
University Press of New England,
One Court Street, Lebanon, NH 03766
www.upne.com
© 2007 by Alan W. Clarke and Laurelyn Whitt
Printed in the United States of America

5 4 3 2 1

Library of Congress Cataloging-in-Publication Data
Clarke, A. W., (Alan W.)
The bitter fruit of American justice : international and domestic resistance to the
death penalty / by Alan W. Clarke & Laurelyn Whitt.
  p. cm.
Simultaneously published in the USA and Canada.
Includes bibliographical references and index.
ISBN-13: 978–1–55553–682–4 (cloth : alk. paper)
ISBN-10: 1–55553–682–4 (cloth : alk. paper)
  1. Capital punishment—United States.   2. Extradition—United States.
3. Human rights—United States.   4. Justice, Administration of—United States.
I. Whitt, Laurelyn.   II. Title.
KF9227.C2C53 2007
345.73'0773—dc22   2007027451

We dedicate this book to our parents,

BUDDY and JO CLARKE &

JACK and NETTIE WHITT,

whose love remains their greatest gift.

Contents

Preface

That international and domestic pressure to halt state execution might intersect and increase the likelihood of bringing the American death penalty to an end was not an idea that came easily or naturally to us. Back in the mid 1980s, Bill Geimer, then professor of law at Washington and Lee University, repeatedly said that the United States would not abolish the death penalty until it was embarrassed into doing so by the rest of the world. At the time, that seemed an impossible prediction, one to be rejected out of hand given the limited role of international law in the debate over capital punishment to that point. Bill, however, proved prescient, and international views are increasingly significant in the death penalty debate.

Thirty years ago the innocence issue seemed similarly unlikely to play a major role in the discussion. Who knew then that the system would prove to be so disastrously flawed? Back then, neither of us would have guessed that either of these issues would have the impact that they now have. We were wrong. International resistance to state execution as a human rights violation has combined with domestic concern over the execution of innocent people to put the American system of capital punishment under greater pressure than ever.

There have long been compelling reasons to oppose the death penalty: the persistence of race, class, and ethnic bias; its profound arbitrariness; its failure to deter more effectively than its alternatives; its exceptional costs. The power of such critiques is itself significantly enhanced by the convergence of the two forces—international pressure and the innocence argument—on which this book focuses. The fact that a significant number of those whose lives the state ends are not only selected on arbitrary and discriminatory grounds, but also are innocent of the crime for which they are being punished only intensifies the gravity of the abuse of state power that constitutes the American death penalty.

We would not have come to our understanding of the issues discussed herein without the support and critique over many years of more people than could possibly be mentioned. We are particularly grateful to those who read and responded to the early rough drafts. These include Hugo Adam Bedau, Richard Lempert, David Lyons, Michael Radelet, Margaret Vandiver, and Mark Warren, all of whom offered invaluable commentary and suggestions. If errors remain in the text, however, they are decidedly, if regrettably, our own.

We are also grateful to Eric Lambert and Oko Elechi, who allowed us to use parts of several articles on which they were co-authors. Our student assistant, Travis Shaw, spent many hours checking sources and preparing the endnotes, and we thank him for his enthusiasm and commitment. To our colleague and program director, Scott Abbott, who continues to support us in myriad ways, but especially through his friendship, we extend our deep appreciation. And finally, we acknowledge the fine faculty of the philosophy department of the College of William and Mary, where we were both first introduced to an issue that neither of us has been able to leave behind.

Acknowledgments

Part of chapter 8 is reprinted (with substantially updated research and rewriting) from *Criminal Law Bulletin*, Volume 38, by Laurie Anne Whitt, Alan W. Clarke, and Eric Lambert, with permission of West, a Thompson business, Copyright 2002. For further information about this publication, please visit www.west.thompson.com/store, or call 800–328–9352.

Other parts of this book have appeared, with substantially updated research and rewriting, in the articles listed below, with permission from each publication. In addition, several of these articles list Eric Lambert and Oko Elechi as co-authors. Eric and Oko have graciously given permission to use these works, and their contributions are gratefully acknowledged.

Alan Clarke, "The Death Penalty in International Law," 60(2) *Guild Practitioner* 86 (Spring 2003).

Alan W. Clarke, Eric Lambert, and Laurie Anne Whitt, "Debating the Death Penalty: The Impact of Innocence," 59(2) *Guild Practitioner* 116 (Spring 2002).

Alan W. Clarke, Eric Lambert, and Laurie Anne Whitt, "Executing the Innocent: The Next Step in the Marshall Hypothesis," 26 *New York University Review of Law and Social Change* 309 (2000–2001).

Alan W. Clarke, Laurie Anne Whitt, Eric Lambert, and Oko Elechi, "Does the Rest of the World Matter? Sovereignty, International Human Rights Law and the American Death Penalty," 30 *Queen's Law Journal* 261 (2004).

Alan W. Clarke, "Terrorism, Extradition and the Death Penalty," 29 *William Mitchell Law Review* 783 (2003).

Laurie Anne Whitt, "Sovereignty and Human Rights," 60(3) *Guild Practitioner* 90 (Spring 2003).

The Bitter Fruit of American Justice

1 : Introduction

Southern trees bear strange fruit
Blood on the leaves
Blood on the root
Black bodies swinging in the southern breeze
Strange fruit hanging from the poplar trees
— "Strange Fruit," Billie Holiday[1]

"Strange Fruit" was a protest of lynching in the American South, written in the hopes of bringing it to an end. Yet American support for a society's right to kill its own citizens has continued largely unabated for over half a century. Despite empirical studies repeatedly demonstrating that execution by the state is discriminatory and arbitrary, that it fails to deter more effectively than other punishments, and that it is vastly more expensive than alternative punishments, Americans have remained strangely unmoved by national and international calls for its abolition. This, however, may be changing; a consensus that has held for some thirty years is being undermined by two recent developments.

The first is internal to the country. The discovery of large numbers of innocent people on America's death rows has plainly shaken public opinion and political resolve on this issue. There is now a profound and growing national unease with capital punishment as awareness settles in that the American justice system actually executes the innocent. The fact that innocent people have been and are being killed in state and federal execution chambers is no longer (if it ever was) an "unreal dream."[2] Worse, for those who would retain the ultimate penalty, there is no basis for supposing that such occurrences are rare, much less that they will or can be eliminated through systemic reforms.

This radical and disturbing certainty is gradually seeping into public consciousness, and political leaders have little choice but to follow. Recognition that the machinery of justice is killing the innocent as well as the guilty has, indeed, already moved the debate—as evidenced by demands for (and implementation of) moratoria, by sagging support in the polls, and by the growth of Innocence Projects in law schools across the country that are vigorously investigating the cases of those condemned to die. The issue of execution of the innocent has figured in international responses to the death penalty as well.

The second crucial factor eroding the pro-death-penalty consensus in America is external to the country, the result of diverse developments internationally, both prior to and in the wake of September 11. Most of the world has repudiated the death penalty.[3] In addition to banning it under domestic law, individual nation-states have committed themselves to treaties abolishing it internationally. Considerable international pressure—particularly in matters of extradition and consular relations—is being brought to bear on the United States to abolish state execution, and this pressure is mounting steadily.

The United States now stands in nearly complete isolation in advocating state executions; the few countries that concur with the practice are among the worst violators of human rights in the international community. With growing adamancy, nation after nation has signaled its dissatisfaction by refusing to extradite persons to the United States in the absence of ironclad guarantees that the death penalty will neither be sought nor carried out. International legal opinions are starting to focus on the fallibility of America's criminal justice system as a compelling human rights reason to refuse extradition without assurances. They also increasingly cite specialized empirical studies demonstrating the risk of executing the innocent, racism in the administration of capital punishment, and the "death row phenomenon" (discussed in chapter 3). Much of the rest of the world is calling for the United States to embrace a higher human rights standard.

Extradition problems adversely affect interests the United States regards as vital, especially its efforts to prosecute those suspected of terrorism. Nor is extradition the only area in which the international community has been bringing pressure to bear to end the American proclivity for state execution. Some nations, such as Mexico, have hired law firms and set up organizations specifically to contest the execution of their nationals in the United States. Other nations are also arguing with increasing firmness that the United States must honor its treaty commitments under the Vienna Convention on Consular Relations (VCCR) (which affords arrested foreigners prompt access to consular assistance). They are vigorously protesting the fact that the United States executes their nationals in defiance of laws requiring consular notification. The consequences for the American death penalty debate are profound. This demand concerning consular access has the potential to undercut numerous capital convictions involving foreign nationals sentenced to death. Moreover, American noncompliance with this treaty in order to avoid reopening these cases has serious consequences. Should the United States continue to ignore its obligations under international law, it will jeopardize its own citizens' access to consular assistance if detained abroad.

Resistance internationally is thus combining with disquiet domestically over an American justice system that gets it wrong all too frequently. The concurrence of these developments recasts the death penalty debate substantially. Domestically, the innocence argument is radically altering the terms of the debate, undermining traditional justifications for capital punishment and weakening the attitudes and positions of even the most adamant retentionists. Internationally, mounting pressures to end state execution are raising the political costs to the United States in ways likely to materially affect the debate. Finally, these international and domestic developments are mutually reinforcing one another in some powerful ways. One remarkable Canadian Supreme Court decision in 2001, for example, relied on the innocence argument to change its extradition policy in death penalty cases.

This book demonstrates why these two seemingly disparate trends are in fact closely connected and how they combine to foster capital punishment's eventual demise. Part I addresses international efforts to convince the United States to relinquish state execution. The second chapter provides a context for understanding resistance to the death penalty nationally and internationally by addressing tensions between human rights and international human rights law on the one hand and the rights of nation-states on the other. From the rise of the modern nation-state after the 1648 Treaty of Westphalia to World War II, individuals had no rights under international law outside of those that nation-states were themselves prepared to grant or protect. As entirely self-determining entities, nation-states enjoyed unqualified rights of nonintervention and noninterference, a status reflected in the rule of non-inquiry.

This traditional, absolutist view of national sovereignty and self-determination has impacted the death penalty debate in significant ways. It is, however, now vigorously contested. Enhanced recognition of human rights in international law inevitably changes our understanding of sovereignty, moving us away from the view that the rights of nation-states are overriding. Moreover, the mutual interdependence of nation-states in the twenty-first century belies the idea that they are wholly autonomous, independent entities whose authority and rights are incontestable within their borders. The implications of this for resistance to the death penalty domestically and internationally are considerable.

Chapters 3 and 4 take up, respectively, the two primary means by which the international community has brought pressure to bear directly upon the American commitment to state execution: through international extradition law and through treaty obligations that attend the Vienna Convention on Consular Relations. Before 1991, capital punishment was seldom an extradition issue, in part because most nations adhered to an inflexible rule of non-inquiry that prevented inquiry into the fairness of another nation's justice system in deciding extradition matters. Expanding views of international human rights law since

World War II have inevitably undercut the rule of non-inquiry. The death penalty has itself become the major impetus for relaxing the rule. Today, in much of the world, extradition is routinely conditioned upon a binding agreement to forgo the death penalty.

Chapter 3 engages the extradition debate in international human rights law, covering the principal international cases from the relevant international human rights courts as well as important decisions from the high courts in Canada and South Africa. It concludes that increased international interest in the death penalty will continue to hamper United States foreign policy and that the erosion of the rule of non-inquiry will begin to have collateral consequences as nations broaden criticism, questioning such matters as military courts, life sentences, and other inequities in the American justice system.

Although it presents itself as the paragon and protector of human rights, the United States has nonetheless refused to ratify three of the six major international human rights treaties. One significant exception to the American penchant for rejecting international treaties and tribunals is the Vienna Convention on Consular Relations, a treaty the United States has signed and ratified. The VCCR provides for consular access to foreign nationals accused of crime. Under it a nation must, without delay, notify such foreign nationals of their rights under the convention to seek the assistance of their nation's consulate, and, if they so request, notify the nearest consulate. Unfortunately, U.S. compliance with these procedures has been the exception rather than the rule for the 120 foreign nationals currently on America's death rows.[4] Chapter 4 examines three major instances of American noncompliance with the VCCR, and of the efforts by the involved countries to see that human rights be respected and international treaty commitments be honored.

Part II critically assesses the current status of the death penalty debate within the United States, arguing that the innocence issue is pivotal in advancing the case against capital punishment. Why have Americans, many of whom are exceptionally chary of state power, supported the ultimate expression of a state's power—the killing of its citizens in the name of justice? Attitudes toward state execution, and much of the support for it by ordinary Americans, have been heavily influenced by what can only be described as myths about the death penalty: beliefs uncritically accepted because they serve to explain and justify a phenomenon already accepted on other grounds. These beliefs are, almost without exception, empirically ill-founded; they do not offer evidence for the justifiability of the death penalty, but are, at best, evidence of a prior conviction that the death penalty is justifiable. Chapter 5 critiques four widely accepted myths that continue to shore up American support for capital punishment: that the death penalty deters homicide more effectively than life imprisonment, that it effectively prevents those who have murdered from murdering again, that it is more cost effective than life imprisonment without parole, and that it is no longer racist in its administration. None of these claims is true. When those who assert them realize this, they must either relinquish their endorsement of killing by the state, or offer other—retributivist—grounds for it; they must, that is, defend it as a means of payback or retribution that society justifiably imposes upon the guilty, who deserve or merit such punishment. There is, as well, a fifth myth about the death penalty, according to which the state does not execute the innocent, because the innocent are rarely (if ever) convicted of capital crimes. The significance of this issue is such that we devote much of the remaining discussion to it.

The sixth chapter reviews attitudinal studies of capital punishment, the various tests of the Marshall hypothesis (which suggests that if Americans had more knowledge about the death penalty they would find it "shocking and unacceptable"), and other poll data. These data indicate that traditional criticisms of the death penalty (appealing to cost; to lack of deterrence; to the presence of racial, ethnic, and class bias) have unfortunately shown limited ability to change people's attitudes notably; desire for vengeance and endemic discrimination within mainstream America may simply be far too pronounced. Despite the moral gravity of these arguments, they have not served to turn a majority of the body politic against the death penalty. And yet the death penalty is unlikely to be abolished until the American public's affirmation of it has been thoroughly shaken. Evidence indicates that the issue of innocence may play a significant role in accomplishing this, since it prompts even the most adamant of retentionists to moderate their position. Those committed to ending the death penalty would do well to draw upon it to demonstrate how innocence lends added moral urgency to standard anti-death-penalty arguments. It is, for example, in a capital punishment system riddled with racial and class bias, that innocent people are convicted of crimes they never committed, find their convictions upheld, their remedies denied, and their lives ended with far greater frequency than anyone has previously supposed.

The innocence argument has decidedly greater force now than it has had at any other time since 1976, when the Supreme Court reinstated the death penalty. A series of recent developments confirms this. They include not only the rise of Innocence Projects across the nation and growing calls for a moratorium, as mentioned above, but also the increase in seeming defections by former retentionists and a sudden spate of doubts in the minds of many apparently wavering supporters. Former Supreme Court Justice Sandra Day O'Connor, for example, who generally supported the death penalty while she was on the bench, recently acknowledged, "If statistics are any indication, the system may well be allowing some innocent defendants to be executed."[5] The execution of a legally and factually innocent person is, she asserts, a "constitutionally intolerable event."[6] Vital segments of the public are becoming aware that judicial executions of innocent people are not merely hypothetical prospects, trotted out by fertile philosophical imaginations to probe the limits of theories of punishment. They are deeply dismaying realities, irrevocable events sanctioned by the state in the name of its citizens. Chapter 7 outlines the rise of the innocence issue beginning with the groundbreaking research by Michael Radelet and Hugo Adam Bedau. It covers the experience of the states with the highest numbers of exonerations and ties in the Marshall hypothesis with the innocence problem, demonstrating that it is highly probable that we have in fact executed, and will continue to execute, innocent people.

Chapter 8 considers the impact of the innocence argument on retentionist positions in defense of capital punishment, arguing that it radically undermines standard justifications for a system of state execution. Utilitarian-based arguments for the death penalty, which attempt to justify it on the grounds that it maximizes social utility, have long been regarded as seriously defective, and the innocence issue only compounds this view. As increasing numbers of death-row inmates are found innocent and released, as public unease with state execution consequently intensifies, and as constitutional safeguards to reduce the likelihood that only the guilty are killed continue to be eroded, no utilitarian can plausibly defend retention of the death penalty. Its negative consequences are simply far too great. Some alternative sanction, such as life imprisonment or life without parole, is the only justifiable recourse for a utilitarian. Since retributivists, unlike utilitarians, are deeply committed to the idea that justice does not allow us to punish the innocent for some greater good, one would expect the innocence argument to seriously impact retributivist-based retentionism. Retributivists cannot morally justify a system that regularly sacrifices the innocent in the interests of executing the guilty. The innocence argument, we contend, vitiates the retributivist case for capital punishment— the most common justification for state execution. Thus, the moral force of the innocence argument is compelling: the sacrifice of innocent people in order to maintain a system of state execution, particularly one which has steadily cast off due process safeguards intended to insure that only the guilty die, is unjustifiable on either utilitarian or retributivist grounds.

Some retentionists have responded to the innocence argument by rejecting capital punishment as currently practiced. They remain, however, fully committed to the death penalty "in principle," and are intent on fixing the faulty system so that state execution may continue. A moratorium may well become a conceptual middle ground in the death penalty debate, strategically adopted by opposing parties for different reasons. Is the call for a moratorium on capital punishment an adequate response to the issues raised by the innocence argument? Chapter 9 argues that it is not. Calls for a moratorium to "fix the system" so that executions may resume fail to appreciate the full force of the innocence argument and cannot be sustained. They also draw on a distinction between accepting a social policy in principle while rejecting it in practice that in this context is spurious. The only way to "fix" the system of capital punishment so as to avoid execution of the innocent is to end it. Efforts can then be directed to fixing the criminal justice system so as to ensure that some alternative punishment is a viable option as a sanction for the most heinous crimes.

Neither are moratoria an adequate response to international pressures to end state executions. The world is rapidly moving beyond moratoria, even beyond limiting executions to wartime military crimes, and is ending the legal basis for capital punishment for all purposes and all crimes. Europe, for example, is now a death-penalty-free continent of eight hundred million people. With Russia's suspension of the death penalty, and Turkey's recent legislation abolishing it, all 46 nations of the Council of Europe have stopped executions. There has not been an execution in all of Europe since 1997. Moreover, forty of its member nations have ratified Protocol 6 of the European Convention on Human Rights, abolishing the death penalty for all but certain limited crimes committed during wartime. Thirty-six European nations have gone further and abolished the practice for any reason and under all circumstances. As the secretary-general of the Council of Europe, Walter Schwimmer, states:

> There is a clear trend toward abolition, often preceded by the institution of a moratorium.
>
> For several years now, no executions have taken place in the area covered by the Council of Europe, spanning from Reykjavik to Vladivostok . . . At a recent conference in Rome, the initiative was taken to aim for abolition even for offenses committed in time of war.
>
> These developments are *not symptoms of an ephemeral trend, but the consequence of a profound belief that the death penalty has no place in a civilized democracy.*[7] (Emphasis added.)

The American public is beginning to comprehend the seriousness of the innocence problem and, in the wake of 9/11, it may finally be beginning to appreciate the nature and scope of international opposition to it. State killing will be abolished; the only question for the United States is when. What is certain is that the moral and political problems that the practice of state execution poses for the United States will not go away and will not get easier. As the abolition movement continues to grow internationally, American isolation will only increase. Intensified interest in human rights feeds interest in, and international opposition to, the death penalty. At the same time, concern about the death penalty broadens understanding of human rights issues and enhances the ability of the international community to deal with them. This has profound repercussions not only for the American system of capital punishment, but also for U.S. foreign policy. As nations feel ever more free to criticize the American justice system, they are freer to reject extradition for reasons unrelated to capital punishment. Thus the death penalty serves as the fulcrum for broader and more searching criticism of, and inquiry into, the American justice system; it is also beginning to affect larger U.S. foreign policy objectives. America's stubborn embrace of the death penalty will continue to hinder its international relations, and it will do so in new and multiple ways. It may well be that America will not abandon its lingering attachment to state execution until the rest of the world shames it into bringing the practice to an end.

PART ONE : International Pressure to Relinquish State Execution

2 : Human Rights and the Erosion of Absolute Sovereignty

> *Boundaries form indispensable protection against violation and violence; but the divisions they sustain also carry cruelty and violence. Boundaries provide conditions of identity, individual agency, and collective action; but they also close off possibilities of being that might otherwise flourish. Boundaries both foster and inhibit freedom; they both protect and violate life.*
> —*William Connolly*[1]

HUMAN RIGHTS VS. THE RIGHTS OF NATION-STATES

International resistance to the American death penalty provides an extraordinarily fertile context for examining underlying tensions between international human rights law—whose subjects are individuals and peoples—and international law—whose subjects have traditionally been held to be states. Following the rise of the modern nation-state, individuals had no rights under international law save those that states were themselves willing to confer or recognize. State sovereignty was construed as absolute and accompanied by unqualified rights of nonintervention and noninterference. This view of the rights of nation-states is reflected in the rule of non-inquiry, addressed in chapter 3, which is central to the debate over extradition and state execution. It has also had at least three significant impacts on human rights. First, it has deprived both individuals and peoples of standing to contest the actions of nation-states. Their rights, and their well-being, are effectively abandoned, left to the mercy of powerful entities whose decisions could neither be appealed nor overthrown. Second, international deference to a concept of absolute sovereignty has discouraged, if not thwarted, efforts by nation-states to critique the judicial practices of other nation-states, including the practice of state execution. And third, the notion that state sovereignty is absolute has shielded certain individuals—particularly the ruling elites within nation-states—from responsibility and accountability for actions violative of the rights of their fellow citizens.

The legitimacy of this understanding of sovereignty is being challenged; with it, long-standing assumptions regarding both the relations among nation-states and the proper limits of state power over individuals are being challenged as well. The post–World War II expansion of international human rights law has contributed decisively to this. From Nuremberg to the creation of the International Criminal Court in 2002, we have witnessed a strengthening trend toward holding the worst violators of human rights accountable. Erosion of the rule of non-inquiry, of the idea that sovereign states must not inquire into the fairness of other sovereign states' justice systems, clearly signals that nation-states are more willing to critique one another's distinctive judicial practices. Similarly, beginning with the International Covenant on Civil and Political Rights, both the intervention of nongovernmental organizations (NGOs) with legal standing and citizen participation in the defense of individual human rights have expanded. National leaders are no longer completely immune from prosecution for human rights violations. Remedies can, on occasion, be sought for such violations, and the scope of action of nation-states is constrained when they are compelled to obey rules not of their own exclusive making.

As concern for human rights, and convictions about the responsibility of the international community to safeguard them, become increasingly commonplace in diverse international fora, both international law and concepts of state sovereignty are being substantively transformed: "The walls of state sovereignty—once thought impregnable in regard to human rights violations—now often appear riddled with peepholes and surrounded by a noisy and hostile crowd."[2] These are not chance trends. Human rights activists and NGOs have plainly used international opinion, together with international legal mechanisms, to speed the breakdown of state resistance and to create and strengthen international human rights norms. Although absolutist views of sovereignty remain in play and are commonly invoked by various states as a protective mantle to deflect criticism and shield them from charges of human rights violations, the legitimacy of such views is contested. They are being eroded, and perhaps displaced, by other conceptions of sovereignty, as well as by other visions of international community. The assertion of state sovereignty, with its concomitant appeal to inviolable rights of noninterference and nonintervention, "no longer automatically trumps other claims of values . . . substantive beliefs in human rights are slowly, but inexorably, coming to trump the procedural beliefs associated with sovereignty."[3] This is most notably the case in Europe, where abolition of state execution is a requirement for admission both to the Council of Europe and to the European Union, and a number of countries have abandoned the practice as a result.

Yet sixty years after Nuremberg and despite these developments, the United States remains fiercely, if selectively, committed to the concept of absolute sovereignty—at least when its own rights and immunities are at issue. This is true in general, and specifically as regards a right to execute. As a result, the country finds itself increasingly isolated within the international community, particularly from those nation-states with which it most closely identifies and whose values it most closely shares—the industrialized democracies of Europe. America's adamant attachment to a no-longer-tenable view of the nature and scope of its rights as a sovereign entity is at odds with its own human rights rhetoric as well as with international human rights law and practice. When it comes to the matter of the death penalty, however, American citizens tend to be quite unaware of the fact that much of the rest of the world regards execution by the state as a grave violation of human rights; that, in the words of U.N. Special Rapporteur Bacre Waly Ndiaye,

> where there is a fundamental right to life, there is no right to capital punishment . . . [G]iven that the loss of life is irreparable, the Special Rapporteur strongly supports the conclusions of the Human Rights Committee and emphasizes that the abolition of capital punishment is most desirable in order fully to respect the right to life.[4]

And there is this added irony for many Americans, especially Republicans and Libertarians, strongly supportive of restricting the powers of the state: the unqualified rights associated with the view that state sovereignty is absolute grant the nation-state exceptional latitude in its treatment of those within its borders. In capital punishment, the immense power of the state is held to justifiably override the most basic of human rights—an individual's right to continued existence. Yet those who most vigorously champion individual liberties over and against the state, tend not to see the practice of state execution in terms of the fundamental tension between state power and human rights that guides their thinking on virtually every other policy issue. To allow the state to kill its own citizens (and in some cases, those of other countries) is to allow it the ultimate power. To do so in a democracy, where such action by the state is undertaken in the name of the people and of justice, is to authorize the exercise of that ultimate power. Members of a democratic, civil society have a commensurate responsibility to interrogate this irrevocable punishment, regularly invoked in their name. That no state should be permitted to have or exercise such power, and that sovereignty—properly understood—neither requires nor sanctions it, is part of our argument here.

STATE SOVEREIGNTY AS ABSOLUTE

State sovereignty, which has dominated the international system for over three hundred years, is now generally regarded as the central organizing principle of world order. For most of this time, the story of sovereignty has been about borders and boundaries—bright-line borders, which are supposedly clear and distinct, hard and fast. It has been, for the most part, a Western story, whose primary author was the seventeenth-century philosopher, Thomas Hobbes, and whose primary text was *Leviathan*.[5] In the literature, this view of the rights of nation-states is most often described as absolute sovereignty, sometimes as territorial or Westphalian sovereignty, and sometimes as thick sovereignty or statism. The scope of such sovereignty was initially limited to a domestic context, to the relation between the ruler and the ruled. Within territorial borders, under this view, the power and authority of the sovereign is absolute, final, and incontestable. Sovereign states are held to enjoy exclusive control over those inside and to be wholly self-determining entities with unqualified rights of nonintervention and noninterference: "No state or group of states has the right to interfere directly or indirectly, for any reason whatever, in the internal or external affairs of any other state."[6] The notion of sovereign immunity—from law, from scrutiny, from justice—is central to this account of the rights of nation-states. Indeed, an indifference to human rights is built directly into the Hobbesian conception of sovereignty, according to which no moral law binds the sovereign, so it is impossible for the sovereign to treat subjects unjustly. The sovereign has the right to lay down any laws that can be enforced, and such laws cannot be unjust: "The law is made by the sovereign power, and all that is done by such power is warranted."[7] Such sovereignty is also monolithic. It cannot be shared or divided: "Sovereignty is one and indivisible, inalienable and imprescriptible."[8]

Diverse accounts of sovereignty generally agree that it is constituted by separation, by bounding one entity off from another. As various state systems developed, the concept of sovereignty began to encompass not just the nature of power and authority within a state, but its political independence from other states. "Sovereignty in the relations between states signifies independence. Independence in regard to a portion of the globe is the right to exercise therein, to the exclusion of any other state, the functions of a state."[9] A sovereign state is not accountable to any outside authority and has no inherent responsibilities to any entity beyond its territory save for those it may voluntarily assume. Absolute sovereignty, as one commentator observes, "renders international relations anarchical, for it makes states wholly autonomous; they are not required to yield or genuflect to any outside authority."[10] While such a sovereign state may enter into relations with other states through voluntary agreements, what obligations it has are spelled out in such agreements; it has no inherent obligations to those outside it.

The cloaking effect of absolute sovereignty makes it a powerful rhetorical tool, commonly invoked when countries, and rulers, wish to defend themselves behind the sheltering shield of Leviathan from charges of human rights violations. Auguste Pinochet, for example, claimed sovereign immunity in response to being charged with crimes against humanity. Far from being a dry expression of legal status, appeals to sovereignty are typically crucial diplomatic moves, taken by politicians intent on expressing and justifying foreign as well as domestic policies. Former attorney general John Ashcroft's frequent invocation of American sovereignty is a case in point. When asked about likely international protest to a pending decision by the Justice Department to seek the death penalty against Zacarias Moussaoui, he responded, "We are a sovereign nation. We make judgments about crimes and the penalties that exist here."[11] Sovereignty, thus, is not merely an empirical claim about the way political power is in fact exercised, but a normative claim about how it should be exercised; it not only describes certain political arrangements, but attempts to justify them, shaping social and political policy.[12]

Perhaps nowhere is the selectivity of America's attachment to this version of sovereignty more pronounced than when it comes to the presence, within its borders, of other nations. At the founding of the country, when the need to establish international legitimacy was acute, things were otherwise. The United States, in treating with Indian nations, regarded their sovereignty and independence as on a par with its own. "Like all other independent nations," an early U.S. attorney general affirmed, "their territories are inviolable by any other sovereignty . . . They are entirely self-governed, self-directed."[13] This changed as the comparative power and territorial ambitions of the United States grew and as its domestic jurisprudence began formulating rationalizations for state actions. From John Marshall's *Cherokee* cases to the plenary power doctrine, and via the mechanism of official Federal Indian Policy, the United States proceeded to assert its power over those within its physical borders, to compromise, qualify, and abrogate the sovereignty of Indian nations. The Marshall decisions "invalidated, for purposes of American law, any conception of the Indigenous nations as sovereigns on a co-equal basis with the United States."[14] Nations whose governance structures had thrived for thousands of years, and whose willingness to treat with a rebellious young nation lent it the international legitimacy it required, were thus paternalistically reduced to "wards" of the enveloping state, "domestic, dependent nations . . . in a state of pupilage,"[15] whose sovereignty "is of a unique and limited character" that "exists only at the sufferance of Congress and is subject to complete defeasance."[16] Today, the United States draws on the mantle of absolute sovereignty to argue vigorously in international fora that it is not accountable outside its borders for its treatment of these nations, since "relations between states and indigenous peoples are purely matters of internal, domestic jurisdiction."[17]

The language of the international law scholar today is no longer the language of sovereignty; rather, it is that of the demise of sovereignty. The sovereign state is increasingly perceived as the problem to be overcome. —Paul W. Kahn[18]

That such a conception of state sovereignty is currently contested and in flux is an understatement. Whenever political and legal theorists must grope widely for metaphors to fit a situation, metaphors that conflict with and contradict one another, something unsettling and unsettled is reliably afoot. The metaphors for sovereignty are without question flying thick and frantically. Sovereignty has been said by various authors to be crumbling, pooling, maturing, diffusing, leaking, evaporating, eroding, shifting, diminishing, fuzzy, misty, obsolete, a shibboleth, a dead duck.[19] Some will not let the word pass their lips, referring to it as "[t]hat 'S' word," whose "birth is illegitimate and [which] has not aged well."[20] Others reach for the literary, calling it "the Banquo's ghost of the academic feast—rattling the soothsayers by reappearing at inconvenient intervals just when many assumed its final departure was at hand."[21] Others have simply sat in frustration and asked whether it is "the word we wish to throw out, or the concept, or the implications of the concept or the word?"[22]

Whatever the outcome, the concept of sovereignty plainly is undergoing transformation, and has been for some time. As already noted, one of the most-oft-cited reasons for this is mounting international concern for human rights. International resistance to the death penalty has simultaneously played a role in this transformation and been impacted by it. The erosion of the rule of non-inquiry, examined in the following chapter, is a reflection at the microlevel of the transformation absolute sovereignty is undergoing at the macrolevel. Its impact, moreover, is not confined to the death penalty, but extends to such other human rights concerns as the use of military courts, the place of women and juveniles in the criminal justice system, and the issue of whether life without parole constitutes cruel and unusual punishment.

Another factor in the transformation of sovereignty has been globalization, "the terrible nearness of distant places,"[23] a multidimensional phenomenon that is bringing disparate parts of the world into contact, and in which the nature and distribution of power in the world is changing in substantive and, often, unforeseen ways. With the rise of transnational corporate entities, of nonstate actors such as NGOs, of critical social movements acting across borders,[24] and with the proliferation of new information-communication technologies, the power of sovereign nation-states is being either bypassed or undermined. Globalization is, however, a phenomenon that may best be described as Janus-faced when it comes to human rights. It has the potential both to significantly enhance and to significantly undermine them. On the one hand, the international community's effort to protect human rights "can itself be seen as an aspect of globalization . . . reduc[ing] the sphere of sovereignty," while, on the other, globalization is attended by powerful nonstate actors fully capable of violating human rights "in ways that were not contemplated during the international human rights movement."[25]

That globalization and international concern for human rights are straining the concept of absolute sovereignty is not surprising, for both defy the notion of inviolable state borders. They are transsovereign events that address, and raise, transsovereign problems—problems that, by transcending borders, escape the control of individual nation-states. The latter include pollution and environmental degradation, crime, infectious diseases, and refugee flows, among others. While some maintain that the nation-state is withering and we must begin to make sense of a notion of "global sovereignty,"[26] others see in globalization the promise of a third revolution in, or transformation of, sovereignty. The previous two, according to law professor Helen Stacy, were efforts to win national freedom from oppressive empires and gave primacy to the demarcation of borders. During the first, the Peace of Westphalia, the Vatican's territorial vassals were transformed into the nation-states of Europe. The second revolution was the partial-decolonization period of the twentieth century, when the aspirations of many former colonies for self-determination were realized. Both revolutions, Stacy observes, "had embedded within them the idea of sovereignty as a strong claim of a new dotted line on the map."[27] Globalization, she contends, now presents us with an opportunity to choose between an account of sovereignty where border demarcation is even more pronounced, or one where it is defined in crucially different ways.

If globalization frustrates the process and point of drawing borders, the development of human rights law has undermined the ability of states to pull sovereignty around them as though it were an immunity cloak, shielding them from charges of human rights violations. According to the 1992 Helsinki Declaration, human rights "are matters of direct and legitimate concern to all participating states and do not belong exclusively to the internal affairs of the state concerned."[28] The degree to which this commitment to human rights permeates international affairs is vividly illustrated by Turkey's bid for membership in the European Union. Its admission was made conditional upon conformance with the Copenhagen criteria.[29] This required abolition of the death penalty and the provision of greater cultural rights for the Kurdish people, an indigenous minority within Turkey's borders. In 2002, Turkey complied, ending state execution and lifting a ban on Kurdish-language education and broadcasts. Further, a series of international humanitarian interventions has recently been heralded as demonstrating that sovereignty no longer functions as "an absolute shield against the world . . . a force field repelling other nation states at the border."[30]

Some have tied developments such as these to the phenomenon of globalization: "the idol of the state must inevitably dissolve in a world that connects people, regardless of borders, through millions of links of integration—ranging from trade, finance, and property, to information links that impart a variety of universal notions and cultural patterns."[31] According to others, it is because we are bound up with one another in complex institutional webs of communication and exchange that moral evaluations of social relations in terms of justice and injustice apply.[32] What is becoming very clear now, if it has not been so in the past, is that sovereignty is bound up with interdependency, and that sovereign power and sovereign rights cannot legitimately be exercised, or recognized, if not responsive to that fact.

So the idea that sovereignty consists of rigid, opaque borders separating discrete territories and interests is being challenged on both moral and empirical grounds—by those arguing that it is normatively inadequate and unable to accommodate the claims of global justice, and by those arguing that it ignores the degree to which current state power is fragmentary and constrained. Absolute sovereignty continues to be invoked by politicians and states intent on insulating themselves from international criticism and accountability, and on shoring up whatever erosion has occurred. The United States, moreover, reliably invokes it to defend what it regards as its sovereign, overriding right to retain state execution as a criminal sanction in the face of charges that such a sanction is, like torture, an unconscionable violation of human rights.[33] Alternatives to this view of sovereignty are, however, actively being forged. The rise of the European Union, and of institutions such as the International Criminal Court, represents a very different view of the way those with power may rule. It is one in which sovereignty entails responsibility and where the legitimacy of criticism of state conduct is not circumscribed by geography, by where territorial borders begin or end. It provides no moral or legal cover for states insisting that their sovereign rights trump human rights. It offers no support for the view that "only domestic 'evolving standards of decency' matter in capital cases,"[34] or that how a particular state treats its own citizens, and the criminal sanctions it may legitimately apply, are its own business and its own business alone.

SOVEREIGNTY AS INTERDEPENDENCY

An impressive array of critiques of absolute sovereignty have been, and are being, formulated by a variety of scholars with diverse disciplinary commitments. Several of these scholars have comparable things to say about what the problem with sovereignty is, as well as about how it might be resolved. We draw on them here in order to help make sense of the permutations the concept of sovereignty is undergoing, to sketch the outlines of an alternative account toward which these critiques seem to be converging, and to draw out the implications of such an account for resistance to the death penalty.

Helen Stacy provides an account of relational sovereignty that proposes that sovereignty is being transformed by a different understanding of the social contract. The social contract must now accommodate "the increasingly complex range of transnational interactions under the conditions of globalization, and also the enlarging role of international human rights norms."[35] Contemporary sovereignty, she suggests, requires responsibility and accountability. It is "becoming conditional upon the ruler discharging responsibilities of care towards the citizen,"[36] responsibilities that extend to the interactions of citizens with the international community and that the international community has a role in assessing. Contemporary human rights cannot be addressed adequately by Hobbesian distinctions between the citizen and the noncitizen, between the "inside" and "outside" of territorial borders. Such distinctions "do not go far enough . . . they remain fixed, with the idea of sovereignty stopping at the border."[37]

The work of a number of indigenous legal scholars and activists who are conducting a reappraisal of the tribal sovereignty doctrine contributes an important element to this alternative account of sovereignty. Their reappraisal, according to Wallace Coffey and Rebecca Tsosie, is "based in the conceptions of sovereignty held by Indian nations and . . . responds to the challenges that confront Indian nations today."[38] Euro-American notions of sovereignty and self-determination, they observe, fail to capture the perspective shared by many indigenous peoples "that human power and agency are limited in very fundamental ways by their relationship to other parts of the natural world."[39] The account of sovereignty they are developing is process-centered and not constrained by "the limitations of a strictly territorial notion of sovereignty."[40] Since sovereignty is "conditioned by the universal moral framework of self-determination," assertions of it "should not insulate a nation from taking responsibility for human rights abuses" within its borders.[41] Interdependence, and the concept of relationship, is fundamental to this account of sovereignty: "[I]t is used to forge connection between Indian nations and other sovereigns, whether Indian or non-Indian."[42] As law professor Craig Scott notes,

> If one listens, one can often hear the message that the right of a people to self-determination is not a right for peoples to determine their status without consideration of the rights of other peoples with whom they are presently connected and with whom they will continue to be connected in the future. For we must realize that peoples, no less than individuals, exist and thrive only in dialogue with each other. Self-determination necessarily involves engagement with and responsibility to others (which includes responsibility for the implications of one's preferred choices for others) . . . We need to begin to think of self-determination in terms of peoples existing in relationship with each other. It is the process of negotiating the nature of such relationships which is part of, indeed at the very core of, what it means to be a self-determining people.[43]

Such reappraisals of the nature and implications of sovereignty by indigenous theorists and activists resonate with discussions by other legal scholars, political philosophers, political scientists, and international relations theorists. Indeed, in some cases, the former are directly informing the latter. Political philosopher Iris Marion Young, for example, draws on indigenous accounts of relational self-determination to argue for "a transformation of the rights and powers of existing nation-states and the assumptions of recognition and noninterference that still largely govern the relation between states."[44] She has also developed a model of governance inspired partly by accounts of the democracy and federalism practiced by the Iroquois. This model envisions a thin level of global governance, which will enable "more local control as compared with the current states system," one in which "locales can relate directly to global authorities in order to challenge and limit the ability of nation-states to control them."[45]

Adeno Addis similarly rejects the idea of a thick, or strongly autonomous, state, arguing that it is neither sustainable nor desirable. He defends a version of thin state sovereignty, in which sovereignty is developed relationally and contingently and is grounded on participation rather than isolation and noninterference. His account stresses the importance of groups in the lives and identities of individuals, rejecting views of sovereignty whose unit of analysis is the abstract individual "unaffected by, and prior to, the community within which it (is) located."[46] The communication revolution has seriously destabilized the traditional view of territorial sovereignty, he contends, curtailing the power of the state and its claim to final authority within its physical borders.

Yet the demise of the state system would be dangerous, since an unregulated international information market would threaten diverse ways of life: "The state may be the only institution . . . capable of minimizing the international tendency to uniformize cultures and individuals."[47] He distances himself from those who regard the state's loss of authority and of border control with alarm, as well as from those who celebrate it. These opposing views, he claims, "misunderstand the ambiguous and even paradoxical nature of territorial boundaries."[48] Louis Henkin makes a similar point:

> [I]f state sovereignty has resisted the human rights movement, and if globalization has begun to threaten state sovereignty, that may sound promising for the human rights movement. But I do not find comfort for human rights in the various forms of globalization. The fact is that human rights, and the human rights movement depend on governments and on the state system . . . I do not see the withering away of the state as a result of globalization . . . In any event, if the state is going to wither away, the time has not come, and will not come soon.[49]

What these critiques share is a conviction that thinking about sovereignty must begin by acknowledging that sovereign entities are interdependent and accountable to one another. They suggest an alternative understanding of sovereignty that, while not inconsistent with the continuation of a state system, does allow for an international system that is not restricted to states, one in which sovereignty implies standing to participate in international regulatory regimes.[50] To construe sovereignty as interdependency is to regard sovereign entities as embedded in and constituted by their relationships, some voluntary or chosen, some (such as geographical proximity) not. Interdependent sovereignty involves an assertion and assumption of responsibility for governing and promoting the well-being of a human community, and for respecting the legitimate claims and interests of all those affected by actions taken in the course of meeting this responsibility.[51] Thus, sovereign states are indeed accountable to those outside their borders, and must consider the interests and claims of all those (individuals, groups, peoples, or states) they impact—whether or not an explicit agreement, contract, or treaty binds them.

The notion of sovereign responsibility replaces that of sovereign immunity within interdependent sovereignty. Sovereign entities have certain responsibilities because they exist in certain relationships, occupy certain roles, and have certain powers. Their control and authority is not unqualified; they can be overridden to protect the rights of others (individuals, groups, peoples, or states). Indeed, following Iris Marion Young's discussion in another context, they can be said not to have rights to noninterference and nonintervention at all, much less unqualified ones, since such rights fail to acknowledge interdependency and the possibilities for domination that threaten interdependent relationships. They do, however, enjoy a right not to be dominated; sovereignty is thus tied to nondomination, to the absence of arbitrary interference.[52] While this involves a presumption of (rather than a right to) noninterference, interference to reduce relations of domination is acceptable and does not violate sovereignty. As Young explains, "[N]ondomination ultimately implies limiting the rights of existing nation-states and setting them into more cooperatively regulated relationships . . . regulating international relations to prevent domination."[53]

Such an understanding of sovereignty is being put in play by the international community as it pursues various forms of resistance to state execution. This view also helps make sense of various recent developments impacting both the state system and human rights. Indeed, the International Covenant on Civil and Political Rights and other human rights instruments are themselves a reflection of interdependent sovereignty. The unique and new aspect of these multilateral human rights treaties is that they enshrine obligations between states and individuals, albeit under the guise of classic "contracts between nations." The growth of international human rights law, for example, does not compromise, limit, or violate sovereignty, but is an opportunity to exercise it. Human rights claims are no longer constrained by geography, membership in a particular group, or territorial borders. They are appropriately addressed to the broader international community as well as to the governing sovereign. Similarly, interdependent sovereignty acknowledges the increased recognition of the right of all peoples to self-determination. States have a responsibility to support the struggles of those peoples who have endured oppression at the hands of powerful nation-states and to redefine the relationship between states and the nations within them to ensure nondomination.[54]

Globalization emerges on this account not as a threat to sovereignty, but as an occasion for states to assume sovereign responsibilities that extend beyond their own "domestic" environments; to control corporate behavior, for example, and to safeguard the rights of those for whose well-being they are responsible. Interdependent sovereignty means behaving accountably across borders and ensuring that other powerful entities (such as corporations) do so as well. It recognizes, moreover, that individuals have allegiances not only to the government in power within their states, but to numerous other entities (such as NGOs) that refuse to be confined within territorial borders.

Construing sovereignty as interdependency, as tied to the acknowledgment and exercise of responsibilities, and as committed to a principle of nondomination may help mold sovereignty into a force for the protection of human rights, rather than (as with absolute sovereignty) a defensive shield to deflect criticism regarding them. It enables the concept of sovereignty, and the state system itself, to better accommodate, safeguard, and advance human rights claims. This is true whether the issue is the treatment of peoples or of individuals within the borders of a nation-state. We noted earlier that the United States relies on the invocation of absolute sovereignty, and of unqualified rights of noninterference and nonintervention, to justify both state execution and its treatment of indigenous nations within its borders. Based on the alternative account of sovereignty sketched here, sovereignty provides no cover for human rights abuses and no justification for oppression. Given the principle of nondomination, the United States cannot arbitrarily interfere "in the activities of those peoples in relation to whom [it claims] special jurisdictional relation."[55] The international community has "a responsibility to interfere with the self-governing actions of a group in order to prevent severe violations of human rights"[56] and to regulate international relations so as to prevent and end relations of domination and serious human rights abuses. Indeed, this seems to be exactly what the European Union has set about doing in making admission of states contingent upon their abolishing state execution and addressing other human rights abuses for which they are responsible, such as the oppression of indigenous nations within their borders.

AMERICAN ISOLATION AND INTERNATIONAL HUMAN RIGHTS LAW

Contemporary international relations are permeated, if not structured, by the tension between appeals to these conflicting understandings of sovereignty; it is a dynamic that largely leaves the United States isolated from, and indifferent to, the rest of the world. America's response to ratified treaties and to the establishment of international tribunals consistently reveals a selective embrace of absolute sovereignty; it is invoked, and its invocation by others is respected, depending on whether U.S. interests are furthered by so doing. The legitimacy of international tribunals and even of ratified treaties is seen as inherently suspect, a threat to the rights (especially the noninterference rights) of a sovereign state. Sovereignty, in this view, confers rights with few, if any, attendant reciprocal responsibilities, and the rights of a sovereign state invariably trump human rights. The United States, for example, habitually fails to obey, or to provide domestic remedies for, violations of international law. As legal scholar Joan Fitzpatrick observes, even ratified treaties such as the International Covenant on Civil and Political Rights and the 1967 protocol relating to the status of refugees, are "regularly violated by the United States, without effective redress, because of peculiar but dominant contemporary views of treaties held by domestic authorities responsible for their implementation."[57] Moreover, the United States regularly limits the enforceability of the human rights treaties that it does ratify with reservations and understandings that conflict with the object and purpose of those treaties. These restrictions are often formally rejected by the international community as violative of international law.

Fear of compromising sovereignty thus construed may help explain the extraordinary and appalling fact that a nation that presents itself as the paragon and protector of human rights has nonetheless refused to ratify three of the six recent major international human rights treaties.[58] Indeed, commitment to state execution has played a determining role in one of these, the Convention on the Rights of the Child, which prohibits state execution of juveniles as a human rights violation.[59] For many years, the United States insisted on its right as a sovereign entity to execute juveniles, and therefore signed but refused to ratify the Convention.[60] Indeed, in 2002 it was the only state in the world known to have carried out executions of juveniles,[61] and one of only two nations still expressly reserving the right to do so.[62] This changed in 2005, however, with the Supreme Court decision in *Roper v. Simmons*, where juvenile executions were finally declared to violate the Eighth Amendment ban on cruel and unusual punishment. The reasoning in the decision is interesting in that it indicates the justices were influenced by international opinion. Writing for the majority, Justice Anthony Kennedy held that "[i]t is proper that we acknowledge the overwhelming weight of international opinion against the juvenile death penalty . . . The opinion of the world community, while not controlling our outcome, does provide respected and significant confirmation for our conclusions."[63] The United States, however, still has not ratified the Convention on the Rights of the Child.

America's resistance to the growing international critique of the death penalty cannot be viewed in isolation from its resistance to international human rights law, and international fora for redress. In distancing itself from such international legal mechanisms generally, and specifically in defending the state's right to execute those within its borders, the United States repeatedly appeals to a concept of absolute sovereignty in which the rights of states to noninterference and nonintervention take precedence over human rights. Since a sovereign entity is not accountable to any entity outside its territorial borders for what goes on within those borders, the American practice of state execution is seen as falling within this protected sphere of sovereign immunity. Thus, the criticism that the death penalty violates human rights is deflected by the American rebuttal that to raise such a criticism is to violate sovereign rights.

As then senator John Ashcroft declared, in objecting to the establishment of an international criminal court, "If there is one critical component of sovereignty, it is the authority to define crimes and punishment."[64]

The United States has also long resisted the jurisdiction of international courts. Always jealous of national sovereignty and suspicious of international judicial fora[65] (at least where human, as opposed to property, rights are concerned),[66] the United States typically does not accede to the jurisdiction of international tribunals.[67] The Bush Administration's failure to support the International Criminal Court (ICC) provides yet another manifestation of its long-standing reluctance to submit to international tribunals,[68] and of its reliance on appeals to sovereignty as a rationale for resisting efforts to bring it into conformity with prevailing human rights standards. Indeed, it took the extraordinary measure of un-signing the 1998 Rome Statute that created the ICC, declaring that it "does not intend to be bound by its signature."[69] What virtually the entire international community has viewed as the shared responsibility of all sovereign states—i.e., safeguarding human rights by creating a mechanism for prosecuting the most serious international crimes—was held by the United States to be a gross breach of sovereignty. "This court strikes at the heart of sovereignty,"[70] Ashcroft asserted in testimony before the Senate Subcommittee on International Operations:

By ceding the authority to define and punish crimes, many nations took an irrevocable step to the loss of national sovereignty and the reality of global government.[71]

Nowhere is the United States more isolated on an emerging human rights issue than on the International Criminal Court. Brought into being over vehement American objections, the ICC entered into force on July 1, 2002.[72] It is probably the best example of the new reach of international law—and of America's "abstention" from international human rights norms out of fear of compromising its sovereignty. The Rome Statute of the International Criminal Court clearly illustrates the human rights standards to which most of the international community has committed itself; it refuses to sanction the death penalty as a punishment, even for the very worst of crimes.[73] In Rome, 120 nations voted to support the creation of such an international forum. Seven states opposed it; the United States was among them, joining "a handful of rogue States and notorious human rights violators such as Iran, Libya, China, and Iraq in voting against the statute for a Permanent International Criminal Court."[74] Israel was the only American ally that voted no.

The role of the United Nations as the central international organization for the creation and maintenance of international peace and justice is widely acknowledged, whatever the dissatisfaction with how well it has fulfilled this mandate. As a legal organ of the United Nations, the International Criminal Court was created in response to the international community's recognition—particularly following the atrocities in Rwanda and Yugoslavia[75]—of the need for a supranational authority to mediate disputes or crimes affecting more than one state. Such an authority eliminates the need for establishing a series of individual, ad hoc tribunals, as happened first in Nuremberg, then in Yugoslavia, and most recently in Rwanda. The ICC, the Yugoslavian tribunal, and the Rwandan tribunal do not include the death penalty as a permissible sanction. According to Amnesty International, a major advocate for its establishment, the ICC will "bring to justice those responsible for war crimes, crimes against humanity and crimes against peace."[76] The ICC is not intended to replace national courts, but to supplement them in specific circumstances. Participating states still retain their power and responsibility for bringing to justice those responsible for international crimes and human rights violations, but the ICC may intercede when states (whether states parties or non–states parties) fail to extradite or to prosecute appropriately those accused of international crimes.[77] As law professor John B. Quigley notes:

> [T]he court must give the state of nationality of a prospective defendant a chance to investigate. If the state of nationality prosecutes, the court must back off. Even if the state of nationality decides not to prosecute, the court must back off. Only if, in the prosecutor's opinion, the state of nationality is covering up a crime rather than acting genuinely would the court assert jurisdiction.[78]

It is in this context that the scope of the ICC's "universal jurisdiction"—that is, its ability to exercise jurisdiction even over nationals of non–states parties reasonably believed to have committed serious international crimes—must be understood. Testifying before the Senate Subcommittee on International Operations, Richard Dicker of Human Rights Watch observed,

> There is nothing novel about such a result. The core crimes in the ICC treaty are crimes of universal jurisdiction—that is, they are so universally condemned, that any nation in the world has the authority to exercise jurisdiction over suspects and perpetrators, without the consent of that individual's state of nationality . . .[79]

Nor, he added, is the "conferral of jurisdiction over nationals of non-State [sic] Parties through the mechanism of treaty law" unusual:

The United States is party to a dozen anti-terrorism treaties that provide universal jurisdiction for these crimes, and empower States Parties to investigate and prosecute perpetrators of any nationality found within their territory. The United States has exercised jurisdiction over foreigners on the basis of such treaties, without the consent of their state of nationality.[80]

What is new in this treaty is that the states within which these major international crimes are committed may now "allow the ICC to proceed in lieu of the state itself."[81]

The sovereignty-based objections that pervaded American opposition to the creation of the ICC are particularly interesting in that they appealed to the idea of legitimate authority. Since in a democracy legitimate authority is conferred by the consent of the governed, to "empower an international institution that is not accountable to the American electorate,"[82] to erect "an international authority with substantive power over individual Americans,"[83] was held to be "fundamentally at odds with the principle of popular sovereignty and self-government upon which the American Republic is founded"[84]:

> [T]he ICC would not be accountable to the people of the United States for its own actions. For example, no action taken by the American people, or their elected representatives, could alter in any way a decision of the ICC. This is extraordinary power.[85]

This argument is curious because it sets up what is essentially a false dichotomy—a staged choice between two mutually exclusive alternatives. It suggests that either we must embrace the idea that states are the legitimate sovereigns or abandon the notion of state sovereignty entirely.

Such a choice is spurious, and required only if the traditional view of state sovereignty is operative. As former Nuremberg tribunal prosecutor Benjamin B. Ferencz told the Rome Conference, "[O]utmoded traditions of State sovereignty must not derail the forward movement."[86] The ICC is an international legal mechanism for protecting human rights; it ensures that those who violate certain of those rights in particularly egregious ways can be held accountable by the rest of the international community and that they—or the state of which they are nationals—cannot successfully invoke sovereign immunity in order to deflect such accountability. The vision of international community embodied by the ICC, as well as that reflected by the use of extradition policy and of the Vienna Convention to protest the American death penalty, is one in which sovereignty entails responsibility and where the legitimacy of criticism of state conduct is not circumscribed by geography, by where territorial borders begin or end. When a sovereign entity consistently violates human rights—especially, as with the death penalty, when it does so as a matter of official state policy—its legitimacy is drawn into question. As Michael Joseph Smith contends,

> The more prevalent the belief that rightful title to rule entails respect for fundamental human rights, the more difficult it becomes for rulers who deny these rights to establish or maintain legitimacy. Ultimately, rulers who deny the legitimacy of human rights will be forced to rule without legitimacy; they will need to rely on fear, coercion, or the absence of viable alternatives.[87]

In a democracy, then, consent of the governed may be a necessary condition for sovereign legitimacy, but it is not the only such condition. The view of sovereignty that undergirds legal mechanisms such as the ICC (and that informs the international community's use of the Vienna Convention and extradition policy to bring the United States into compliance with prevailing human rights standards), makes this clear. The cardinal virtue of such a view of sovereignty "is that it allocates responsibility as well as authority."[88] Such responsibility is assumed by interdependent, sovereign entities existing within an international community whose members are connected by, and interreliant upon, numerous and growing structural processes. These are not only economic in nature, but include the types of political, legal, and juridical processes discussed here—as well as such instruments as extradition treaties and the Vienna Convention on Consular Relations and such institutions as the International Criminal Court and the European Union. These interconnections, shared institutions, and jointly-binding instruments give rise to shared responsibilities to remedy social injustices and end human rights violations.[89] They also offer, as we have seen in the case of the death penalty, vital means of addressing and remedying such violations.

The isolation of the United States within the international community with regard to the death penalty is growing complete. Americans might well be troubled to learn that the United States is out of step with an emerging worldwide consensus that the death penalty, even for the most heinous terrorist, "has no legitimate place in the penal systems of modern civilized societies."[90] Over the last 40 years, 97 countries abolished capital punishment, either in law or in practice, for an average rate of nearly two and a half abolitions per year. As of 2005, 129 nations were abolitionist in law or in practice, with only 68 retaining the death penalty.[91] The rate of change continues to accelerate, and these abolitions are more comprehensive than was previously the case. Initially, many nations abolished capital punishment for so-called ordinary crimes (such as murder during peacetime), while retaining the death penalty for wartime crimes and treason. Now nations are increasingly abolishing the death penalty for all crimes. As abolition grows broader and deeper, retentionist nations become increasingly isolated.

While isolation on a single international issue does not necessarily pose significant undesirable consequences for a resisting nation-state, these strong international trends carry with them potent and adverse legal, diplomatic, and practical consequences, as we explain more fully in the next two chapters. In 2003, the Council of Europe's Parliamentary Assembly president, Peter Schieder, stated that the Parliamentary Assembly "believes that everyone's right to life is fundamental and goes beyond geographical borders."[92] The entire Council of Europe now constitutes a death penalty–free zone.[93] Further, nearly all of the world's major democracies have abolished capital punishment. The United States, Japan, India, and South Korea alone retain it.[94] With few exceptions, state execution flourishes within autocratic countries commonly associated with egregious human rights violations; only China and Iran consistently execute more often than the United States.[95] So in executing its own citizens, America keeps company with some of the world's worst human rights abusers, and Americans are, for the most part, wholly oblivious of this. Moreover, just as nations that execute tend to be human rights abusers, American states that execute tend to be those with the worst historical civil rights records. It is predominately the former slaveholding states with long records of lynching that persisted well into the modern era that regularly execute. Similarly, these few American states carry out the majority of American executions, just as less than a handful of members of the international community carry out the vast majority of state-sanctioned killings. Four nations, China, Iran, Saudi Arabia, and the United States, accounted for 94 percent of all known executions in 2005.[96]

The isolation of those few jurisdictions that endorse state execution in the face of overwhelming rejection of it as a grave human rights violation is increasing, and increasingly costly. American ambassadors are frequently confronted on the issue, which is beginning to impact U.S. relations with all of Europe. Indeed, no single human rights issue more consistently, and adversely, affects American diplomatic relations with the countries of the European Union. These diplomatic pressures are more than mere abstractions. As scholars have pointed out, "U.S. diplomats abroad are increasingly called into meetings to answer foreign criticisms of the death penalty" and "important bilateral meetings with our closest allies are now consumed with responding to repeated official challenges to this practice."[97]

The consequences of these criticisms reach beyond time-consuming diplomatic protests; they adversely impact substantive cooperation as well. Felix G.

Rohatyn, former U.S. ambassador to France, recently wrote in the *New York Times:*

> [N]o single issue was viewed with as much hostility as our support for the death penalty. *Outlawed by every member of the European Union, the death penalty was, and is, viewed in Europe as a throwback to the Middle Ages.* When we require European support on security issues—Iran's nuclear program; the war in Iraq; North Korea's bomb; relations with China and Russia; the Middle East peace process—our job is made more difficult by the intensity of popular opposition in Europe to our policy.[98] (Emphasis added.)

Harold Hongju Koh, former assistant secretary of state for democracy, human rights and labor, and a Yale law professor, reports, "Important meetings between America and its allies are increasingly consumed with answering official protests against the death penalty."[99] Ambassador Rohatyn and Professor Koh are correct in seeing this as a major and continuing impediment to American diplomacy. In 2005, the president of the European Parliament, Josep Borrel, called for the abolition of capital punishment, saying, "Most unfortunately, in the U.S. the 1000th execution was carried out. The fact that it almost coincided with Human Rights Day makes this fact particularly poignant . . . For us in Europe, the right to life is an inalienable right. No one ever loses their right to life, no matter what they have done." He added that the "European Union has a duty to convince Americans to end the practice."[100] Indeed, the secretary general of the Council of Europe, Walter Schwimmer, has stated that the American death penalty "is our greatest concern."[101]

The international community is using every means it has to bring America into compliance with prevailing human rights standards. These include refusing to cooperate judicially with the United States, refusing to extradite without raising questions about the fundamental fairness of American sentencing practices, and insisting that the United States honor its commitments under the Vienna Convention. These states are rejecting the traditional view of sovereignty as absolute, and acknowledging the interdependence of the international community, together with the sovereign responsibilities that entails. State sovereignty, even American sovereignty, no longer implies the kind of opacity to outside scrutiny imbedded in the rule of non-inquiry; it is consistent with accountability to the international community. If America is to heed the lesson of its own persistent rhetoric of human rights, it will need to set aside the rhetoric of sovereign immunity and end the practice of state execution.

3 : Extradition
Holding the United States to a
Higher Human Rights Standard

This act will not stand. . . . We will find those who did it. We will smoke them out
of their holes, we'll get them running, and we'll bring them to justice.
—George W. Bush, referring to the events of September 11, 2001.[1]

EXTRADITION AND THE DEATH PENALTY

Law changes slowly, tarrying at society's rearguard, mocking Oliver Wendell
Holmes's complaint that "[I]t is revolting to have no better reason for a rule of
law than that it was laid down in the time of Henry IV."[2] International extradition of capital defendants is a swiftly changing exception in the law, with wider
ramifications affecting not only the death penalty, but also a broader human
rights critique of the U.S. justice system.

Extradition is the judicial process by which people who are charged with
crimes are brought from the jurisdiction where they are found to the place where
the crime was committed and where, ordinarily, trial is most appropriate. The
process is quite complex, subject to international treaties and well-barnacled
principles tracing from the Peace of Westphalia in 1648. Unlike the relatively
simple process of bringing a person from one U.S. state to another to answer
serious criminal charges, international cooperation is necessary to send a person
from one country to another. Politics, national pride, and differing perceptions
of human rights all enter into this otherwise treaty-bound process.

Extradition of a fugitive to stand trial or face imprisonment in another nation, and the related ability to secure evidence across borders, is increasingly
important to a globalizing world where people, money, and crime flow without regard to national boundaries. However, human rights norms provide an
important countervailing check and are affecting international relations and
law, including extradition law: much of the rest of the world has become reluctant to extradite persons facing the death penalty. This change may seem
small, but it both undermines the perceived fairness of death penalty administration and opens up broader human rights concerns.

If other nations can refuse to extradite in capital cases unless the United
States agrees to waive the death penalty, then they can also balk at extradition
in cases where American punishments offend international norms or where
U.S. courts (such as post–9/11 military tribunals) fail to enforce fundamental

international norms. Thus, the use of capital punishment results in international pressure in other areas, and has diplomatic and legal consequences as other nations more boldly question the practice of state execution and American commitment to human rights.

America's stubborn embrace of the death penalty will unquestionably hinder international relations in new, multiple, and largely unpredictable ways. It may well be that America will not abandon the ultimate penalty until the rest of the world compels an end to the practice. Thus, the problem of extraditing people who face execution is a manifestation of a much larger problem and has broader consequences than one might at first imagine.

EXTRADITION AND HUMAN RIGHTS

For nearly two hundred years, from the first extradition treaty between the United States and Great Britain in 1794, until 1991, extradition practice remained almost entirely unaffected by capital punishment.[3] Most nations considered the fairness of neither trial nor punishment. Now, in much of the world, extradition is routinely conditioned upon agreement to forgo the death penalty. Moreover, what began in 1991[4] as a halting, limited impediment to extradition in *some* potentially capital cases is now solidifying into a rigid international rule barring *all* extradition requests absent an agreement to waive capital punishment. Many abolitionist nations will deny extradition even for an al-Qaeda terrorist, unless the receiving nation gives assurances barring the death penalty.

The reasons for complying unconditionally with extradition requests, regardless of the ferocity of punishment or the unfairness of the trial, reach back to seventeenth-century notions of the nation-state as the sole actor in international law. Under this view, individuals had no remedies under international law because it was for the states to take up the cases of their citizens abroad. As one eminent scholar observed, this was "far from satisfactory from the individual's point of view,"[5] because it was left to the state to take up his case; the country might fail to do so for reasons unrelated to the merits, or it might do so slowly and ineffectually.[6] Thus, the individual was wholly at the mercy of the state, which might well be unresponsive and insensitive.

Individuals were not subjects of international law and could not be prosecuted for human rights violations. Even heads of state and officials conducting an unjust war escaped prosecution under international law. This practice was so thoroughly embedded in international law that the few odd exceptions illustrate, if not prove, it, such as Napoleon Bonaparte's exile to Saint Helena in 1815 and the victorious allies' unsuccessful attempt to prosecute Kaiser Wilhelm II after World War I.

Thus, nations did little to pursue human rights objectives through international law. Wrongdoers were left to the courts of the various nation-states and individuals had no redress under international law.[7] Often, nations either lacked interest in the individual citizen or had conflicting interests, and thus failed to protect their citizens from another nation's human rights abuses. Most nation-states had even less interest in general human rights abuses—even genocide—where their own citizens were not involved.

Prior to World War II, noninterference in the affairs of others, as noted in chapter 2, was one of the strongest norms of international law. Domestic interests are at their strongest when it comes to regulating a nation's judicial system. Moreover, criminal law and punishment within the larger judicial system are among the most strongly defended islands of noninterference. While commercial law has long bent to international mercantile needs, the criminal law has not done so and has been considered exempt from international scrutiny. Thus, the human rights revolution and resistance to capital punishment run headlong into one of the strongest and best defended areas of traditional, absolute sovereignty—the right of a nation to run its criminal justice system free from the influence of, and interference by, other nations. Extradition in capital cases is part of this trend toward applying international human rights norms to individuals and away from an unqualified view of the nation-state as sole actor under international law.

THE RULE OF NON-INQUIRY

The general rule of noninterference applies to extradition law through the rule of non-inquiry.[8] Under this rule, nations faced with an extradition request focus narrowly on the specific extradition treaty without determining whether the receiving nation will act fairly. These issues often are confined to questions such as: is the person being requested correctly identified? Is there reason to believe he or she committed a crime in the requesting nation? Is the act a crime in both nations? Is it among the class of crimes contemplated by the extradition treaty? Is it a political crime? Beyond these limited concerns, the nation fielding the request does not inquire about the adequacy of the requesting nation's justice system or its treatment of offenders—hence the rule of non-inquiry. Since fairness itself is not in issue, the fairness of a particular punishment, such as the death penalty, is not considered (in the absence of specific treaty language permitting consideration).

Of course, there have been exceptions to this rule. For example, Portugal abolished capital punishment in 1867 (later reinstated it and then again abolished it) and negotiated an extradition treaty in 1908 with the United States, which contained mandatory language denying extradition in capital cases unless assurances were given barring the death penalty.[9] Plainly, this was an anomaly, like the application of quasi-criminal international law to Napoleon or Kaiser Wilhelm II.

Subject to a narrow exception barring extradition to a nation where torture or inhumane treatment is likely, the rule of non-inquiry has been and continues to be a cornerstone of American extradition policy. The rule outlined by Justice Oliver Wendell Holmes in 1911 remains, to this day, the American position on extradition.

> It is common in extradition cases to attempt to bring to bear all the factitious niceties of a criminal trial at common law. But it is a waste of time. For while of course a man is not to be sent from the country merely upon demand or surmise, yet if there is presented, even in somewhat untechnical form according to our ideas, such reasonable ground to suppose him guilty as to make it proper that he should be tried, good faith to the demanding government requires his surrender . . . *We are bound by the existence of an extradition treaty to assume that the trial will be fair.*[10] (Emphasis added.)

The rule of non-inquiry applies equally to all countries with extradition treaties with the United States and is not limited to countries with stellar or even modestly fair judicial systems. The rule against inquiring into another country's justice system, likewise applies to inquiring about the severity of a punishment, including the death penalty. Thus, in the death penalty context, the United States has traditionally expected other nations to extradite persons back to the United States. It also means that (assuming the existence of a valid extradition treaty) the United States will extradite a suspect to a country that might impose capital punishment.[11]

While America is not alone in adhering to the rule of non-inquiry, it is becoming increasingly lonely. Intensified interest in human rights feeds interest in, and international opposition to, the death penalty; at the same time, concern about the death penalty broadens understanding of human rights issues and enhances the ability of the international community to deal with them. This has repercussions not only for the American capital punishment system, but also for its foreign policy. As nations feel ever more free to criticize America's justice system, they are freer to reject extradition for other human rights reasons. Also, the problem of extraditing terrorists, who may be eligible for the death penalty or arguably unfair trials, is beginning to impede larger American foreign policy objectives.

Jens Soering's murderous rampage in Virginia, killing his girlfriend's parents, might well have been just another vicious double homicide, with little repercussion beyond the immediate parties. Had he been caught, convicted, and executed in the United States, his case might have merited only the odd passing footnote, just another capital case out of thousands since reinstitution of the death penalty in 1976.

Instead, Soering, a German national, fled to and was captured in Great Britain, setting off an international chain of events, with continuing reverberations today that limit America's ability to extradite in capital cases, put additional pressure on the machinery of death, and call into question the fairness of the American justice system. The *Soering* case provides the intellectual underpinning for many human rights–based objections to extradition under international law. It may well be one of the most cited international cases and is the most important international extradition case of the twentieth century.

Jens Soering, aged eighteen, suffered from severe mental illness, which lessened but did not eliminate "mental responsibility for his acts."[12] His personality became submerged into that of his profoundly disturbed and delusional girlfriend, who persuaded him to kill her parents.[13] Both the United States and Germany sought to extradite him for the two homicides occurring in Virginia. (Germany, unlike the United States, can try its citizens for acts committed abroad.) Since Germany lacks capital punishment, extradition to that country would have eliminated the possibility of a death penalty sentence for Jens.

Although Germany was not allowed to extradite Soering for trial, the fact that it pursued such an uncommon strategy showed the increasing European aversion toward the death penalty. Germany would not likely have interfered in what was otherwise a minor extradition matter between the United Kingdom and the United States, but for the possibility of the death penalty for one of its nationals. The case also demonstrates a heightened sensitivity toward consideration of international human rights norms in extradition matters, and a concomitant erosion of the rule of non-inquiry.[14]

The United Kingdom–United States Extradition Treaty in effect at the time allowed the United Kingdom to deny extradition unless assurances were given that the death penalty would not be carried out. The Virginia prosecutor would only say that he would tell "the judge at the time of sentencing that it is the wish of the United Kingdom that the death penalty should not be imposed or carried out."[15] Nonetheless, the prosecutor intended to seek the death penalty. Despite this nonassurance, the United Kingdom decided to allow the extradition to the United States and the case wound its way to the European Court of Human Rights.[16]

The then-governing law, the 1953 European Convention for the Protection of Human Rights and Fundamental Freedoms, not only did not abolish capital punishment, but also allowed it under certain narrow circumstances.[17] Moreover, the United Kingdom had not, as of the *Soering* case, ratified Optional Protocol 6 (requiring abolition) to the Convention on Human Rights.[18] Thus, despite Amnesty International's friend-of-the-court efforts, *Soering* did not present a promising case for an absolute rule against capital case extradition.

Nonetheless, *Soering* offered difficulties for the court. Article 3 of the Convention on Human Rights provides that "no one shall be subjected to torture or to inhuman or degrading treatment or punishment."[19] While the death penalty might not be a direct human rights violation under this convention, it was an open question whether its administration constituted "inhuman or degrading treatment or punishment."

Jens Soering presented a sympathetic case for this sort of thinking. He was young, highly suggestible, and suffered from a mental disorder that likely would have provided a partial defense (short of the all-or-nothing insanity defense) in Great Britain, though not in Virginia. One factor counting heavily against extradition, unless assurances barring the death penalty were given, was that if he were sentenced to death he could expect to spend six to eight years on death row, giving rise to the "death-row phenomenon." The death row phenomenon, as a bar to capital punishment, was later fleshed out in 1993 by Great Britain's Judicial Privy Council (which serves as Jamaica's highest court) in *Pratt v. Jamaica*, where the court encountered prisoners who had languished for sixteen years in terrible conditions on Jamaica's death row.

> There is an instinctive revulsion against the prospect of hanging a man after he has been held under sentence of death for many years. What gives rise to this instinctive revulsion? The answer can only be our humanity; we regard it as an inhuman act to keep a man facing the agony of execution over a long extended period of time.[20]

The notion that the length of time spent on death row can constitute cruel and unusual punishment may strike many Americans as peculiar, since in the United States inmates' appeals take time. Nonetheless, it is a concept that has gained sympathy in international courts, and it plays an important role in maintaining international pressure against the death penalty.[21]

The prosecutor's tepid assurance that he would advise the judge of the United Kingdom's position while continuing to pursue execution, left little doubt that the death penalty, and the death-row phenomenon, remained a realistic possibility. In retrospect, it now seems obvious that U.S. interests would have to give way, but it remained to be seen just how problematic for American foreign policy this case would become.

The European Court of Human Rights held that extradition under these conditions would constitute inhuman or degrading treatment. The death penalty was not an absolute bar to extradition, but extradition courts were to engage in a balancing process to determine whether and under what circumstances capital punishment was appropriate. It is this balancing approach that is so problematic from the U.S. viewpoint, because it opens the way to questioning other human rights problems.

The *Soering* case is important for two reasons. First, in undercutting the rule of non-inquiry, it not only calls death penalty cases into question, but it gives international and domestic courts a basis for greater scrutiny of other kinds of cases. This type of scrutiny can, for example, extend to post–9/11 military tribunals, life imprisonment without the possibility of parole, and juvenile and women's prisons. Second, the capital case rule is gradually becoming unconditional. For an increasing number of abolitionist nations, the rule is: no extradition without assurances barring the death penalty. This, in turn, undercuts the perception of the evenhandedness of American justice: the likelihood of execution turns on the morally irrelevant fact of where the fugitive is caught, rather than on individual guilt. Ordinarily, punishment hinges upon the circumstances of the crime and the individual committing that crime. Coincidental circumstances surrounding a fugitive's capture, in this context, means that whether someone is eligible for death is solely the result of whether he or she must be extradited to a nation that imposes state execution. Thus, at least in this circumstance, evenhanded application of the death penalty becomes impossible.

THE U.S. POSITION AND ATTEMPTS TO BYPASS EXTRADITION

Except in narrow circumstances involving the Convention against Torture and Other Forms of Cruel, Inhuman or Degrading Treatment or Punishment, America continues to adhere to the rule of non-inquiry.[22] It objects when other nations implicitly criticize the American justice system by conditioning extradition on U.S. willingness to forego capital punishment. Former U.S. attorney general John Ashcroft outlined the American position in his response to Europe's refusal to extradite al-Qaeda members facing the death penalty: "I believe the law, which is clear in relation to capital punishment in the United States, is a law that we ought to be able to enforce."[23] From the U.S. perspective, then, international balkiness on extradition violates American sovereignty, impedes U.S. law enforcement, and obstructs foreign policy goals in pursuing terrorists. Moreover, in cases where it has to seek extradition, the United States not only must increasingly provide assurances on the death penalty, but must sometimes forego military tribunals,[24] and occasionally has been unable to extradite at all.[25]

The U. S. Supreme Court, in United States v. Alvarez-Machain, permitted American law enforcement officials to avoid extradition issues by kidnapping fugitives found in other countries.[26] Obviously, abduction is not always practicable, and in any event its use has caused so many foreign policy difficulties that it is not likely to become a common way to circumvent extradition.[27] As a result of the "storm of international protest" provoked by the decision,[28] the government's ability to abduct fugitives without extradition has been greatly limited.

Department of Justice guidelines now prohibit federal officers from kidnapping suspects in other countries without advance approval. Moreover, after the Supreme Court's decision, the Mexican government suspended U.S. Drug Enforcement Administration activities in Mexico, and later negotiated a treaty with Washington (not yet ratified) that prohibits transborder abductions.[29] Finally, an American bounty hunter and his brother, who abducted and returned a fugitive, were charged and ordered to stand trial by a Mexican judge.[30]

The recent backlash against extraordinary renditions (whereby a person captured in one country is transported to a third country, presumably to avoid application of U.S. legal protections) is likely to make the kidnapping of fugitives more difficult. The press has widely reported that the CIA has resorted to extraordinary renditions to send suspected terrorists to other countries, where they are tortured for information.[31] This has raised a firestorm of protest. While extraordinary rendition is not quite the same thing as kidnapping in lieu of extradition, nonetheless, no independent nation could long tolerate this kind of intrusion without political backlash. The inquiries arising in Europe and Canada over this issue, and their own complicity therein, will likely affect kidnappings of any kind. Abductions, regardless of whether returning a fugitive or "rendering" a terrorist, may be a dying tool; and it surely will not be useful in most capital cases, where international scrutiny is at its highest.

Deportation can provide another way to circumvent formal extradition procedures in potentially capital cases. Some countries do allow deportation in lieu of extradition, but they are unlikely to do so in capital cases. The use of deportation in this context is likewise coming under criticism, and may not be an option under the laws of some nations. The South African Constitutional Court, for example, has held that deportation may not be used in lieu of extradition. The case, Mohamed v. President of the Republic of South Africa, arose out of the al-

Quaeda bombings of U.S. embassies in Africa and involved potential capital punishment in the United States.[32] It is likely to be particularly influential in other Commonwealth countries,[33] making deportation as an end-run around extradition increasingly difficult. Additionally, the United Nations Human Rights Committee weighed in on the issue in *Judge v. Canada* (discussed below), prohibiting deportation in capital cases and potentially affecting most, if not all, abolitionist nations.[34]

Finally, deportation or expulsion, in the absence of a threat to national security, must permit formal case review. Otherwise, summary deportation violates Article 13 of the International Covenant on Civil and Political Rights (ICCPR).[35] Given that most nations have ratified the ICCPR, using deportation as a way to avoid formal proceedings violates international law.

Because kidnapping and deportation are not likely to be effective, or lawful, extradition will continue to be the primary method of bringing criminal suspects to the United States. Thus, erosion of the rule of non-inquiry in potential capital cases will continue to be an impediment both to law enforcement and to the U.S. government's foreign policy objectives.

EUROPEAN EXTRADITION IN CAPITAL CASES

Europe has become a death penalty–free zone. In all of Europe (including the formerly communist countries and Russia), only Belarus continues to execute. Both the European Union (twenty-five nations) and the Council of Europe (forty-six nations, ranging from Iceland in the Atlantic to Russia's Pacific coast, and Scandinavia on the Arctic to Turkey on the Eastern Mediterranean)[36] now prohibit absolutely extradition in all potentially capital cases unless assurances are given barring the death penalty. This occurred in two stages.

First, there were a series of cases beginning in 1991 from various European courts denying extradition in death penalty cases, with most allowing extradition only after assurances were given that the death penalty would not be sought. Gradually, it became harder and harder to extradite in capital cases. As a result of piecemeal litigation, the presumption against returning individuals to a country where they faced the death penalty became stronger and stronger, until extradition from Europe in capital cases, absent assurances as to the death penalty, became practically impossible.

Second, treaty law came to recognize what had in practice already come about. In 2001, the European Union adopted the Charter of Fundamental Rights, which bars extradition where there is a serious risk of being subjected to the death penalty. And in 2003 the European Union signed an extradition treaty with the United States that allowed the member states of the European

Union to "grant extradition on the condition that the death penalty shall not be imposed on the person sought."[37] No European Union member-state retains the death penalty, and E.U. members now routinely refuse extradition unless capital punishment is prohibited.

Similarly, the Council of Europe's Resolution 1271[38] states:

> The Assembly, which has declared itself to be strongly opposed to capital punishment and which has succeeded in ridding Europe of the death penalty, tolerates no exceptions to this principle. Therefore, prior to the extradition of suspected terrorists to countries that still apply the death penalty, assurances must be obtained that this penalty will not be sought.
>
> The Assembly also insists on the fact that member states should under no circumstances extradite persons who risk being subjected to ill-treatment . . . being subjected to a trial which does not respect the fundamental principles of a fair trial, or in a period of conflict, to standards which fall below those enshrined in the Geneva Convention.

Two things should be plain. At least as to Europe, no one will be extradited if he or she faces the death penalty. This rule is unqualified. Moreover, the erosion of the rule of non-inquiry has expanded beyond death penalty cases. Fair trials and fair treatment, even in a time of conflict, are expected, and extradition will not be forthcoming where those conditions are not met. Thus, the small death penalty exception to the rule of non-inquiry has expanded, and it now impacts prosecutions stemming from the war against terrorism. One cannot be absolutely certain whether this might have occurred without *Soering*'s response to the U.S. death penalty, but one cannot avoid making the connection.

CANADA'S REVERSAL ON EXTRADITION

The policy of seeking assurances before extradition in capital cases has spread beyond Europe to many other nations, most notably Mexico, Canada, and South Africa. What began as an equitable balancing approach has become a nearly conclusive rule, not just in Europe, but also among most abolitionist nations.

The Canadian example is instructive. Notwithstanding a treaty that allowed the Canadian government to seek assurances in capital cases, the Supreme Court of Canada in 1991 permitted extradition to the United States in two cases, *Reference Re Ng Extradition* and *Kindler v. Minister of Justice* without such assurances.[39] The minister of justice had complete discretion in the matter, and the Canadian courts would not interfere. In both cases, the accused were extradited to the United States, where each faced capital punishment.

Both cases proceeded, after the fact, to the United Nations Human Rights

Committee, which held that the death penalty did not create a per se bar to extradition in capital cases.[40] The Human Rights Committee's decision distinguished *Soering*, where the suspect's age and mental condition had militated against extradition. The Human Rights Committee held that the minister had not erred in the *Kindler* case,[41] but reached the opposite result in *Ng*, where the accused faced a painful death by cyanide asphyxiation.[42] Thus, in 1991 the rule remained a fluid balancing approach that permitted at least some extraditions in the face of a potential death sentence.[43]

The most startling and clearest indicator of the direction of death penalty extradition law after *Soering* is unquestionably the Canadian Supreme Court's dramatic about-face only ten years later, in *United States v. Burns*.[44] Two Canadian citizens, Burns and Rafay, faced capital murder charges in Washington State. The minister of justice ordered extradition without seeking assurances. A unanimous Canadian Supreme Court reversed, holding that while the Canadian Charter of Rights and Freedoms did not create an absolute rule barring extradition of death-eligible persons, nonetheless, "in the absence of exceptional circumstances . . . assurances in death penalty cases are always constitutionally required."[45] The court declined to speculate on what might constitute "exceptional circumstances." This is as close to a conclusive presumption as one can get without actually having it. *Burns* did nominally approve the "balancing process," but, by 2001, it had moved to a rationale that is far more compatible with an absolute rule than the equitable fact-balancing rule of *Soering*.

The largest part of the *Burns* opinion turns on "the factors that appear to weigh against extradition without assurances that the death penalty will not be imposed."[46] Most of the reasons for refusing to extradite in this case revolve around matters that could not be adequately addressed by any retentionist nation and, indeed, revolve around trends that are only likely to cut more and more against capital punishment. The court wrote,

> It is, however, incontestable that capital punishment . . . engages the underlying values of the prohibition against cruel and unusual punishment. It is final. It is irreversible. Its imposition has been described as arbitrary. Its deterrent value has been doubted. Its implementation necessarily causes psychological and physical suffering. It has been rejected by the Canadian Parliament for offences committed within Canada.[47]

Much of the opinion focuses on Canadian and international initiatives to abolish the death penalty. Very little of this supports ad hoc determinations that would even occasionally permit the extradition of someone who faced the possibility of capital punishment. Indeed, the court pointed out:

> [I]n 1948, the year in which the Universal Declaration of Human Rights was adopted, only eight countries were abolitionist. In January 1998 . . . 90 countries retained the death penalty, while 61 were totally abolitionist . . . and 27 were considered to be abolitionist de facto . . . a total of 102 abolitionist countries. These general statistics mask the important point that abolitionist states include all of the major democracies except some of the United States, India and Japan . . . 85 percent of the world's executions in 1999 were accounted for by only five countries: the United States, China, the Congo, Saudi Arabia and Iran.[48]

Most of the analysis dealt with the fact that innocent people are being convicted of capital crimes. The court noted the repeated calls for moratoria, the Illinois experience (where there had been thirteen exonerations of death-sentenced inmates), and research disclosing a two-out-of-three error rate in the capital punishment system.[49] This is important because, unlike some other administrative critiques of the death penalty, execution of the innocent is not a flaw that can possibly be remedied. When one looks at administrative problems in any judicial system, one generally reviews things that are correctable. If fixed, the objection disappears. If due process is being denied, it can be put right. Presumably, speeding up the process could lessen the "death-row phenomenon," but that would almost surely increase the numbers of miscarriages of justice. It is hard to imagine a judicial system that did not convict the innocent, and in death penalty countries, this means sometimes executing the innocent.

In 2003, the United Nations Human Rights Committee (UNHRC) may have concluded the matter when reversing its earlier balancing approach in *Ng* and *Kindler*, it ruled against Canada in *Roger Judge v. Canada*.[50] Judge had escaped to Canada after having been sentenced to death in the state of Pennsylvania. Canada deported him, thus circumventing formal extradition procedures. The Human Rights Committee ruled that Canada, by failing to require assurances that the death penalty not be carried out, had violated the International Covenant on Civil and Political Rights:

> For countries that have abolished the death penalty, there is an obligation not to expose a person to the real risk of its application. Thus, they may not remove, either by deportation or extradition, individuals from their jurisdiction if it may be reasonably anticipated that they will be sentenced to death, without ensuring that the death sentence will not be carried out.[51]

Thus, assuming that Canada accepts this authoritative decision by the UN Human Rights Committee's ruling, it joins the Council of Europe and the European Union in prohibiting extradition in potentially capital cases unless there are assurances that the death penalty will not be imposed. This ruling applies to all nations that are party to the International Covenant on Civil and Political Rights and that have also abolished capital punishment, and not just to the fifty state parties to the Second Optional Protocol to the International Covenant on Civil and Political Rights, Aiming at the Abolition of the Death Penalty.[52] Indeed, Canada at the time of *Judge* had not yet signed the Second Optional Protocol, yet the ruling applied explicitly to Canada. This remarkable turnabout demonstrates the speed with which international opinion and law is changing with respect to capital punishment.

Human rights researcher Mark Warren points out that the real significance of the *Judge* decision goes far beyond its influence on Canadian extraditions and deportations, as important as that may be to the United States. "More than 150 nations are now parties to the International Covenant on Civil and Political Rights,[53] including virtually every country that has abolished the death penalty in law or in practice."[54] Thus, the rule against extradition in capital cases, unless assurances are given, is becoming a rule of international law and is likely to be accepted by a majority of the world's nations. *Judge* may well become one of the most important decisions ever made by the United Nations Human Rights Committee.

Finally, in November 2005, Canada signed the Second Optional Protocol. This commitment to worldwide abolition, combined with the Human Rights Committee's decision in *Judge*, makes it exceedingly unlikely that the Canadian minister of justice will ever be able to find "extraordinary circumstances" leading to extradition without assurances in capital cases, as permitted under *Burns*. Moreover, cases from around the world suggest increasing hostility to the death penalty, and the rule prohibiting extradition to countries that employ execution, absent assurances that it will not be used, is becoming unconditional. This trend gives nations like Canada the ability to resist U.S. pressure.

SOUTH AFRICA: A SPECIAL CASE

South Africa provides an important example of this trend away from extradition unless the death penalty is abandoned. Many African nations have abolished the death penalty in the last few years, making that continent one of the fast-changing areas in this respect.[55] Even there, the South African example stands out. The South African Constitutional Court abolished the death penalty in 1995, only a few years after the demise of apartheid.[56] Progress on abolition, however, did not end with that landmark case.

In a potentially capital case involving an al-Qaeda member, the court announced an absolute rule against either extradition or deportation in lieu of extradition.[57] Khalfan Khamis Mohamed, a member of al-Qaeda, was sought by the United States because of his role in the embassy bombings in Kenya and Tanzania. Found in South Africa, he was deported to the United States. Because immigration authorities treated the matter as a deportation, no assurances of any kind with respect to the death penalty were sought. A codefendant, Mahmoud Mahmud Salim, was extradited to the United States from Germany, which sought and received assurances against imposition of the death penalty.

The South African Constitutional Court held that "the handing over of Mohamed to the United States government agents for removal by them to the United States was unlawful."[58] Since Mohamed had already been deported to the United States and was in fact in the middle of his capital murder trial, the court's options were limited; it ordered "the full text of this judgment to be drawn to the attention of . . . the Federal Court . . . as a matter of urgency."[59] The U.S. district court judge ruled that Mohamed could present the South African court's ruling to the jury at the penalty phase of trial to show that the other equally guilty defendant's life would be spared.[60] The jury was not able to reach a unanimous verdict on the life or death issue, and Mohamed was sentenced to life imprisonment.

While the South African Constitutional Court ultimately relied on the South African constitution, it analyzed international extradition law in capital cases at length. Importantly, the court laid down an unqualified rule not dependent on any fact balancing or other ad hoc determination. While this decision is not binding on other nations or on international human rights tribunals, its reasoning is likely to be highly influential[61] and is yet another indication both that the rule against extradition from abolitionist countries is becoming unequivocally firm and that the rule of non-inquiry is becoming less rigid.

MEXICO

Mexico is a particularly interesting example of how the erosion of the rule of non-inquiry has proceeded beyond the death penalty. Mexico abolished capital punishment for all ordinary (nonmilitary) crimes in 1976 and does not ordinarily imprison for life without the possibility of parole. Mexico has refused extradition (absent assurances) in capital cases since 1978, and from 2001 to 2005 it also sought assurances that extradited prisoners not receive life imprisonment without the possibility of parole. Not surprisingly, given its long border with the United States, Mexico presents a particularly nettlesome problem for its northern neighbor, in that fugitives often flee to Mexico, thus avoiding both life imprisonment without the possibility of parole and the death penalty.

In 2005, the Mexican Supreme Court reconsidered its position on life imprisonment, and reverted to extraditing in life-without-parole cases.[62] Mexico's aversion to capital punishment, however, remains solid—and, also in 2005, it removed the last vestiges of the death penalty for some remaining military penal code crimes. (Mexico last executed for ordinary crimes in 1937 and the last military execution occurred in 1961).[63]

Mexico, unlike South Africa, sometimes resorts to deportation instead of extradition, and this can be used to avoid restrictions that might otherwise halt extradition.[64] Deportation, however, does not appear to have been used in capital cases, and is unlikely to affect significantly the practice of seeking assurances in such cases.

As nations such as Canada, Germany, South Africa, and Spain,[65] turn away from life imprisonment without the possibility of parole, the practice of seeking assurances in such cases may spread. This could cause greater scrutiny of other U.S. penal practices, which are generally harsher than those of most other democracies. If so, the small exception to the rule of non-inquiry created by *Soering* will have become indeed problematic. Other countries, such as Colombia,[66] Costa Rica,[67] and Spain,[68] continue to refuse to extradite in cases involving life imprisonment unless the United States agrees to a lesser punishment. While these countries do not have the numbers of fugitives that Mexico has, the issue continues to live on and is further evidence of the erosion of the rule of non-inquiry. Whether or not this erosion would have happened regardless of capital punishment, it seems that revulsion occasioned by American executions has hastened that effect. It is undeniable that this trend—whether viewed as good or bad—places restrictions on the wars on terror and drugs that the current Bush administration does not want.

THE REST OF THE AMERICAS

Two major international treaties on the death penalty apply to the Americas. The Second Optional Protocol to the International Covenant on Civil and Political Rights, Aiming at Abolition of the Death Penalty, which applies worldwide, and the Protocol to the American Convention on Human Rights to Abolish the Death Penalty.[69] Both provide for total abolition but allow wartime exceptions. Moreover, the American Convention on Human Rights limits the death penalty to "serious crimes" and provides that "the death penalty shall not be reestablished in states that have abolished it." Each of these treaties provides cover for abolitionist nations seeking to limit extradition in potentially capital cases. Moreover, the Inter-American Convention on Extradition requires assurances against capital punishment, life imprisonment, or degrading punishment.[70]

This covenant has been ratified by five abolitionist nations (Costa Rica, Ecuador, Panama, Haiti, and Venezuela) and two retentionist nations (Antigua and St. Lucia).[71] Assuming that this treaty gains additional parties, the United States can expect increased difficulties in capital and life-imprisonment cases in its own hemisphere. In any event, the clear trend is away from extraditing where execution is a realistic possibility, and life without the possibility of parole is also under attack.

Costa Rica provides an example of just how entrenched many nations are on this point. Russell Winstead, who was accused of the vicious robbery and murder of an elderly woman in Kentucky, eluded authorities by fleeing to Costa Rica. Hopkins County Commonwealth's Attorney David Messamore had to agree to waive both the death penalty and life without parole in order to secure Winstead's return:

> Unless a miracle happens, the only way he can be extradited to the United States for trial on murder would require a waiver of those two options as punishment . . . And I have been told by the (U.S.) Secretary of State's office that if I did not do that, then he would be in Costa Rica forever. They wouldn't return him.[72]

Plainly, the Costa Rican position took Kentuckians and their officials by surprise.

In one highly publicized (and discomforting) case, the Dominican Republic required and received assurances that the death penalty would not be imposed on Alejandro de Asa Sanchez, who stood trial for murder, assault and narcotics trafficking. The Justice Department attempted to renege and sought to proceed against Sanchez capitally. U.S. District Judge Jack Weinstein criticized the government's position saying, "[W]hen a person is extradited with the limitation imposed by the extraditing state that a conviction will not result in a death sentence, federal courts will honor the request."[73] Nonetheless, he ordered briefing and the Justice Department, facing a no-doubt embarrassing loss, backed down and decided to honor its agreement with the Dominican Republic. One can imagine extraditions grinding to a halt had the United States not kept its word.

The Organization of American States involves all thirty-five nations of the Americas. Of these nations, only the United States, Guyana, Guatemala, and Belize (as well as many of the island nations of the Caribbean) retain the death penalty. The abolitionist nations (like Costa Rica and Colombia) that refuse to extradite where a life sentence might be in play will certainly also refuse to extradite in capital cases unless appropriate assurances are given.

Even more telling, eight nations in the Americas—including Canada, and Venezuela many countries in Latin America—are abolitionist for all crimes, including treason and crimes during wartime. The movement in the Americas against state executions is far more advanced than most U.S. citizens realize. The American Convention on Human Rights contains language protecting against "cruel, inhuman, or degrading punishment," and is similar to Article 3 of the European Convention for the Protection of Human Rights and Fundamental Freedoms, the subject of the *Soering* case. This could result in further limitations on extraditing in capital cases.

Moreover, even the Caribbean, the hemisphere's last major bastion of capital punishment outside of the United States, may be changing. The Judicial Committee of the Privy Council has struck down as unconstitutional the mandatory death penalty statutes of the Bahamas, St. Vincent and the Grenadines, St. Lucia, Grenada, St. Kitts and Nevis, Dominica, Belize, Antigua, and Barbados.[74] While capital punishment remains in effect in this region, executions have been stalled, and there is pressure for change. Only Trinidad and Tobago, Saint Kitts and Nevis, and the Bahamas have hanged anyone in over a decade[75] and no one has been executed in the Bahamas since January 2000.[76] If these nations finally relinquish the ultimate punishment, U.S. isolation in its own hemisphere will be nearly complete, and extradition without assurances in capital cases may become regionally impossible.

ASIA, THE PACIFIC ISLANDS, AND THE MIDDLE EAST

Much of Asia, the Pacific Islands, and the Middle East retain capital punishment and continue to extradite death-eligible persons to the United States without question. Indeed, death penalty support is stronger in Asia than in any other region. According to the 2000 Gallup International Millennium Survey, 63 percent of Asians supported capital punishment, while only 21 percent opposed and it, 16 percent did not know. Asia sees more executions than any other, with China, Iran, and Saudi Arabia leading all other nations in 2005.[77] Exceptions include some of the America's closest allies in the region, including Israel, Australia, and New Zealand, which do not have capital punishment and will not extradite to those nations that do. Many of the Pacific Island states also lack capital punishment, as do both Cambodia and Nepal. Moreover, a number of Asian countries have not executed anyone in decades and are considered abolitionist in practice.[78]

The whispers of change are percolating through the continent of Asia. Uzbekistan will abolish capital punishment beginning January 1, 2008. A moratorium on executions covers much of that part of central Asia that was formerly part of the Soviet Union. South Korea has not executed anyone since 1997, and its president has called for abolition. Likewise, India's president has called for abolition(India's last execution occurred in August 2004).[79] There have been persistent calls for abolition in Japan and Taiwan. As Japan's minister of justice put it, "From the standpoint of the theory of civilizations, I believe that the general trend from a long-term perspective will be to move toward abolition."[80]

Even the historically pro-death penalty Middle East may see slow change. First, Islamic scholars are beginning to lay the groundwork in Shari`a (traditional Islamic religious law) for a broader conception of human rights generally,[81] and for a much narrower ambit for capital punishment.[82] Second, political change seems possible: Jordan, for example, appears to be moving toward abolition.[83]

Finally, the Philippines has (again) abolished the death penalty. After the fall of the Marcos dictatorship in 1987, it was the first Asian nation to abolish state execution. After a wave of violent crime, the death penalty was reinstated in 1994 and executions resumed until 2000, when the president imposed (and later lifted) a moratorium. Then in early 2006, President Gloria Macapagel-Arroyo pledged to commute the sentences of more than twelve hundred death-row inmates and pushed legislation to again abolish capital punishment. This prompted applause from the European Union, Amnesty International, the Catholic Church, and other groups[84]—and anguish from some anti-crime groups.[85] Finally, in June 2006, the Philippine Congress approved a bill repealing capital punishment and President Arroyo signed the bill into law.[86]

Even China has responded to international pressure and adopted new procedural rules that will likely curtail executions,[87] although even with this change it will undoubtedly remain the world's leading executioner. The death penalty will probably recede slowly from this region, leaving the United States even more isolated and increasingly unable to extradite freely in capital cases. Nations may abolish capital punishment and yet extradite capital defendants without assurances; abolition does not automatically equate with refusal to extradite. But nations abolishing the death penalty are emboldened to restrict extradition and most undoubtedly will.

ABOLITIONIST PRESSURE MOUNTS

Europe, most of the Americas, and increasing portions of Africa and Asia no longer extradite in capital cases. As these numbers grow, the only way the United States will be able to extradite in these cases will be to offer assurances that the death penalty will not be imposed. To the extent that these changes in international law reflect policy and attitudinal transformations around the world, they will pose even greater problems for the United States. *Soering* weakened the rule of non-inquiry, and its logic cannot be confined to capital cases. Inquiry into the fairness of another nation's judicial and penal systems is broadening to encompass other human rights issues, and includes scrutiny of military courts and of juvenile and women's prisons.[88] For example, as we have seen, Germany's highest constitutional court allowed the extradition of a suspected al-Qaeda operative only on the conditions that he not face the death penalty, that he not be tried by a military tribunal, and that he not be interned in a camp like Guantanamo Bay.[89]

The death penalty increasingly isolates the United States; makes extradition in capital cases more difficult, exposes the entire criminal justice system to international scrutiny, and impedes the wars on terrorism and drugs, which recent administrations have embraced. While these problems will not, by themselves, end state execution, they do make the affair more difficult.

4 : Honoring Treaty Commitments
The Vienna Convention on Consular Relations

> *[T]here is resistance to international law and enforcement, cries of "sover-*
> *eignty," even by countries that respect human rights and have effective national*
> *systems for their enforcement. The United States, too, invokes sovereignty as*
> *the text (or pretext) for resisting international governance, for non-cooperation,*
> *for "isolationism," for unilateralism, not the least on human rights issues.*
> *—Louis Henkin*[1]

Friction between the international community and the world's last superpower
has steadily mounted over the last decade. America pays a steep price for evad-
ing world opinion. In a steadily globalizing world, even the United States is
obliged to consider the views of others, and it must at least appear to keep its
word by honoring its treaty commitments. Even the appearance of keeping
one's word imposes constraints; treaty violations cannot be so blatant as to be
obvious to all. While progress is erratic, the human rights revolution nonetheless impacts all nations. This has been unquestionably true in the American response to pressure from members of the international community seeking to
provide consular assistance to foreign nationals facing the death penalty.

For the first time in history, a U.S. president has ordered state courts to
comply with a decision of an international court. In 2005, President Bush ordered state courts to "give effect to the decision [of the International Court of
Justice] . . . in cases filed by the 51 Mexican Nationals" who were on various
state death rows.[2] The first state court to consider the president's memorandum has rejected the order, holding that President Bush lacked the power to
order a state court to abide by the decision of the International Court of Justice.[3] That decision will certainly be appealed to the United States Supreme
Court, and since the issue of presidential power is involved, it seems likely that
the appeal will be heard.[4] Thus, the extent to which this country will comply remains to be seen, but the fact that there is an effort to comply is new and important. The story of how America went from full resistance to partial, attempted compliance—with international pressure continuing—has important
implications for capital punishment.

There are four reasons for this shift from outright defiance to partial compliance. First, few other seemingly domestic issues have so nettled U.S. relations with some of its closest allies. It is one thing to oppose the United States

on a major international issue such as the Iraq war or American support for Israel. Some Americans may not like the criticism, but they do understand that national interests sometimes differ. It is quite another thing to intervene actively in what (at least to Americans) appears to be a domestic criminal justice issue. (The fact that these nations have treaty rights agreed to by the United States, or that capital punishment is seen by many to be a human rights issue, is lost on some.) Worldwide antipathy to the death penalty and worldwide perception that state execution constitutes a human rights issue, are plainly seen here, as traditional allies such as Canada and Mexico push hard to keep their nationals off American death rows—in part by invoking treaty rights to consular protection for their nationals who face the U.S. death penalty.

Second, despite setbacks in the U.S. Supreme Court, the issue of honoring America's treaty commitments on consular access to defendants facing state execution could modify some of the most onerous procedural rules facing persons seeking to avoid a death sentence. Anything that can mitigate the administration of capital punishment in the United States is significant. That foreign pressure may play such a role is unprecedented.

Moreover, this issue has the potential to magnify the U.S. public's perception of the inequities in the present American capital punishment system. If consular assistance results in fewer death sentences for foreigners by increasing the likelihood of fair trials, Americans may come to question the fairness of the death penalty when it is imposed on their fellow citizens. Whether this occurs or not, anything that publicizes specific problems with capital punishment has long-term value more generally.

Finally, and most importantly, the issue of consular relations has profound implications for Americans traveling abroad. As the *Detroit Free Press* put it,

> Most Americans would be justifiably appalled if a U.S. citizen in a foreign country were charged, convicted and executed for a capital crime without being advised of a right to contact the U.S. Embassy for legal help. Such due process is guaranteed under the international Vienna Convention; the United States demands it be accorded to U.S. citizens detained abroad.
>
> Yet, in a disturbing number of cases, American states are executing foreign nationals without advising them of these rights. This is occurring over the protests of their countries, human-rights organizations and even the U.S. State Department. Such practices don't bode well for Americans detained abroad.[5]

Thus, despite its seeming obscurity, the Vienna Convention on Consular Relations (VCCR) plays a key role in international resistance to capital punishment. Moreover, the vigor with which nations have pushed the issue demonstrates the significance of capital punishment as an international human rights issue; it also demonstrates the political force that the issue has in many other nations.

THE VCCR'S SIGNIFICANCE FOR INTERNATIONAL RELATIONS

The VCCR is a comprehensive, multilateral treaty governing consular relations between nations, with 170 nations party to the convention.[6] As such, it is one of the most widely accepted and most important treaties in the world. Its Optional Protocol Concerning the Compulsory Settlement of Disputes provides for jurisdiction in the International Court of Justice (ICJ or World Court) for the binding resolution of disputes over the meaning of the treaty's provisions.[7] The United States ratified the VCCR in 1969 and is bound by its terms. It also ratified the Optional Protocol and, until President Bush withdrew from it in 2005,[8] was also bound by the decisions of the World Court. Thus, from 1969 to 2005 the World Court had jurisdiction over disputes under the VCCR between the United States and other parties to the Optional Protocol.

Article 36 of the VCCR provides for consular access and assistance to any foreign national who is "arrested or committed to prison or to custody pending trial or is detained in any other manner." The foreign consulate must be notified that its national has been detained if that individual so requests, and the person detained must be informed "without delay of his rights." Those rights of the detainee include the right to communicate with the consulate and to receive consular visits. Consulates have a parallel right "to converse and correspond with him and to arrange for his legal representation." Thus, foreign nationals who have been arrested have the right to seek consular assistance and to be informed of that right without delay; and, unless the detainee objects, the consulate has the right to know when any of its nationals have been charged with a crime. The benefits of the VCCR are reciprocal and plainly advantageous to all nations; citizens can travel the world knowing that consular assistance from their own country will be available if they are charged with a crime or otherwise detained. However, if a nation persistently fails to meet its own obligations under the VCCR, one might wonder whether its citizens abroad would be afforded full protection under the treaty.

Indeed the U.S. government, despite its resistance to compliance, has conceded as much. In an important friend-of-the-court brief to the U.S. Supreme Court, the United States argued that the President's order to state courts to comply with an order from the World Court (discussed in detail below) "serves to protect the interests of United States citizens abroad."[9] It continued: "Consular assistance is a vital safeguard for Americans abroad, and the government has determined that, unless the United States fulfills its international obligation [to comply with the World Court's order] its ability to secure such assistance could be adversely affected."[10]

The United States was the first beneficiary of the Optional Protocol when it successfully sued Iran in the World Court in 1979 over the taking of American citizens hostage at the United States embassy in Tehran. Until the United States withdrew from the jurisdiction of the World Court, American adherence to the Optional Protocol was the one exception to the rule that the United States does not accede to the jurisdiction of international courts in human rights matters. As Joan Fitzpatrick notes, this adherence was "a rare instance in which the treaty obligations of the United States, affecting individual rights, were subject to binding international adjudication."[11] This must be distinguished from trade and commercial matters, where the United States does support and generally accede to the jurisdiction of international tribunals such as the World Trade Organization.[12]

Notwithstanding U.S. withdrawal from the Optional Protocol, President Bush continues to recognize that the United States must be seen to be complying with the VCCR so that U.S. citizens can continue to receive consular assistance abroad—thus, the order to state courts to comply. Apparently, the United States wishes to be seen as complying with the treaty obligations even as it resists strict compliance. This desire to convey the appearance of lawfulness before the court of world opinion requires that the United States walk a fine line, maintaining a semblance of lawfulness while it reneges on its legal obligations.

In hindsight, this conflict over consular relations appears to have been entirely foreseeable. Because of the status of the VCCR under U.S. law, challenges to Article 36 violations in the domestic courts were not only possible but virtually inevitable. The U.S. Constitution declares that ratified U.S. treaties "shall be the supreme Law of the Land; and the Judges in every State shall be bound thereby. . . ."[13] Many treaties (including the VCCR) are deemed to be self-executing, meaning that they require no implementing legislation after ratification and that the federal courts are responsible for interpreting and enforcing their terms.[14] The Supreme Court has long held that a self-executing treaty is on par with an act of Congress "whenever its provisions prescribe a rule by which the rights of the private citizen or subject may be determined."[15] When those individual rights are of a nature to be enforced in a court of justice, that court resorts to the treaty for a rule of decision for the case before it, as it would to a statute.[16] Moreover, since Article 36 appears to confer specific rights on individual foreigners under arrest, a serious violation of those rights by law enforcement can become the subject of judicial review and potential remedy.

Notwithstanding President Bush's declaration that the United States "will always be the world's leader in support of human rights,"[17] for the 120 foreign nationals on U.S. death rows as of October 5, 2006 compliance with the Vienna Convention on Consular Relations has been the exception rather than the rule.[18] U.S. law enforcement officials rarely tell foreign nationals who are criminal defendants of their rights under the VCCR, and, as a result, they rarely get timely access to the consular assistance that they are entitled to—assistance that in some cases makes the difference between life, death, and complete exoneration. This failure causes much of the world to see America as an "international scofflaw."[19] It also undermines America's attempt to cast itself as an exemplar of human rights virtue and evinces the selective and "hypocritical" nature of its commitment to international human rights treaties.[20]

One of the first clear indications of American noncompliance with the VCCR came from Angel Breard's death sentence and subsequent execution in 1998 by the state of Virginia. Breard, a citizen of Paraguay, was convicted in Virginia of rape and capital murder. He was not advised of his right to consular notification under Article 36 of the VCCR, nor was his trial lawyer aware of the treaty obligation. Not surprisingly, the issue of violations of the VCCR was not raised in any Virginia state court proceeding,[21] and the Virginia Supreme Court did not address it.[22] Breard raised the issue in his federal habeas corpus petition,[23] but the federal district court refused relief, holding that the issue had been procedurally defaulted, that is, lost because the defendant had failed to raise the point in a timely manner at the trial court.[24]

Procedural default is a complex legal rule, the intricacies of which are beyond the scope of this book. Understanding of the general concept, however, is necessary to appreciate what happens in cases where the United States refuses a remedy for violation of the Vienna Convention on Consular Relations. The procedural default rule refers to the forfeiture of a claim due to the failure to assert that claim in a timely fashion, either at trial or on appeal, in a criminal proceeding. If state criminal and appellate courts deny all claims that have been, for any reason, procedurally defaulted, then federal courts will likewise refuse to hear the claim on federal habeas corpus.

A procedural default can occur at any level, and once a claim is lost, it is lost forever. For example, a state trial court can hold that an objection to evidence has been lost because of the trial lawyer's failure to contemporaneously object when the evidence is first offered at trial. If the state appellate courts uphold that ruling (and many would), then the federal habeas courts will do so as well. In some states, incontrovertible evidence of innocence acquired as little as three weeks after the trial will not suffice to overturn a death sentence. Thus, in Virginia, evidence of innocence[25] presented more than twenty-one days after the trial cannot be heard in any court, state or federal.[26] The rule is said to promote efficiency and finality. A case is tried once, appeals are allowed; and then, except for habeas corpus, it is over, and anything that was not timely raised during this process is, subject to very narrow exceptions, irretrievably lost. Miscarriages of justice sometimes go unrecognized as a result, but that is often seen by the courts as an acceptable price for a reasonably efficient, and generally fair, system of justice.

As we will see, the procedural default rule has come to trump the VCCR. Many countries, including common law countries with legal systems similar to America's, do not have such a rigidly enforced rule. For example, in Canadian jurisprudence, the failure to timely object to evidence is only one of many factors taken into account in determining whether to grant an appeal.[27] Thus, rigid enforcement of the rule, without an exception for honoring one's treaty obligations, baffles even America's closest friends. They see the rule as a device used by the United States to avoid keeping its word. Adding to the irritation, the rule does not provide any remedy for the treaty violation. Where there is no remedy, there is little incentive to comply. Allies and enemies alike can see this, and have reason to view the entire regime of consular relations as undercut by American intransigence on this point.

Breard continued his appeals, and Paraguay attempted to intervene in the U.S. federal courts. The *Breard* cases were combined and disposed of by the U.S. Supreme Court on the day of his scheduled execution. The Court denied both petitions, and Breard was executed that same evening. His issues, including the violation of the Vienna Convention, had been lost—procedurally defaulted. Justices Stevens, Breyer, and Ginsburg all dissented, decrying the haste with which the Supreme Court acted. In Justice Breyer's words, the issue of violation of the VCCR warranted "less speedy consideration."[28]

Breard was dead, but Paraguay continued the fight before the World Court.[29] However, it withdrew its petition when the U.S. government issued a formal apology. That apology, while not correcting the problem, reveals America's failure to honor its commitment under the treaty, and its desire to appear to comply with the Vienna Convention, in order to protect Americans traveling abroad:

> [The] failure to notify Mr. Breard [of his rights under the Convention] was unquestionably a violation of an obligation owed to the Government of Paraguay.

The Government of the United States of America fully recognizes the violation of the Vienna Convention in this case, and conveys its apologies to the Government and people of Paraguay.

Recognizing that United States compliance with the requirements of the Vienna Convention must improve, the Government of the United States has undertaken efforts to better educate officials throughout the United States of the consular notification requirements. . . . *We fully appreciate that the United States must see to it that foreign nationals in the United States receive the same treatment that we expect for our citizens overseas. We cannot have a double standard.*[30] (Emphasis added.)

Two aspects of *Breard* suggest that the case was of greater importance than it might otherwise seem from the formal response. First, in an unprecedented move, then secretary of state Madeline Albrecht had urged the governor of Virginia to stay the execution because "ignoring the international court could be seen as a denial by the United States of the significance of international law . . . and thereby limit our ability to ensure that Americans are protected when living or traveling abroad."[31] While the governor did not comply, this recognition at the highest level of government that adherence to the treaty is in its own national self-interest suggests a greater importance to the issue than is evidenced by the mere post-execution apology given to Paraguay.

Second, it is not clear that an apology was the only price paid for Breard's speedy execution. As Mark Warren points out:

In exchange for the apology, Paraguay withdrew its case at the ICJ; just days later, Washington removed Paraguay from its trade piracy blacklist. Paraguayan authorities publicly denied any connection between the two events. In private, however, officials reportedly confirmed that a deal had been brokered whereby the United States avoided certain defeat at the ICJ and Paraguay was spared U.S. economic sanctions for not cracking down on the counterfeiting of brand name consumer goods worth one hundred million dollars annually.[32]

If the United States thought that it had staved off humiliating defeat before the World Court, it was mistaken. The payment to Paraguay only put off the inevitable and, as we will see, the problem persists, notwithstanding U.S. withdrawal from the World Court's jurisdiction. While the Vienna Convention on Consular Relations is not exclusively, or even primarily, concerned with state execution, plainly this issue is driven by the specter of foreign nationals facing the death penalty without the benefit of their treaty-given rights. The price to be paid diplomatically, for what is widely seen as a major human rights violation, is greater than would otherwise be the case for a relatively minor series of treaty violations. While many in the public are not aware of this price attached to capital punishment, the diplomatic community has long been well aware of it and has sought to mitigate the harm abroad caused by it.

The procedural default issue will also continue to cause problems. The Supreme Court in Breard held (upholding the lower court decision mentioned above), among other things, that the Vienna Convention conflicts with the later U.S. Antiterrorism and Effective Death Penalty Act of 1996 (AEDPA), which requires that issues be presented to the state courts or be procedurally defaulted.[33]

Neither Breard nor his lawyer knew about the VCCR, and they did not raise an objection concerning the violation of his consular rights in the Virginia courts. The United States follows a rule that if a treaty and a federal statute conflict, the later in time controls. Thus, a later-promulgated treaty trumps an inconsistent statute. Conversely, if a statute conflicts with an earlier treaty, the statute overrides the treaty (even if such override causes the United States to breach its international obligations under that treaty). Given the Supreme Court's interpretation that the AEDPA conflicted with the VCCR, it followed that the VCCR had been superseded as to this point. The procedural default rule, then, had priority over the Vienna Convention and overrode it, thus cutting off Breard's claim that the Convention had been violated. Breard's ignorance of his rights (due to Virginia's failure to inform him) resulted in forfeiture of the claim. Thus, responsibility for the state's failure to comply with the treaty is deftly turned against the foreign national—who is the party least able to avoid the problem in the first place.

This is Kafkaesque. Because neither Breard nor his lawyer was aware of Virginia's violation of international law, Virginia was exonerated and Breard was executed. The U.S. courts' continued rigid enforcement of the procedural default rule put the country on a collision course with International Court of Justice decisions in the LaGrand[34] and Avena[35] cases, discussed below, which rejected application of the procedural default rule to violations of the Vienna Convention.

After Breard, Virginia executed a Mexican national, Mario Murphy, who also was not afforded proper consular notification under the Vienna Convention. Although the United States apologized for the treaty breach, Mexico, unlike Paraguay, did not let it rest there and sought an advisory opinion from the Inter-American Court of Human Rights. At the time, Mexico was in a peculiar position. It recognized the jurisdiction of the Inter-American Court,[36] but had not then become a party to the Optional Protocol.[37] The reverse was true for the

United States, which recognized the compulsory jurisdiction of the World Court concerning violations of VCCR, but did not recognize the jurisdiction of the Inter-American Court of Human Rights. Thus, as to the United States, any opinion by the Inter-American Court had no legal weight.

The opinion of the Inter-American Court of Human Rights, among other things, held that the VCCR confers individual "rights upon detained foreign nationals," the denial of which "is prejudicial to the due process of law" and, in these circumstances, violated Murphy's "right not to be deprived of life 'arbitrarily.'"[38] The United States ignored the adverse advisory opinion.[39] This opinion, however, laid the groundwork for a confrontation before the International Court of Justice, whose jurisdiction the United States did, until recently, recognize, and which could issue authoritative opinions on alleged violations of the Vienna Convention on Consular Relations. As we will see, both Germany and Mexico are determined to see that the United States honors its obligations under international law and this, in turn, increases the diplomatic cost of ignoring world opinion on capital punishment.

CONTINUED U.S. NONCOMPLIANCE: GERMANY

In 1999, despite repeated protests by the German government, Arizona executed two German brothers, Walter and Karl LaGrand. After Karl's execution, but before Walter's, the German government sought and received a provisional ruling from the International Court of Justice requiring, among other things, that "the United States should take all measures at its disposal to ensure that Walter LaGrand is not executed pending the final decision in these proceedings."[40] Germany also attempted to file suit in the U.S. Supreme Court, but that Court refused to enforce the World Court's order, citing Eleventh Amendment concerns.[41] Arizona took the position that the World Court order was merely advisory and did not create a legally binding obligation. It thus ignored the World Court's stay and Walter was executed.

The International Court of Justice followed its provisional ruling with a binding judgment, which vividly demonstrates the nature and degree of pressure the international community is exerting upon the United States. The ICJ held specifically in *LaGrand (Germany v. United States of America)* that the United States must, as the necessary remedy for any future VCCR violation, provide "review and reconsideration" of the conviction and sentence. As we will see below, the United States' narrow interpretation of the meaning of "review and consideration" in large part prompted Mexico to bring its own claim before the ICJ in *Case Concerning Avena and Other Mexican Nationals (Mexico v. United States)*.

Moreover, the ICJ also held that its provisional orders are binding, not merely advisory, thus creating "a legal obligation for the United States"[42] and making Walter's execution illegal under international law insofar as it violated the court's order. Third, it held that, contrary to strenuous U.S. objections, the Vienna Convention creates individual rights,[43] which makes it enforceable by the foreign individual as well as the foreign government. Fourth, it held that state procedural default rules cannot trump a foreign national's rights under the Vienna Convention.

U.S. courts have generally ignored or evaded the World Court's *LaGrand* decision.[44] These cases demonstrate how hard it still is to translate international law into successful domestic relief within the United States. But U.S. evasion of international law has had diplomatic and political costs, as evidenced by President Bush's 2005 directive that state courts give effect to a recent World Court decision on some of the same points.[45]

The *LaGrand* decision also clarifies the court's power to issue binding provisional measures in order to prevent a country from acting before the World Court has had an opportunity to rule. When the court ruled that the state of Arizona "should" stay LaGrand's execution, the word "should" must be read as a legal command, a "shall." Clearly, if the World Court's orders were merely advisory, such that countries *could* carry out an action before a ruling, then the court's rulings would be merely precatory and of little practical effect.

Indeed, lest there be any continuing confusion on the part of the United States, the provisional order in *Avena*, discussed below, admonishes that the United States "*shall* take all measures necessary to ensure that [three Mexican nationals] are not executed pending final judgment in these proceedings." (Emphasis added.)[46] It may be that the word change from "should" to "shall" indicates some impatience with the American position. In any event, American resistance has resulted in the court dropping the polite diplomatic fiction that its provisional orders are merely precatory; they constitute legal requirements that ought to be obeyed.

U.S. NONCOMPLIANCE: MEXICO

Mexico, which as of the provisional ruling in *Avena* case in 2003, claimed to have fifty-four of its citizens on various death rows in the United States,[47] refused to accept persistent U.S. noncompliance with international law, and sought to hold the United States to its obligations under the Vienna Convention. Mexico began proceedings in the World Court, arguing that death-row prisoners of Mexican nationality had been denied their right to obtain consular help from their own government.

While Mexico and the United States agreed that "review and reconsideration" was required under *LaGrand* to give "full effect" to the treaty rights under the VCCR, one of the major disputes between the *Avena* parties was whether "review and reconsideration" could be achieved by means of clemency proceedings alone, as the United States contended, or necessarily required effective judicial review, as Mexico asserted. This was the issue of continuity between the two cases: what did the *LaGrand* court actually mean by "review and reconsideration"?

Mexico claimed (and its actions have confirmed) that had it known about its citizens' facing charges in the United States, it would have assisted in a variety of ways. In death penalty cases this includes aggressively seeking out evidence, often in Mexico, for the penalty phase of trial in mitigation of sentence. Mexico asserted just as vigorously that it would have advised and explained legal rights to detainees at the time of their arrest. That argument was essential to Mexico's claim that advisement and notification without delay must occur immediately and prior to any interrogation.

Capital trials divide into two phases: a guilt phase and, if the defendant is found guilty of a capital offence, a penalty phase, where the issue is whether the defendant receives a death sentence or some term of imprisonment (in most states, life without the possibility of parole). At the penalty stage, the prosecution submits "aggravating facts" tending to argue for death, and the defense has the opportunity to offer mitigating evidence that might move the jury toward leniency.[48] This can include evidence of childhood traumas, upbringing, and other matters that might help both to humanize the defendant and to place the crime in a context that might persuade the jury to vote for life rather than death.

It is difficult to overemphasize just how important the latter service is. Skilled death penalty lawyers often use mitigation specialists, who attempt to construct a defendant's life history in ways that humanize the defendant and make an otherwise inexplicable act comprehensible. This type of evidence, in the hands of a competent lawyer, often makes the difference between life and death. Mexico's willingness to search out and interpret hard-to-find evidence from (in defense counsel's perspective) a foreign country is a crucial component of consular assistance. It also helps to explain why both state execution and consular assistance are considered by many to involve important human rights concerns that are not always fully appreciated by Americans.

Mexico would have secured first-rate legal counsel for Mexican defendants, as well as experts to analyze the scientific evidence. As was pointed out in a brief filed in the case of Mexican national Osbaldo Torres,

[Torres's trial lawyer] seems not to have realized that the Mexican Government stood ready and willing to assist her—that it would have supplemented the modest fee she was getting from an impoverished family; that it would have helped with the investigation she needed to do here and in Mexico; that Mexico—if the Court had refused funding—would have hired investigators, experts, and second counsel. In short, she seems to have been completely ignorant of the fact that *Mexico cares deeply about the welfare of its citizens, just as this country cares about the welfare of any United States citizen abroad,* and that, had she only asked, Mexico would have done its best to ensure that Mr. Torres not be sentenced to death.[49] (Emphasis added.)

This kind of assistance makes a big difference in death penalty cases, where poor lawyering by appointed counsel seems to be the norm. Just having a well-paid and competent lawyer for the trial can make a decisive difference to a capital defendant.[50] Once one has a decent lawyer, having expert witnesses to deconstruct the state's account can provide a crucial edge. Mexico was then, and continues to be, willing to put more than lip service into its opposition to capital punishment. Not only was the Mexican government helping its citizens who were already on U.S. death rows, but it was also committing to assist all Mexicans facing a capital trial in a U.S. court.

Plainly, the cost to the United States is no longer merely diplomatic. Nor is it confined to the communication of hostile opinions by other nations. The United States is on notice that the Mexican people, through their government, will make the execution of Mexican nationals as difficult as possible. This will, among other things, make trials of Mexican defendants more costly, and can only exacerbate the already glaring inequities and maladministration inherent in the U.S. death machinery. As a result, Mexican criminal defendants in America have a better opportunity to establish innocence than many other similarly situated defendants, and, if convicted of a capital felony, they have a better chance of persuading the jury that life imprisonment is the appropriate sanction. They also have a greater chance of avoiding capital charges in the first place. Mexico intervenes vigorously to try and persuade prosecutors not to seek death, often with remarkable success (the prospect of facing the legal resources of another nation, at trial and beyond, changes the equation significantly for many prosecutors).

Mexico's efforts support its assertion that consular assistance is not a mere formality, that the failure to accord it is not "harmless error." That consular assistance can make the critical difference in the outcome of cases goes far toward demonstrating the legal prejudice suffered by the initial violation. Moreover, Mexico, by its actions, has demonstrated the reason why the VCCR, with its mutually reciprocal provisions, can be vitally important to the citizens of all nations, including American citizens traveling abroad.

As a first measure, the World Court ordered the United States to halt the execution of three Mexican nationals who most immediately faced execution, and set the matter for hearing and resolution. U.S. State Department lawyers unsuccessfully argued that a ruling on the merits for Mexico would amount to "a sweeping prohibition of capital punishment of Mexican nationals in the United States,"[51] and "would constitute a wholly unprecedented and unwarranted interference with the sovereign rights of the United States."[52] Whether or not the ruling interferes with its "sovereign right" to execute not only its own citizens but those of other countries, the United States found itself in the unprecedented position of being ordered by an international court to halt the executions of at least three, and potentially more than fifty, Mexican nationals. Although the World Court's order was only binding on the parties, its reasoning could also affect the nationals of other nations because of probable violations of the VCCR.

The Merits of *Avena*

In 2004, the International Court of Justice decided *Avena*'s merits, holding, among other things, that the United States could not apply its procedural default rule to violations of the VCCR. The potential importance of this cannot be overstated. People on death row are there in part because they had bad lawyers. The person on death row who can afford to have an excellent lawyer is rare indeed. These weak lawyers omit evidence, pertinent objections, and focused legal arguments, often to the defendant's detriment. When competent postconviction counsel reinvestigates the cases, it is often too late, because of the procedural default rule, to resurrect the omitted issue. Thus, there is a close connection between ineffective lawyering and the procedural default rule: less able lawyers are the very ones most likely to omit (or default, or forfeit) an important issue. It is this curious catch-22 in U.S. law that ran afoul of the VCCR. Lawyers who did not know about, and who failed to raise, the issue before the trial court, thus defaulted on an important issue that, had it been raised, might well have resulted in exoneration for some and life sentences for others.

However, the *Avena* court did not set aside the convictions. Rather, with respect to those three Mexican nationals whose judicial avenues had been exhausted, the World Court ordered "the United States of America to provide, by means of its own choosing, review and reconsideration of the convictions and sentences of the Mexican nationals."[53] What this might mean for U.S. courts is not entirely clear. At a minimum, these foreign nationals were due a judicial hearing of some sort to determine whether or not they had been prejudiced by the violation of the VCCR. Given Mexico's intention to aggressively reinvestigate these cases, it seems that at least some of these foreign nationals on death row were likely prejudiced in their trials.

Moreover, the court said, the United States cannot satisfy its obligation under the Vienna Convention by resort to its clemency procedures, because "the clemency process, as currently practiced within the United States . . . is . . . not sufficient in itself to serve as an appropriate means of 'review and reconsideration.'"[54] Thus a court, not a political official, must determine in each case whether "the violation of Article 36 committed by the competent authorities caused actual prejudice to the defendant."[55] This remained true even of the three cases in which judicial review had run its course, leaving no further judicial avenues under U.S. law.[56] Finally, the World Court held that "review and consideration should be both of the sentence and of the conviction."[57]

Thus, the United States could not cite the death-row inmate's opportunity to seek clemency to rectify the treaty violation. Nor would a new sentencing hearing satisfy the court's ruling. This is important because it means that, under the World Court's ruling, even the cases of foreign nationals whose appeals had run their course, and who had no further access to the courts under domestic law, would have the right to another hearing before a court on both guilt and sentencing issues. Moreover, in order to comply with the World Court, the domestic court would have to modify its procedural default rule. Not only would this slow the process down and make it more expensive, but it also would require a change in domestic law as to both the right of access to the court system and the courts' application of a domestic legal rule (that is, procedural default). While, as we will see, the U.S. Supreme Court did not agree with the World Court in this, the ruling nonetheless has had an important impact on American policy insofar as the president has directed state courts to comply.

As Mexico seeks to spare its nationals from the death penalty, it will no doubt push in all political, diplomatic, and judicial fora available to it. For example, in 2002, Mexico's president Vicente Fox stunned the Bush administration, and Texas governor Rick Perry, when he canceled his trip to President George W. Bush's ranch in Crawford, Texas. Perry had spurned Fox's requests to stay the execution of Mexican national Javier Suarez Medina. Perry could have granted a thirty-day stay for further consideration of the case, but he rejected Fox, and Medina was executed. Some sixteen nations joined Fox with court briefs or letters seeking relief for Medina.[58] Given the close relationship between Fox and Bush, and President Bush's many attempts to improve relations with Mexico, this diplomatic snub surely hurt. Moreover, support for the Mexican position from other nations contrasts with the near-isolation that the United States finds itself in.

Mexico, as we have seen, operates the only foreign capital-assistance program in the United States. "Through the consular assistance programs, Mexican consular officers try to ensure the general fairness of proceedings and to enhance the quality of legal representation at trial; they serve as 'cultural bridges' for their detained nationals, assist in amassing vital mitigating evidence,"[59] and have already provided decisive assistance in capital cases.[60] Moreover, the Mexican government also funds a Mexican Capital Legal Assistance Program, which complements consular assistance in capital cases.[61] This is unprecedented. Nations do not ordinarily set up formal legal-assistance programs, outside of general consular assistance, for their nationals facing criminal prosecution in another nation.

This demonstrates that the VCCR is being transformed into a vehicle for expressing an increasingly-worldwide distaste for and displeasure with the American death penalty. It also illustrates the extent to which other nations can and will intervene in the U.S. domestic criminal justice system on an important human rights issue. This, in turn, may also be a reflection of domestic politics in Mexico, as well as in other nations whose nationals face American capital punishment. For example, the execution of Irineo Tristan Montoya in 1997 "was met with protests from authorities and citizens in Mexico."[62] The execution "fanned a national wave of sorrow and solidarity,"[63] and in response, Ruben Beltran, a top official at the Foreign Relations Secretariat, visited Washington and said, "Mexico opposes the death penalty, by principle."[64]

Citizens of many other nations without capital punishment also regularly protest American use of state execution. As the *International Herald Tribune* reports:

> When Bush has traveled abroad, anti-death-penalty protests have regularly greeted him. They did in Germany in May, for instance. When the United States lost its seat on the United Nations Human Rights Commission last year, the death penalty was cited as one reason.
>
> Other countries, including Britain, Thailand and Canada, have lodged sharp protests when their own nationals, or dual nationals, faced being put to death in the United States.[65]

Thus, political winds from afar come home to affect U.S. policy on capital punishment in ways that most Americans never see or quite comprehend. Human rights concerns play a role in official governmental protests of U.S. capital punishment. Popular opposition to the death penalty allows politicians in these countries to move forcefully and effectively when confronting the United States.

Some Americans resent foreign intrusion into the U.S. capital punishment machinery. For example, after *Avena*, Oklahoma's governor commuted Osbaldo Torres's death sentence.[66] Predictably, clemency triggered a negative response from the victim's family. The victim's brother said, "I knew it was going to be all politics . . . I'm upset that we let the Mexicans come over here and have more power than us."[67] While this reaction from a family member may be understandable, it does ignore the facts of the case. Shortly after the governor granted clemency, the Court of Criminal Appeals of Oklahoma expressly found:

> [T]he Mexican government takes its consular obligations to its citizens very seriously, particularly when those citizens are capital defendants in another country. The Mexican government has a tradition of active assistance extending back to the 1920s, and provided extensive assistance to capital defendants in 1993, the year of Torres's arrest. Had the consulate been contacted, it would have monitored Torres's case, consulted with and offered assistance to his attorney, and helped gather evidence, particularly in preparation for the second stage of trial . . . Among consular officials' most important duties are the gathering of mitigation evidence and locating mitigating witnesses in Mexico and the United States. After belatedly entering into Torres's case, Mexico hired two bilingual investigators, two gang experts, a mitigation expert and a neuropsychiatrist, to assist in developing mitigating evidence for the appellate process.[68]

It appears doubtful that Torres would have been on death row but for Oklahoma's violation of the VCCR. Moreover, Torres continues to claim that he is innocent of the death penalty,[69] and his lawyer has confirmed that Torres may continue to fight the conviction.[70] Whether Torres is in fact innocent of the death penalty[71] is unknowable at this point, but given his life term, there will be an opportunity to address any evidence of innocence that might be forthcoming. While the statement above by the brother of the victim may be understandable, the president of the American Society of International Law provides a different assessment, suggesting that legal issues overcame politics in this case.

> An Oklahoma court did a brave thing a few months ago: it held, under considerable time pressure, that international law applicable in the United States required a stay of execution of a criminal defendant and an eviden-

tiary hearing on the remedy to be provided for a violation of international law by Oklahoma authorities. The effect of decisions of international tribunals on U.S. domestic proceedings sometimes is a political issue in this country, and the Oklahoma Court of Criminal Appeals . . . deserve[s] recognition for treating it instead as a serious legal matter and addressing the issues with full consideration of the important principles involved.[72]

The problem for the United States will likely grow sharper as other nations make similar demands on behalf of their nationals on America's death rows. Honduras, for example, has already sought commutation for two of its nationals on death row in Oklahoma,[73] and has intervened in the capital trial of one of its nationals in California.[74] At the very least, the World Court order in *Avena* is a major embarrassment for the United States, demonstrating the country's failure to honor its international obligations under the Vienna Convention, and its readiness to justify that violation by appeals to an overriding sovereign right to nonintervention.

U.S. RESISTANCE: *SANCHEZ-LLAMAS V. OREGON* AND *BUSTILLO V. VIRGINIA*

The U.S. Supreme Court agreed in 2005 to hear two cases involving prisoners claiming that their convictions were tainted by the failure to afford consular assistance. That Court continued to follow the *Breard* precedent and rejected a portion of the World Court's rulings in *LaGrand* and *Avena*, while ducking the important issue of whether the Vienna Convention on Consular Relations creates judicially enforceable rights. While this rejection of international law may be understandable given domestic resistance to international law,[75] it does appear to put the Supreme Court at odds with the president's directive for courts to "give effect to" *Avena* "in accordance with general principles of comity."[76]

The two cases involved a Mexican national, Moises Sanchez-Llamas, and a Honduran national, Mario Bustillo.[77] Sanchez-Llamas was convicted in Oregon of several serious offenses, including attempted murder, and sentenced to 201½ years in prison. Bustillo was convicted in Virginia of murder and sentenced to 30 years in prison. Both cases involved violations of petitioners' consular rights, and the two cases, combined on appeal, raised three important issues:

1. Does the Vienna Convention create personal rights (as opposed to rights held by the government alone) that an individual criminal defendant may raise, either at trial or in postconviction proceedings, in contesting the conviction or sentence?

2. Does a violation of the Convention require the suppression of an incriminating statement? (Under U.S. law, incriminating statements can be excluded from the evidence under certain circumstances, usually involving a violation of a person's rights under the Fifth Amendment to the Constitution to be free from self-incrimination. This is an aspect of the "exclusionary rule." This case, then, raises the issue of whether this particular treaty violation triggers the exclusionary rule.)

3. Does the doctrine of procedural default (the loss of an issue because the lawyer failed to properly or timely raise it) apply to the failure to raise a violation of the Vienna Convention? (The problem here concerns the state's failure to tell the defendant of his or her right to consular assistance, as Virginia failed to do in the *Breard* case. In this respect, the court is being asked to either overrule or distinguish *Breard*, so as not to apply it to these cases. The question, then, revolves around the defendant's failure to tell the trial court about the state's failure to tell him of his rights in the first place, which *Breard* held to be procedurally defaulted. Thus, under *Breard*, the burden is effectively flipped, with the defendant penalized for the state's mistake.

The Court ducked the first issue, assuming without deciding that the Vienna Convention does create rights that the individual (as opposed to his or her home country) may raise in court. This avoided a direct conflict with the World Court on this point, thus leaving this important issue for another day.

The Court also held that a violation of the VCCR does not require suppression of an incriminating statement. This, too, does not directly contradict the World Court's rulings in *LaGrand* and *Avena*. While the dissenting justices made a strong argument that "suppression may sometimes provide an appropriate remedy" for a violation of the VCCR, the majority did not agree. Among other things, the majority pointed out that, absent a violation of the U.S. Constitution, the Supreme Court lacks the power to correct state court decisions with which it might disagree. Furthermore, the VCCR does not specifically mention suppression as a remedy, and in these circumstances the court felt that the "failure to inform a defendant of his Article 36 rights [under the Vienna Convention] is unlikely . . . to produce unreliable confessions."[78] The Court did leave some room for a defendant to argue that a violation of his rights under the convention resulted in an involuntary confession, which could be excluded as unreliable. However, given the history of this issue in courts that have often found highly coercive confessions to be "voluntary," it is not clear at this point just how much of an opening this is.

The Supreme Court also held that state procedural default rules could prevent reconsideration of cases where the defendant had been tried and sentenced without being afforded the opportunity for consular assistance. (Recall that *Avena* had barred use of state procedural default rules in consideration of cases where the VCCR had been violated.) This is the more interesting and compelling issue, because it appears that Bustillo may actually have been innocent of the murder for which he was convicted and sentenced. Moreover, the Honduran government, like the Mexican government, was prepared to assist Bustillo in asserting his innocence at trial. While some eyewitnesses had tied Bustillo to a brutal murder, others testified that Bustillo did not wield the fatal baseball bat; that another Honduran (Sirena), who shortly thereafter fled to Honduras, committed the murder. The prosecution ridiculed the suggestion that another, conveniently absent, Honduran existed at all, much less that he had committed murder, and the jury apparently agreed. The prosecution, however, failed to turn over evidence that the police had stopped Sirena near the scene of the crime with "what appeared to be red ketchup stains on his shirt and pants," as well as other potentially exculpatory evidence.[79] In addition, Sirena had "admitted to friends, in surreptitiously videotaped conversations, that he was the one who killed [the victim] Merry."[80] Courts are understandably suspicious of confessions when they are discovered after another person has already been convicted of the crime. However, the fact that these confessions were secretly videotaped, combined with other witnesses tying Sirena to the crime, makes this a particularly compelling case for recognizing a highly probable miscarriage of justice.

Finally, and most importantly, considering the purpose of the Vienna Convention, the Honduran consulate stated that under these circumstances "it would have: (a) provided a photograph of Sirena to prove his existence; (b) supplied immigration records showing that Sirena had entered Honduras the day after Merry died; and (c) attempted to contact and interview Sirena in Honduras."[81] This goes to the heart of a foreign national's consular rights. Like Mexico, Honduras was willing to give its citizen the kind of help that might well have proved his innocence, or at least have caused the jury to have concluded that there was a reasonable doubt.

Notwithstanding the evidence of innocence and the Honduran willingness and ability to help demonstrate it, the Supreme Court found that Bustillo suffered no legal prejudice and went on to conclude that the World Court's interpretations of the law were not "intended to be conclusive on our courts."[82] *Avena* was thereby held not to apply to Bustillo's case, with the Court concluding that "[o]ur holding in no way disparages the importance of the Vienna Convention . . . It is no slight to the Convention to deny petitioners' claims under the same principles we would apply to an Act of Congress, or to the Constitution itself."[83] Domestic law, under the majority's view, thus trumps international law.

Justice Ginsberg concurred in the majority's holding, because "critical for me, . . . his attorney at trial was aware of his client's rights."[84] However, since the majority's reasoning did not turn on this point, *Bustillo* will apply to all cases involving the VCCR, and not only those where the lawyer erred. *Bustillo* is not an isolated case. As demonstrated in chapter 7, American courts routinely use procedural labyrinths to deny relief, arguing that finality and efficiency take precedence over virtually every other consideration.[85]

The dissent argued that the VCCR creates individual rights that a defendant may enforce, and that it is in America's own self-interest to give more respect to international law and the rulings of the World Court. The dissent would have allowed the VCCR to sometimes provide a domestic remedy, in those rare cases where domestic law afforded no avenue for vindicating rights, where prejudice to the individual defendant can be shown. The dissent also pointed out that the majority's approach "simply rejects the notion that [the VCCR] sets forth any relevant requirement,"[86] that it "leaves States free to deny effective relief for Convention violations, despite America's promise to provide just such relief,"[87] and that it

> risks weakening respect abroad for the rights of foreign nationals, a respect that America, in 1969, sought to make effective throughout the world. And it increases the difficulties faced by the United States and other nations who would, through binding treaties, strengthen the role that law can play in assuring all citizens, including American citizens, fair treatment throughout the world.[88]

The last clause of Article 36 of the VCCR provides that, while states will apply their own domestic laws, "the said laws and regulations must enable *full effect* to be given to the purposes for which the rights are intended" (Emphasis added). It is difficult to see how the failure to provide *any* remedy for a treaty violation can be squared with this language. Under the facts of several of the cases thus far seen, there were clear treaty violations, and home governments were prepared to provide substantial support in cases where the outcome would likely have been different. These were not mere technical violations; they touched the core of the treaty, though they were without remedy or effect.

PEERING THROUGH THE GLASS DARKLY

The dissent is no doubt correct in its assessment that the majority opinion in *Sanchez-Llamas* and *Bustillo* effectively guts the Vienna Convention by leaving the issue entirely to the state courts. This ruling, combined with the United States' withdrawal from the Optional Protocol, thus ending World Court jurisdiction as to consular disputes involving the United States, limits how this issue can play out for death-row inmates in the immediate future.

However, when one reflects upon how much was accomplished by the issue of consular access, how it continues to nettle U.S. foreign policy, and how it continues to undercut the death penalty, one sees the true effect of international pressure on capital punishment. President Bush's memorandum directing state courts to "give effect to the decision" of the International Court of Justice in the Case Concerning Avena and Other Mexican Nationals mitigates and undercuts the Supreme Court's ruling on procedural default.[89] According to the government's friend-of-the-court brief in another case involving similar issues, the president's memorandum directs state courts to suspend those same procedural default rules in appropriate cases involving violations of the Vienna Convention. State courts must now decide whether to comply with the president's unprecedented order[90] or (as did the Court of Criminal Appeals of Texas) to use the Supreme Court decision to justify continued defiance of the World Court's order.[91] This tension between the Supreme Court and the executive branch raises difficult separation-of-powers questions, which may ultimately be addressed in the likely appeal of the Texas court's order. But this conflict itself only underscores the importance and difficulty of these issues, even as it makes accurate prediction of their outcome impossible.

While some states may continue to strictly enforce their procedural default rules, others may well follow international law and relax their default rules for death-row inmates whose consular rights have been violated. In the long run, this relaxation will likely have the effect of undermining procedural default rules more generally in capital cases. If a state, in response to international pressure and the president's directive, grants relief to a foreign-born death-row inmate who has not raised a procedurally defaulted claim, this will provide fuel for other death-row inmates with equally worthy non–treaty-related claims. Moreover, relaxation of these default rules in one place can encourage law reform more generally. Human rights concerns can thus influence law reform in ways that are not easily predictable but that seem, after the fact, to have been inevitable. Thus, even a limited change in the law in this area is significant in that it can recast the terms of the death penalty debate more generally.

Death penalty opponents abroad, as well as foreign-born death-row defendants, continue to fight. No one expects other nations to end the pressure to save the lives of their nationals just because of an adverse ruling in the U.S. Supreme Court. To the contrary, in fact, diplomatic and other pressures will undoubtedly be brought to bear if, and when, a state decides to go ahead with the execution of a foreign national whose rights under the VCCR have been denied.

Moreover, international law is beginning to affect domestic law in ways that would have been quite unimaginable even a few years ago. While some state courts appear to be avoiding *Avena*,[92] others are struggling to come to grips with it. Most remarkably in the latter regard is the decision of the Oklahoma Court of Criminal Appeals, discussed above. Few death penalty lawyers would have predicted, even a decade ago, that international law would ever have the slightest effect on any capital case. Furthermore, even the partial limiting of the procedural default doctrine in these cases is important. The procedural default doctrine has probably prevented retrial of more capital cases tainted with significant error than any other legal doctrine.[93] Even if only a few states modify their rules, it would represent a significant victory for human rights advocates.

Local authorities in the United States will no doubt become better at advising foreign-born defendants of their rights under the VCCR. Countries like Mexico that aggressively provide consular assistance will be able to see that their nationals receive better legal assistance from the beginning, thus giving them a decided advantage over others charged with capital offences. This, in turn, raises fairness questions, since the United States continues to provide substandard lawyers to its own citizens charged with capital crimes. Americans are likely to conclude that justice is not being done if foreign nationals receive superior legal assistance when facing the death penalty. While there may be a short-term backlash, in the long run these persistent fairness questions undermine the death penalty's legitimacy. Also, fairness questions do (eventually) have political impact. One Oklahoma governor denied clemency in a capital case, despite a consular notification violation, because it would "would presume greater rights for foreign nationals that, in my judgment, are not warranted,"[94] while a later governor granted clemency to Osbaldo Torres.[95] Local politics prevailed in the first instance; international law and world opinion prevailed in the second.

Sandra Babcock, the American lawyer representing Mexico in *Avena*, has stated that she expects the United States will comply with the World Court order, and the president's directive is a step in that direction. Failure to do so would send the impression, as one writer put it, that the United States "didn't care about the rule of law."[96] The United States is being forced to recognize, gradually and perhaps reluctantly, that it cannot expect other nations to respect human rights and international treaty commitments if it refuses to reciprocate. When former United Nations high commissioner Mary Robinson was asked whether more powerful countries should be held to a higher human rights standard because they are more influential, she replied, "I would hold them to the *same* standard of human rights. But the responsibility to uphold that standard is greater if you have more power and influence" (Emphasis in original).[97]

CONCLUSION

Americans won a major victory in the World Court when that court ruled that the Iranian takeover of the United States embassy in Teheran was illegal, and awarded monetary damages. The United States scored politically and diplomatically in that case. Now, having lost before that same World Court, the United States has withdrawn from its jurisdiction—it does not wish to play anymore. The first cost of this decision is to prevent any recourse to the International Court of Justice when the tables again turn. If another nation violates an American's consular rights, there will be no judicial forum to redress that violation. This renders Americans more vulnerable abroad, while also limiting the nation's diplomatic options in the case of a violation. At the same time, this decision will only increase foreign pressure on the United States to end the death penalty. It is a short-term withdrawal from the rule of law, with long-term adverse consequences.

Moreover, this snarl over consular relations reveals both the intensity and expanse of much of the world's determination to see the end of capital punishment and to protest its continued existence in the United States. The battle is far from over. Diplomatic pressure will continue. More importantly, international law and international human rights norms will increasingly affect the United States and its policy on capital punishment. The United States can hide from, but it cannot completely escape, the rest of the world.

PART TWO : Domestic Resistance to the Death Penalty

5 : Death Penalty Myths
Science Confronts Conventional Wisdom

It ain't what you don't know that gets you into trouble.
It's what you know for sure that just ain't so.
—Mark Twain[1]

Conventional wisdom has a muddled reputation. We follow it because it usually works. We know many things almost by osmosis; we do not need to touch a hot stove burner to know what that might mean. Nonetheless, such "knowledge" is not always accurate. Our most strongly held beliefs can be distorted, misguided, or, even worse, false. Over two thousand years ago, the Greek mathematician and philosopher Eratosthenes calculated the earth's circumference; yet, until comparatively recently, people mostly saw a flat earth. Capital punishment is one area where our instincts fail, where some of our strongest beliefs turn out to be wrong.

The five most prevalent myths about the death penalty are:

1. The death penalty deters violent crime.
2. Execution is the most effective way to keep a murderer from killing again.
3. Racism has been eliminated from the modern capital punishment system.
4. It costs less to execute someone than it does to imprison someone for life without the possibility for parole.
5. Innocent people are never, or rarely, convicted of capital crimes, much less executed for crimes that they did not commit.

Not everyone subscribes to all or even some of these bits of conventional wisdom; recent polls show an increasing awareness that capital punishment does not do all that its advocates claim. Nonetheless, these are common notions, held by many otherwise knowledgeable people. For example, both candidates in the 2000 presidential election supported the death penalty for its supposed deterrent effect. Moreover, then governor George Bush proclaimed his confidence in the Texas criminal justice system, and claimed that it had not executed innocent people. While a candidate's pronouncements may not always reflect their true beliefs, they do suggest sufficient public acceptance to make them politically safe. Each myth, therefore, merits scrutiny.

Conventional thinking is particularly immune to contrary facts where crime is concerned. The nature of wrongdoers is something we all think we have a feel for, and anything that contradicts that mind-set is suspect. Moreover, social science rarely attains the predictive accuracy that the natural sciences can attain, so skepticism seems more acceptable. But the conclusions of many social science studies, using multiple methods, should not be dismissed out of hand. In this regard, few areas have received greater attention than capital punishment. In this chapter we will cover the empirical evidence that increasingly rejects each myth.

DETERRENCE AND THE DEATH PENALTY

Deterrence is based on the notion that people rationally weigh consequences. If we catch and fine speeders, there should be fewer speeders. Detection and conviction, followed by widely publicized punishment, should reduce crime.

Unless we catch substantial numbers of wrongdoers, the threat of punishment will be correctly perceived as remote, and deterrence will be lost, or at least muted. Moreover, we must not only prosecute, but convict substantial numbers of offenders. Without convictions, the threat will be similarly lost. So detection, prosecution, and conviction of malefactors remain the initial (and likely most important) problems for law enforcement. Without these, deterrence is illusory.

Next, punishment must be sufficiently stern to impress wrongdoers with the gravity of the offence. Criminologists differ on what the right amount of punishment may be for a given crime. Then, too, criminologists often disagree with elected officials, whose interests are not allied with what deters crime but, rather, what establishes "tough on crime" credentials. Thus, prosecutors prosecute, judges judge, and legislators legislate not on what works against crime, but on what works with the voting public.

Most criminological studies show that the first factor—the realistic threat that if crime is committed it will be detected and successfully prosecuted—is far more important than the severity of punishment.[2] If criminals do not fear getting caught, the severity of the punishment will be of much less relevance. Nonetheless, there is general agreement that punishment must be sufficiently severe for deterrence, despite genuine disagreement over how much punishment would suffice.

Finally, deterrence must do more than simply stop a particular person from reoffending. The detection, prosecution, and punishment of crime must be sufficiently publicized so that people know what is prohibited. Most of us know someone who has been convicted of drunk driving or speeding, so we hear about what happened in that case. And who is not familiar with "if it bleeds it leads" journalism and court TV? One way or another, people come to know what is prohibited and have some idea of the consequences of misconduct.

Deterrence theory is further divided into specific deterrence (punishment to stop a given person from reoffending) and general deterrence (we see another being punished and decide to avoid that conduct). Moreover, the law's deterrence function is sometimes distinguished from its educative function: some people know what the law proscribes without being deterred.

Prompt detection and punishment does reduce crime overall. There is, however, a large body of scholarly research that demonstrates that deterrence (or rational choice) plays a relatively minor role in predicting or suppressing crime. Other factors, such as "racial heterogeneity, poverty, and family disruption," perform larger roles).[3] Thus, while deterrence plays a role in reducing crime, it is relatively small.

Capital punishment is complicated by the fact that the choice is not between death and no punishment, but between death and some other punishment. The question of how much punishment suffices looms large in this debate. Does the death penalty deter more than some other severe punishment—such as life imprisonment, perhaps without the possibility of parole? Do people fear death more than lifelong loss of freedom?

Americans are nearly evenly divided on the question of whether the death penalty deters people from committing crimes,[4] and a strong majority of death penalty supporters believes it deters murders and other violent crimes.[5] Criminologists, whose job is to study such matters scientifically, disagree. A well-constructed study by Michael Radelet and Ronald Akers found that 95.5 percent of the experts surveyed disagreed that the death penalty is a stronger deterrent to homicide than long prison sentences.[6] Moreover, 86.5 percent of those same criminologists felt that abolition of the death penalty would have no significant effect, one way or the other, on murder rates.[7]

Experts can be wrong; even agreement among top scholars does not prove the point. That is why it is important to examine the evidence. Fortunately, there are few more thoroughly investigated areas. Most studies fail to find any deterrent effect; a few find that executions may actually increase homicides. There are some studies that purport to find a deterrent effect; all are massively flawed and have been widely criticized.

Historical Arguments

Skepticism about deterrence has long animated the death penalty debate. Cesare Beccaria, an Italian philosopher, politician, and economist of the Enlightenment, argued lack-of-deterrence as early as 1764 and called for abolition. Historian Douglas Hay has pointed out that in eighteenth-century England, "transported convicts were so little afraid that they often returned to England to pick pockets on hanging days."[8] Reformers of the era argued that the death penalty "paradoxically weakened the enforcement of the law"[9] by terrifying juries and prosecutors, "who feared committing judicial murder."[10] Dr. Benjamin Rush, a signer of the Declaration of Independence, crusaded against capital punishment, insisting that it "did not serve as a deterrent."[11] After a particularly gruesome, botched Canadian hanging in 1869, a local paper reported on a stabbing that same evening, "pointedly adding, 'Hanging men for stabbing does not seem to prevent that work.'"[12]

In nineteenth-century America, the death penalty's lack of deterrence became a part of the legislative debate. As early as 1841, a report prepared for the New York legislature (which body came close to abolishing capital punishment)[13] argued that the death penalty failed to deter crime "first, because the death penalty unleashed rather than harnessed those passions that caused crime, and, second, because imprisonment was most likely more effective as a deterrent."[14]

Michigan abolished the death penalty in 1846. Rhode Island followed in 1852, and Wisconsin did so in 1853. Although little was made of the deterrence argument in Michigan's successful abolition,[15] by 1868, arguments made before the Minnesota legislature included the statement that crime had not increased in Michigan, Rhode Island, or Wisconsin since abolition.[16]

Research

COMPARATIVE STUDIES. Early-twentieth-century researchers approached deterrence in two ways. Some compared homicide rates in neighboring jurisdictions with and without the death penalty; others compared homicide rates before and after abolition. A variety of innovative strategies have been employed, including comparisons of countries or states before and after abolition, contiguous state comparisons, regional comparisons, and even county-by-county comparisons.

As early as 1925, sociologist Edwin H. Sutherland found that in every "comparison that can be made . . . the homicide rate is lower [where] the death penalty is illegal."[17] Among other things, he looked at the available statistics and concluded that there "is no evidence that murder will increase if the death penalty is abolished and will decrease if it is restored."[18] Similarly, in 1952, after reviewing the evidence, Karl F. Schuessler concluded that "[t]he fact that men continue to argue in favor of the death penalty on deterrence grounds may only demonstrate man's ability to confuse tradition with proof, and his related ability to justify his established way of behaving."[19]

Another of the earliest and perhaps the most influential of these scholars, Thorstin Sellin of the University of Pennsylvania, grouped states into regions containing three contiguous states, each with one abolitionist state and two retentionist states. This, he hoped, would negate cultural, economic, or other factors that might skew the results. Sellin failed to find evidence of deterrence.[20] Moreover, his method has been replicated many times using a variety of comparisons, and yet not one such study has found any deterrent effect for the death penalty.

One way to overcome the criticism that cultural, economic, or other differences may account for the generally lower homicide rates in abolitionist states and countries is to compare small sections of a country that are culturally, economically, and socially similar. In a very clever study, Keith Harries and Derral Cheatwood matched adjacent counties from abolitionist states with adjacent counties in retentionist states.[21] After locating 393 matched pairs of similarly situated jurisdictions, with capital punishment being the only obvious distinguishing factor, the authors found that "what correlations do appear between capital punishment variables and violent crime are positive. As one increases, so does the other." The authors, while reserving judgment, conclude, "[T]he data certainly fit a brutalization model better."[22]

The argument that capital punishment not only fails to deter, but actually serves to increase, violent crime is controversial, and the authors were right to reserve judgment on that. Nonetheless, one cannot help but be impressed by the fact that, in most cases, abolitionist countries, states, and counties tend to have lower violent crime rates and lower murder rates than similarly situated retentionist jurisdictions. When Peterson and Bailey compared abolitionist states with retentionist states for the period 1980 to 2000, they found that death penalty states always have higher rates of murder and non-negligent manslaughter (ranging from 1.4 to 2.0 times higher over the 21-year period).[23] If the death penalty really deterred, one would expect the opposite—that capital punishment states would, at least some of the time, have lower rates.

Moreover, the gap in murder rates between death penalty states and non–death-penalty states is getting larger.[24] Thus, a decrease in murder rates cannot be attributed to capital punishment. At best, capital punishment does nothing to affect murder rates; if the brutalization hypothesis proves accurate, however, it may make Americans less safe.

Nonetheless, cross-sectional studies can be criticized in that sociological, demographic, economic, or other differences between the areas of comparison may distort the data. Even careful and creative studies matching the tiniest jurisdictional blocks cannot completely overcome this criticism.

STUDIES OVER TIME ("TIME SERIES"). To remedy this, researchers have followed jurisdictions before and after abolition. By looking at a single place over time, researchers mitigate cultural and socioeconomic bias: a single jurisdiction does not ordinarily change quickly enough for such differences to distort the picture. While these things do change, this method is less subject to the same criticism, and it plainly provides useful information.

Many studies have looked at murder, homicide, or violent-crime trends over time. Some recent ones have attempted to control for other socioeconomic variables. None of the studies has demonstrated a deterrent effect. Some have suggested brutalization: the hypothesis that the death penalty may increase murder and violent crime. The idea is that "executions brutalize members of society such that potential offenders are inspired by the execution,"[25] thus legitimizing murder. Studies on this, by Ruth D. Peterson and William C. Bailey, appear persuasive, but not conclusive.[26]

The evidence led former attorney general Janet Reno to say: "I have inquired for most of my adult life about studies that might show that the death penalty is a deterrent. And I have not seen any research that would substantiate that point."[27] For Reno as well as for most criminologists, the cumulative weight of these many studies has been decisive.[28]

ECONOMETRIC FALLACIES. Beginning with Isaac Ehrlich in 1973, a variety of economists using complex econometric models have claimed to find that the death penalty has a deterrent effect. Ehrlich's original research was wholly discredited. His research aggregated national data, lumping abolitionist states with retentionist states. It also suffered from a variety of other defects, including the fact that the years he chose to study were the only years for which a deterrent effect could be found. When the time frame changed, the deterrent effect disappeared. Other researchers were unable to replicate Ehrlich's findings, and they were rejected as unfounded by the prestigious National Academy of Sciences in 1978.[29]

Later researchers have refined Ehrlich's technique, with some claiming to find a deterrent effect. Indeed, some claim that each execution deters up to eighteen murders.[30] Economists—not criminologists—conducted these studies, and each used econometric strategies for estimating a deterrent effect. The mathematics involved is quite complex, but "all suffer from an important and avoidable error: they examine the relationship between death penalty variables and total non-negligent homicide."[31] Thus, each study, while purporting to use sophisticated, multiple-logistic regressions to control for all other confounding variables, stumbled on the most elementary problem of them all. By aggregating murders that could not possibly result in execution, these studies risked falsely concluding that changes over time in homicide rates are caused by variations in threatened or administered rates of execution. The inclusion of all homicides assumes that the deterrent effect of execution is highly inelastic across a very heterogeneous set of circumstances and individuals of varying capacities. Adding in so many noncapital cases risks creating an ocean of artificial deterrence.[32]

Thus, when Jeffrey Fagan, Franklin Zimring, and Amanda Geller extracted capital homicides from non-death-eligible homicides, they found no marginal deterrent effect.[33] The numbers of death-eligible cases did not go down (relative to non-death-eligible cases) as the threat of execution went up, nor did it go down when the risk decreased. Moreover, there were not more death-eligible cases in non-death-penalty states than there were in states that execute, nor was there any evidence for deterrence when death penalty states and non-death-penalty states were compared over time.[34]

The attempt by economists to control for multiple variables in order to test the deterrence hypothesis was admirable. However, econometric studies that compared execution risks to all homicides lost sight of the fact that executions are unlikely to deter rational actors who do not commit capital murder and whose crimes are not thus eligible for the death penalty. The most relevant group for which to test the deterrence hypothesis is composed of people who commit crimes for which the death penalty is a possible sanction. If a deterrent effect is not found there (and Fagan, Zimring, and Geller failed to find such an effect even in Texas, which executes more than any other state),[35] then it is unlikely to exist anywhere.

Another problem with each of these studies is that they all rely on highly skewed data: there is Texas, with many executions each year, and there are the rest of the states. A few states execute one or two a year, and many execute no one in most years. Thus, the drop in murder rates correlates with Texas executions, but this is surely a confounded correlation, like the correlation between ice cream sales and drownings in hot weather.

As one prominent statistician put it, "[C]laims of deterrence are a statistical artifact"[36] of this skewed data. Indeed, another prominent statistician calls these attempts to use econometric modeling on this type of data "junk science."[37] Yet another points out that such "mathematical complexity does not make for good social science."[38]

Moreover, these economists appear to put more weight on criminals' rationality than modern social science finds justifiable. Relatively few murderers make the kind of cold calculation required by this theory. Furthermore, it would be extraordinary if each execution could prevent eighteen additional homicides. If that were so, one would expect that countries with very low homicide rates could reduce those rates to nearly zero. Canada, with about one-third of the U.S. homicide rate, should have seen its rate skyrocket with abolition. Yet nothing of the sort occurred. Would 15 fewer executions cause 270 more Texas murders? Thus, these types of ultracomplicated computations lack facial plausibility. While some research results can seem implausible yet be true, the lack of surface plausibility of these econometric studies, in the face of so much contrary evidence, ought to raise one's level of suspicion. Healthy skepticism is called for.

Criminologist Jon Sorensen and attorney Rocky LeAnn Pilgrim in *Lethal Injection* point out that urban homicides have gone down at a far greater rate than rural homicides. When the drop in Texas's homicide rate is compared with that of New York (which has not executed anyone since 1963) and of California (which executes at a far more leisurely pace than Texas), one finds nearly identical drops in homicide rates. As they point out, "[E]ach state experienced historically large drops in homicide rates in their major urban centers."[39] Contrary to the understanding of those who believe in deterrence, New York—not Texas—had the largest drop. They conclude that the "decrease in homicide rates in Texas . . . is not the result of increases in the number of executions."[40] A variety of factors may be causing the drop in homicide rates; they suggest that increased imprisonment may be the most likely factor.

If Texas's high number of executions were responsible for the recent drop in the murder rate, one would expect the effect to show up most strongly in Houston, which has been responsible for "more death sentences and executions than any other county in America."[41] Yet, despite sophisticated efforts to find such a relationship, no credible evidence could be found that executions decreased the Houston murder rate.[42]

The killing of police officers is asserted to be one of the strongest arguments for capital punishment. Proponents argue that the death penalty deters criminals from shooting it out with police officers; that if criminals know that they will face capital punishment upon killing a law enforcement officer, they will be more likely to surrender, or at least not use lethal force in their attempt to escape. This hypothesis also founders upon the reality of empirical research. An interesting study by Geoffrey Rapp concluded that the death penalty may make police officers less safe, and, in any event, it provides no marginal deterrence over lengthy imprisonment.[43]

Professors John J. Donohue and Justin Wolfers provide the most sustained critique of these econometric attempts to prove that the death penalty deters.

After analyzing such studies' data from a variety of analytical perspectives, they conclude that "the evidence for deterrence is surprisingly fragile, and even small changes in specifications yield dramatically different results."[44] In summary, they point out:

1. It is very difficult for researchers to control for all factors that might affect causation. If important analyses are omitted, then the mathematical model may predict causation where none exists—confounding variables may make a correlation seem relevant when it is not. For this reason, we look to comparison groups to see if the hypothesis of causation is plausible. States and countries that have the death penalty should show different patterns of murder rates from those that do not have capital punishment. As Donohue and Wolfers state, "If the execution rate is driving the homicide rate, then one should not expect to see a similar pattern in the homicide time series for these comparison groups"[45] that are without capital punishment. But in every comparison that can be made, no correlation consistent with deterrence appears. Canada has about one-third as many homicides (and one-third the variation in homicide rates) as the United States. Canada has had no death penalty since 1976, and its homicide rate has gone up and down almost in lockstep with that of the United States. If the death penalty deterred homicide, one would expect that Canadian homicides would have gone up relative to those in the United States, once the United States restarted capital punishment in 1977.

   The sum total of these comparisons suggest that these massive mathematical models all suffer from a similar flaw—they fail to take into account the real factors that drive homicide rates, and erroneously see the drop in homicide rates in the immediate past as resulting from executions. Thus, using slightly different methods, Donohue and Wolfers make the same point that Sorensen and Pilgrim make: these models fail to capture accurately what is going on. They confuse the drop in homicides everywhere with the high execution rates in a few states and therefore lose sight of reality.

2. All of these new econometric models supposedly indicating a deterrent effect for capital punishment rely on mathematical models so complex as to be beyond the ability of all but a few specialists to understand. But if these models were correct, they would be relatively stable—changes in minor specifications in the model should not yield radical changes in outcome. Yet Donohue and Wolfers demonstrate that very minor

changes in specifications (that should result in little or no change in outcome) result in major changes in outcomes, sometimes moving from a strong deterrent effect to an equally strong antideterrent (or brutalization) effect.

3. Each of these new models is dependent on the years over which the mathematical model is applied. When the same model is applied over a longer time frame, the supposed deterrent effect again disappears.[46]

Statisticians make many other, more technical, criticisms of these new econometric attempts at modeling reality. They are junk science precisely because they confuse correlation with causation and then hide that confusion behind a blizzard of data and complex algorithms. They do not have the validity of the other simpler, less sophisticated studies. Ted Goertzel of Rutgers put it best:

When junk science is released to the media by scholars at prestigious universities, and published in reputable refereed journals, people become understandably skeptical about the value of social science research. A few years ago *The Economist* (May 13, 1995) published a tongue-in-cheek editorial announcing that "74.6% of sociology is bunk." Cynics wondered if the estimate might not have been low. But it is important not to throw out the baby with the bath water. There is good solid work being done in sociology, criminology and other social sciences, although it may not make it into the journals that value statistical complexity over reliable findings. The most reliable work uses simpler statistical techniques that do not require so much adjustment and standardizing of the data. This has the great advantage that . . . the work can be read and used by people who have not devoted years of their lives to learning obscure econometric techniques.[47] (Emphasis in original)

Criminologists as a group are generally quite skilled in interpreting statistical studies, and for "many criminologists the capital punishment and deterrence question is a dead issue."[48] While one can find politicians, lay persons, and even a few economists who believe that the death penalty deters, the one group with the most expertise almost uniformly rejects the deterrence hypothesis.

STUDIES ON BRUTALIZING EFFECT. There have been a number of recent studies attempting to assess whether the death penalty in fact brutalizes, such that it actually increases the risk of violence. In 1998, William J. Bowers and Glenn L. Pierce set out to test systematically whether executions encourage more homicides. They reasoned that if brutalization were to play a role, evidence of it would be most pronounced right after an execution, and that the effect would be greater where the execution was highly publicized. Their study of New York State from 1906 to 1963 found that the murder rate does go up after executions.[49] This suggests that the death penalty may do the opposite of what rational-choice, or deterrence, adherents argue.

More recent studies have had mixed results. In 1998, William C. Bailey, studying Oklahoma's reinstatement of the death penalty, found a significant increase in killings involving strangers, as well as results consistent with a brutalization effect for all homicides.[50] On the other hand, John K. Cochran and Mitchell B. Chamblin looked at California executions and found it a wash—argument-based murders of strangers increased and non-stranger felonies decreased.[51] Further, Jon Sorensen, Robert Winkle, Victoria Brewer, and James Marquart[52] analyzed Texas data and concluded that there was no evidence to support either a deterrence hypothesis or a brutalization theory.

Whether the death penalty increases violent crime is uncertain; there have not been enough scientific studies to prove the point. Moreover, when criminal justice experts were surveyed, two-thirds rejected the brutalization hypothesis.[53]

The idea of a brutalization effect may at first seem counterintuitive. How can a more severe punishment possibly increase violent crime? Surely, something must be wrong with the science? A moment's reflection will show this to be not so odd after all. Most people reading this have much to look forward to in life and much to lose by misbehavior. Others, with less to look forward to, can gain a kind of fame by infamous crime.

Former prosecutor Joel Clarke tells of prosecuting a fourteen-year-old boy convicted of murder. Why did he kill? He wanted to be like two infamous death-row inmates, later executed. One of the authors once represented a death-row inmate who expressed pleasure at the publicity he was getting after his capture. For some, the death penalty may be a spur to a kind of otherwise-unobtainable fame. Then, too, some people perhaps have a death wish. It is thought that serial killer Ted Bundy moved to Florida to commit his murders because he wanted to be executed. Not all people are deterred by the same things, and some may even be attracted to the passing fame of the gallows or a way out of this life.

Anecdotes do not prove, but do illustrate, the point. More research should be done. One fact, however, is clear from the research, and undercuts one of the strongest arguments in favor of capital punishment: the death penalty is not an effective deterrent.

INCAPACITATION AND THE DEATH PENALTY

It is quite true that the dead never kill. Most people assume that this ends the discussion. However, many people fail to realize that most murderers generally do not kill again: this is not a crime that ordinarily generates repeat offenders. To say that execution prevents repeat killings is to avoid the more important question of whether that person would have killed again had he or she not been executed.

Capital punishment does not usually lend itself to scientific experiments. In such a matter, we cannot ethically just change a variable and then measure the results of those changes. Consider the deterrence issue. How would one set up an experiment? Make the death penalty the punishment for capital murders occurring on Monday, Wednesday, and Friday—with life in prison the punishment for murders occurring during the rest of the week? It is hard to imagine an ethical experiment that would test capital punishment's most serious issues. For these reasons, most death penalty studies rely on less easily understood methods, whose very complexity breeds doubt. Incapacitation provides a rare exception.

Furman v. Georgia[54] emptied America's death rows in 1972. In that case, a badly fractured U.S. Supreme Court held that the death penalty as then administered was so arbitrary that, in the words of Justice Stewart's concurring opinion,

> [t]hese death sentences are cruel and unusual in the same way that being struck by lightning is cruel and unusual . . . the Eighth and Fourteenth Amendments cannot tolerate the infliction of a sentence of death under legal systems that permit this unique penalty to be so wantonly and so freakishly imposed.[55]

Only two of the justices would have found the death penalty cruel and unusual punishment under all circumstances. A plurality found it unconstitutional as then administered, and allowed the states to modify their statutes to attempt to find a constitutional death penalty; but those already on death row had their sentences commuted. Some, but not all, of the new statutes passed in response to *Furman* were upheld by the Supreme Court in 1976, thus reinstating the death penalty in the United States.[56]

Following those with commuted sentences to see what they, in fact, did provides a reliable guide to whether death-sentenced people are likely to reoffend. In this case, the "real world" itself provides the elements of a natural experiment: sufficient numbers of prisoners with commuted death sentences, without other biasing factors, such that reasonable inferences are possible.

The research on this is powerful, easy to understand, and startling. James Marquart and Jon Sorensen[57] tracked down, and obtained records on, 558 of the approximately 613 persons on death row whose death sentences were undone by the *Furman* case in 1972.[58] During the fifteen years of the study, some had been paroled, some remained in prison, and a few had returned to prison for parole violations or other crimes. Of those 558 formerly-death-sentenced prisoners, 98.7 percent did not kill again, either in or out of prison, and recidivism rates were in general low.[59] Of the 1.3 percent who killed again, only one killed while out on parole. Marquart and Sorensen's findings are consistent with other research on capital offenders. All such studies find a low rate of recidivism. Moreover, as other research has established, "among all convicted felons, murderers are the best parole risks."[60]

Contrary to conventional wisdom, murderers rarely kill again,[61] and tend not to recidivate. We tend to overestimate the danger these people present and to underestimate their prospects for rehabilitation. Murderers are generally older when paroled (thus they may have aged out of the crime-prone years); they had been "good convicts"; they were often first-time offenders and their crimes were more often situational or crimes of passion.[62] A person whose only major crime is a murder triggered by an emotionally charged situation (often between family or friends) is less likely to repeat the offence than many others.

The reason we overestimate the rate of recidivism among murderers may be psychological. Some of us tend to think of murder as a great threshold, and once it is crossed, all social inhibitions are forever set aside. One can see that such thinking ignores the role of unreasoned passion in most murders. Such "commonsense" assumptions, based as they are on a false notion of criminal psychology, lead us astray. Outside of Hollywood and those few crimes played up endlessly by the press, repeat killers are rare.

Of the pre-Furman group of 558 convicted capital murderers, 5 were innocent of the crimes that put them on death row and were later exonerated.[63] Innocence is a greater problem than anyone had realized until recently, making it likely that there were even more who were innocent, but whose innocence was never discovered. We fail to discover the extent of the criminal justice system's errors, and this is magnified in capital cases by an increased reluctance to admit error. The incapacitation argument stands or falls on the idea of saving innocent lives: we kill so that the killer will not again kill. But we have a system that kills many to save few, and that takes as many (or more) innocent lives as it saves.

It may be that mental health professionals are better at assessing dangerousness, but they still are not very good at it. Even when actuarial methods are used, we get it wrong in most cases. So it is unsurprising that life-and-death decision making is so flawed and that juries are unable to predict who will or will not be violent.

Capital murderers may be somewhat more likely than the general population to kill. Yet trained mental health professionals are not accurate in predicting future dangerousness. Even under the best clinical conditions, predictions of dangerousness are barely better than coin flipping.[64] Sociologists Michael Radelet and James Marquart point out that even those in the highest category, "young men with long histories of violence, have a much higher probability of future nondangerousness than they do of future dangerousness."[65]

Finally, the advent of laws establishing life in prison without the possibility of parole has taken the wind out of the argument that a murderer will be released to prey on the public again. Thirty-seven of the thirty-eight death penalty states now have the option of life without parole.[66] In those states, someone found guilty of a capital crime will never be released.

If incapacitation is the goal, capital punishment relies on predictions that cannot accurately be made, and assumes that the murderer will be released back into the public. Neither the assessment of dangerousness, nor the assumption of release, is based on fact. Citizens are entitled to protection. However, one must ask, what protection does the death penalty actually provide and at what cost to the lives of wrongly charged innocent citizens?

RACE AND THE DEATH PENALTY

> One of you two is gonna hang for this . . . Since you're the nigger, you're elected.
> —Police officer to Clarence Brandley, convicted 1981, exonerated 1990[67]

Progress has unquestionably been made in lessening racial discrimination in the United States. Lynching is rare, and prosecuted vigorously. In the eyes of the law, separate no longer means equal. The above quotation, however, illustrates that racism's legacy remains.

Most studies of race and the death penalty have, unsurprisingly, focused on African Americans and white persons of European descent. Relatively few Hispanics have been executed (67) and they make up only 10.4 percent of prisoners on death row. Native Americans are lumped into a generic category of "other," which comprises 2.3 percent of all executions as well as 2.3 percent of people on death row.[68] The 14 Native Americans who had been executed as of March 2006 are too few for meaningful statistical comparison, although one state—Oklahoma—executed 6 of the 14.[69] By comparison, blacks, who are about 12.3 percent of the population,[70] constitute nearly 42 percent of people on death row, and 34 percent (350) of all modern executions have been carried out on African Americans, thus generating numbers large enough for statistical comparison.

Racial discrimination in death sentencing is neither as pronounced nor as pervasive as it was during the early part of the twentieth century. Prior to *Furman v. Georgia* in 1972, the death penalty discriminated strongly against black defendants, particularly in the South. Death as a punishment for rape of a white woman was almost exclusively reserved for black men; whites were rarely punished for killing a black person.[71]

Race-of-defendant discrimination is now smaller, more isolated, and detectible in some places and in some circumstances (but not all). However, modern death penalty research demonstrates strong race-of-victim discrimination. In most jurisdictions, the killers of white people stand a much greater chance of receiving the death penalty, and black killers of white people stand the greatest probability of all. This effect is so strong that "[r]ace is more likely to affect death sentencing than smoking affects the likelihood of dying from heart disease"[72]

According to one of the leading researchers, David Baldus (whose team has investigated this issue in more places than anyone else),

> The race-of-victim influence was found at all stages of the criminal justice system process, although there were variations among studies as to whether there was a race-of-victim influence at specific stages. The evidence for the race-of-victim influence was stronger for the earlier stages of the judicial process (e.g., prosecutorial decision to charge defendants with a capital offense, decision to proceed to trial rather than plea bargain) than in later stages. This was because the earlier stages were comprised of larger samples allowing for more rigorous analyses. However, decisions made at every stage of the process necessarily affect an individual's likelihood of being sentenced to death.[73]

Some of these studies have found that a black defendant who kills a white victim will be four times more likely to receive a death sentence than a white defendant who kills a black victim. Moreover, "cases involving Black defendants and White victims are treated more punitively than cases with all other defendant/victim combinations."[74] The lesson is not only that the American justice system values white lives over black lives, but that American prosecutors and jurors are especially offended when a black person kills a white victim.

This racial multiplier in death penalty sentencing is, with only one exception (discussed below), found in all states with capital punishment. Southern states are not alone; it is found in the Northeast, the West, and the Midwest. Even in liberal California, researchers Glenn Pierce and Michael Radelet found that after "controlling for all other predictor variables, those who kill non-

Hispanic African Americans, are 60 percent less likely to be sentenced to death than those who kill non-Hispanic Whites."[75]

While race-of-perpetrator (as opposed to race-of-victim) effects are weak, it turns out that some black murderers appear more death-worthy than others. A stunningly simple, yet powerful, study reanalyzed the Baldus data to look not only at race, but also the effect on courts of defendants "whose appearance was perceived as more stereotypically Black."[76] After controlling for "a wide array of factors," the authors found that "defendants whose appearance was perceived as more stereotypically Black were more likely to receive a death sentence than defendants whose appearance was perceived as less stereotypically Black."[77]

The authors suggest that "jurors are influenced not simply by the knowledge that the defendant is Black, but also by the extent to which the defendant appears stereotypically Black."[78] Race remains more insidious than previously suspected. Some (perhaps many) Americans value white lives over black lives, punish more severely those whom society believes to be most stereotypically violent—and associate violence with morally irrelevant features such as lips, nose, hair texture, and skin tone.

Nebraska was the only state in which Baldus did not find a race-of-victim effect, and it was unusual in several ways. First, the study did find a strong socioeconomic effect. After controlling for all relevant factors concerning the defendant's culpability, the Baldus team found that "defendants in high socioeconomic status victim cases were more than five times as likely to receive a death sentence as those in low socioeconomic status victim cases."[79] Thus, even where no strong race effects could be found, death sentences were imposed on the morally repugnant and legally irrelevant grounds of class.

Moreover, racial effects were found in some areas of Nebraska, but these simply washed out when the state was considered as a whole. So the failure to find racism in death sentencing to a statistically significant degree there does not mean that race was not a factor; it only means that the signal was not strong enough statewide to detect it.

Nebraska was one of those states in which the judge, not the jury, sentenced defendants. The U.S. Supreme Court ruled in *Ring v. Arizona*[80] that a jury must find all of the facts upon which a death sentence is predicated.[81] This means that a judge cannot sentence someone to death because of evidence not presented to, and found to be factual by, a jury. Nebraska did not wait to see how its statute might fare under this new ruling changing its law to provide for jury sentencing. It remains to be seen what effect, if any, this will have on older Nebraska cases where the judge did the death sentencing.

Finally, while racism may be an inevitable feature of capital punishment (as it is an ubiquitous part of society), it is possible to reduce its presence. As David Baldus points out, the fact that some jurisdictions have reduced systemic discrimination to the point where it cannot be detected by modern statistical methods demonstrates that this discrimination can be lessened, although not eliminated.[82] Indeed, if the study cited above, demonstrating that jurors react to the extent to which defendants appear to be "stereotypically black," is valid, it is difficult to see how jurors' racism can be eliminated without first eliminating it in society as a whole. However, limiting capital punishment to the very worst murders, Baldus suggests, would lessen some of the most jarring disparities.[83]

Constricting the death penalty's application would not end racism in capital punishment. It would, however, reduce the numbers on death row and soften some of the worst problems. This would do more than save money and reduce racism. Abolition of the death penalty in most of Europe and Canada was presaged by a reduction in its use. If the pace of executions were slowed, the public might eventually conclude that it no longer needed this ultimate punishment. Baldus's suggestion might seem unsatisfactory to both abolitionists and retentionists; it could also be a tentative step toward a more rational system that eventually stops needing capital punishment.

The U.S. Supreme Court in *McCleskey v. Kemp*[84] held that statistical evidence showing systemwide racial bias in death sentencing does not prove that race was the deciding factor in any given case; it does not prove that a particular defendant received an unfair trial and this kind of evidence is, according to the Court, constitutionally insufficient to prove discrimination in a particular case. While undoubtedly true, this kind of evidence is routinely used in other contexts, such as employment discrimination cases. For example, a woman claiming to have been passed over for promotion can make use of statistics demonstrating that the employer disproportionately promotes men. That sort of statistic finds everyday use in America's civil courts. Only the death-row inmate is held to a higher standard of proof.

Justice Brennan's dissent in *McCleskey* pointed out that race was more likely than not the dominant factor, and "surely we would not be willing to take a person's life if the chance that his death was irrationally imposed is more likely than not."[85] That, however, is exactly what the courts do. By ruling out evidence of disparate impact of race in death sentencing, the Supreme Court has removed the courts from this issue. Because of *McCleskey*, lower courts cannot even consider statistics demonstrating that in a given case, race, rather than evidence, was the most powerful explanatory variable. In order to prove that race was a factor in these cases, a petitioner would have to get a statement by the prosecutor or the jurors admitting that they decided the case based upon race. This is not evidence that is likely to surface often, thus shutting the court-house door to the most powerful evidence available.

Many citizens may think that the courts are policing racial discrimination in the capital punishment system. They are not. The argument that race must not be much of a problem because, if it were, the courts would set it right, is false. Racism is the capital punishment system's dirty secret, hidden at all costs, and never acknowledged.

Studies of race in capital sentencing are not the only measures of racism within the system. As recently as June 2005, the Supreme Court in *Miller-El v. Dretke*,[86] reversed a capital case because of overwhelming evidence that a Dallas prosecutor had struck black jurors from the jury pool for no better reason than a dislike of black jurors in capital cases. It had been official policy to strike black jurors and then to offer pretexts in justification. Until *Miller-El*, most courts accepted the practice.

The Capital Jury Project has collected in-depth information on the behavior of capital juries in Alabama, California, Florida, Georgia, Indiana, Kentucky, Louisiana, Missouri, North Carolina, Pennsylvania, South Carolina, Tennessee, Texas, and Virginia.[87] These include the states that most often execute. That research concludes:

> The statistical evidence reveals that White male jurors were far more likely than African-American male jurors to think of the African-American defen-dant as dangerous to others and far less apt than their Black counterparts to see the defendant as sorry for what he did. White women were much less likely than Black women to acknowledge the defendant's emotional distur-bance. Concerning the tendency to identify with the defendant, African-American male jurors were significantly more likely than others to imagine themselves in the situation of the defendant's family, to imagine them-selves as a member of the defendant's family, to be reminded of someone by the defendant, and less likely than others to see the defendant's family as different from their own. And, as the Court supposed, the evidence shows that White jurors of both genders are much less receptive to arguments and evidence of mitigation than African-American jurors who served on the same Black-defendant/White-victim cases.[88]

While this may not be the overt, blatant racism of the past, it remains a sys-temic bias that selects people for death for reasons wholly unrelated to guilt, and it explains why prosecutors strive to strike black jurors.

Moreover, the type of studies pioneered by Baldus might not detect subtle race-of-defendant bias, even while finding the stronger race-of-victim bias. It may be that the signal is just not strong enough to show up given present methods of detection. Baldus and colleagues are, after all, struggling with large numbers of variables in a complex system. As good as these methods are (and most experts agree that the Baldus methodology is superb), there are both statistical and pragmatic constrictions on what these kinds of studies can do. Inevitably, on the other hand, their methods have gotten more sophisticated over time. This may explain why a later study, by Baldus and others, with findings from Philadelphia, did find strong evidence of race-of-defendant discrimination in capital cases.[89]

The notion that the death penalty is intimately intertwined with race is bolstered by its strong historical connection with slavery and lynching. As Jack Greenberg pointed out two decades ago:

Since at least 1967, the death penalty has been inflicted only rarely, erratically, and often upon the least odious killers, while many of the most heinous criminals have escaped execution. Moreover, *it has been employed almost exclusively in a few formerly slaveholding states*, and there it has been employed almost exclusively against killers of Whites . . .[90] (Emphasis added.)

Other research supports this view. As of November 1, 2006, nearly 82 percent of all post-Furman executions occurred in southern states,[91] and both qualitative and quantitative studies have repeatedly shown the linkage between both slavery[92] and lynching[93] and the death penalty. As Franklin Zimring points out, "[M]odern executions are concentrated in those sections of the United States where the hangman used to administer popular justice without legal sanction."[94] Recent research, using multiple logistic regression to factor out possible confounding variables, supports the connection between historic lynching and the modern death penalty.[95] Given the well-established historical fact that lynchings were predominately perpetrated upon southern blacks by southern whites, the linkages between the death penalty, slavery, and lynching seems clear. It is not a linkage that most death penalty proponents wish to acknowledge.

It is no longer possible to pretend that capital punishment laws apply equally to all people. Blacks killing whites face a greater risk, regardless of culpability; stereotypical appearances do matter—the more "black" one looks, the greater the risk; white jurors are more punitive toward black defendants and less able to appreciate mitigating circumstances; prosecutors continue to try to stack juries with whites; the linkages to slavery and lynching are plain.

While any one of these factors may not be conclusive, the combination of studies, all pointing to race as the most important factor in who lives and who dies, is compelling.

SURPRISING COSTS OF THE DEATH PENALTY

Many people do not consider the monetary cost of capital punishment. Surely a chemical drip costs less than life imprisonment. How could execution possibly cost more than imprisonment?

Capital punishment not only costs more—it costs much more. It took more than a quarter of a billion dollars for California's 11 executions—nearly 23 million dollars per execution![96] California is an extreme case, but a well-constructed study done in North Carolina, by Phillip J. Cook and Donna B. Slawson (for the Terry Sanford Institute of Public Policy at Duke University), demonstrated that it cost 2.16 million dollars more to prosecute a case capitally per death penalty imposed than for life without parole. In the Cook and Slawson study, the cost of a year in prison in a maximum-security cell was estimated to be $23,039. Assuming that the prisoner lived for 40 years (prison lives tend to be short, so 40 years is a reasonable estimate), a life prisoner in a maximum-security prison would cost less than a million dollars. Since most prisoners do not stay in maximum-security facilities for nearly that long, the average for most prisoners would undoubtedly be less than that. Cook and Slawson concluded:

> The extra cost to the North Carolina public of prosecuting a case capitally, as compared with a noncapital prosecution, is more than $216 thousand per death penalty imposed. This estimate takes into account the likelihood that the jury will actually impose the death penalty, and if so, that the appellate courts will return the case to Superior Court for retrial or resentencing.[97]

Texas, because it executes so frequently, should be more efficient than most, but even there each capital case costs about three times what it costs to imprison a person for forty years—thus, far more than it costs to keep that same person in prison for life.[98] No state has found a way to make executing cost less than life imprisonment.

The immediate (and wrong) reaction is that the excess cost is attributable solely to appeals—just reduce the appeals to cut costs. This, however, ignores the innocence problem; cutting appeals inevitably increases miscarriages of justice. There are two reasons why miscarriages increase as appeals are cut. First, as we will see in chapter 7, most discoveries of innocence occur in spite of the system. Volunteers reinvestigate the cases, unearth the mistake, and bring it to the court's attention. Appeals provide the time necessary to find the system's errors. Speeding up executions decreases the likelihood of discovering the error at all, much less in time to save the life of an innocent person. Secondly, appeals do sometimes assist in the discovery of error. Cases are returned for retrial, new and better lawyers are appointed, and error is uncovered. Thus, appeals, and the time they take, are an essential component in discovering miscarriages of justice.

Appeals, however, are only one small part of the expense; reducing them would only result in modest savings, while increasing the problem of the innocent at the gallows. Capital trials are longer and more complex. Not only are there more expert witnesses and lawyers, but the entire process takes longer, requiring more of the judge's time, more court personnel, and the like. Moreover, capital cases are more likely than other cases to go to trial rather than to plea bargain. "Because death is different, death penalty cases go to trial ten times more often than do other felony cases."[99] So not only are they more expensive per case, there are also proportionately more of them.

Prosecutors have a relatively low success rate in these cases. Every time the jury returns a life verdict, instead of death, the excess cost of these capital trials must count against the system's true cost; Americans also pay for the imprisonment of the now-convicted defendant. Finally, two-thirds of all capital verdicts are overturned on appeal or in state or federal postconviction legal proceedings, such as habeas corpus.[100] Many of these cases will return to the trial court for another expensive trial or sentencing. Some of these people are innocent and will ultimately be exonerated. Others will end up with life imprisonment, even after multiple, expensive hearings. All of this adds to the costs.

Moreover, the appellate process costs more in capital cases. States have to hire lawyers to work on these cases, and the convicted capital offender will have a postconviction lawyer, who will often be paid for her work. Appellate judges spend more time on these cases than any other. Housing the death-row inmate in a super-maximum death-row facility will, in most states, also be an added burden; and even the execution costs more than one might think. When one considers the reasons for all of these costs, one sees that it is impossible to create an execution system that will save money.

These costs come at the expense of roads, police, schools, health care, and the like. For example, New York State reinstituted the death penalty in 1995. Since then, the state has paid over 170 million dollars on its capital punishment system, without executing a single person.[101] New York's highest court invalidated that state's death penalty, and legislators have decided (for the time being) that the costs are not worth the effort. To true fiscal conservatives, the costs may prove decisive in the death penalty debate.

INNOCENCE

The last, and possibly most important, myth is that the American system of justice remains nearly infallible; that the American system of capital punishment only executes criminals who richly deserve their fate. As with the other myths, this one is likewise untrue. Because of its importance, however, we deal with it later, in a chapter of its own.

Modern research reveals capital punishment's striking lack of usefulness. There is little credible evidence that the death penalty deters violent crime, and it may even have a brutalizing effect on our society, thus making Americans less secure. It does not incapacitate effectively, perhaps killing as many, or more, innocent people as it saves. It is racist and it costs more than life imprisonment. The notion that the death penalty is an effective crime policy serving a greater good is a chimera chasing a ghost.

6 : Attitudes toward Capital Punishment: Do Facts Matter?

[T]he question with which we must deal is not whether a substantial proportion of American citizens would today, if polled, opine that capital punishment is barbarously cruel, but whether they would find it to be so in the light of all information presently available.
—Former U.S. Supreme Court Justice Thurgood Marshall[1]

INTRODUCTION

Americans have not always enthusiastically supported capital punishment. In 1965, polls showed 47 percent opposed to the death penalty and only 38 percent in favor. Support remained tepid until the *Furman v. Georgia* decision in 1972, ending capital punishment as unconstitutional as it was then administered. At that point, support for the death penalty, as reflected by the polls, began a more-than-two-decade upward surge. By 1973, nearly six people out of ten supported capital punishment. *Furman*, seen by some as unduly activist and undemocratic, created a backlash, and that, combined with rising crime rates and other socioeconomic factors, led to ever-stronger support until, by 1994, fully four out of five Americans supported state execution.[2]

These hardening attitudes were reflected in both politics and the law. By 1976, only four years after *Furman*, thirty-five states had passed new death penalty laws. Many of these new laws were found to be constitutional in three cases decided on the same day, *Gregg v. Georgia*,[3] *Proffit v. Florida*,[4] and *Jurek v. Texas*.[5] Plainly, state legislatures and state governors sensed the new attitude toward capital punishment, as did the Supreme Court.

By the 1980s, one candidate for governor in Alabama could run on a pledge to "fry them 'till their eyes pop out"[6] and another in Texas could run an ad "in which he walked along a panel of huge photos of men executed during his term as governor."[7] Michael Dukakis lost a double-digit lead in the polls and lost the 1988 presidential race, in part because of his negative answer to the question of whether he would support the death penalty if his wife were raped and killed. Similarly, Mario Cuomo lost the 1994 New York governor's race in which the winner, George Pataki, repeatedly attacked Cuomo's vetoes of capital punishment legislation.

Moreover, judges (like Rose Bird of California) perceived to be overly lenient on capital punishment were voted out of office, and governors in death penalty states commuted far fewer death sentences than had previously been the case.[8] Courts became increasingly hostile to death-row inmates' legal claims.[9] Capital punishment seemed popular, good policy, and good politics. Dissenters struggled in near isolation.

Slowly, since the mid-90s, attitudes have softened. Death penalty support dropped to 64 percent by 2000,[10] and has since hovered at about the two-thirds mark. More importantly, when respondents are given the option of sentencing capital offenders to life imprisonment without the possibility of parole, the number of death penalty supporters drops significantly. In a May 2006 Gallup Poll, a plurality of 48 percent favored life without parole, while 47 percent favored the death penalty.[11] All death penalty states except for New Mexico now provide for life imprisonment without the possibility of parole.[12] Polls that simply ask a generic "Are you for it or against it?" question provide a less accurate measure of death penalty support. Thus, true death penalty support is thinner than support measured by generic polls that fail to address the life-without-parole alternative.

Death penalty advocates also seem less enthusiastic. No longer do politicians focus so strongly on this one issue, and courts appear to be somewhat more critical in their approach to death penalty cases.

There is now an active and growing moratorium campaign spreading throughout the United States. So far, 143 local governments nationwide have called for a moratorium on the death penalty, and at least 14 death penalty, states have considered legislation establishing a moratorium on capital punishment.[13] While supporters continue in the majority, dissenters are being heard; their opposition is both a factor in, and a consequence of, changing attitudes.

There are regional differences. In some states, support has dropped to levels not seen since the 60s. A recent New York State poll showed 46 percent opposed to reinstating the death penalty; only 42 percent were in favor.[14] And when life imprisonment without parole is given as an alternative, New Yorkers are even more dubious about capital punishment, with 53 percent preferring the former and only 38 percent favoring capital punishment.[15]

Texans and other southerners tend to be more supportive of the death penalty, but even in Texas support is not as strong as it once was.[16] In Alabama a majority now supports a moratorium on executions "until questions about fairness and reliability are studied."[17] Support is declining overall, and this dwindling majority appears less and less enthusiastic.

The reasons for regional differences in attitudes include complex socio-economic disparities, including crime rates, homicide rates, and the perception thereof,[18] but the presence of an active death penalty also plays a role. Texas has by far the nation's busiest execution chambers, killing nearly thirteen people per year since its first post-*Furman* execution in 1982.[19] New York State has not executed anyone since the Eddie Mays electrocution in 1963.[20] Moreover, the Northeast accounts for less than 1 percent of all executions, while the former states of the old Confederacy account for 69 percent.[21] Not surprisingly, death penalty support tends to be highest where execution is most used; death penalty support generally drops after abolition.[22]

While death penalty support has gone up and down since the 1960s, we know little more than that about earlier attitudes. Early polling methods were flawed in that they only asked whether a person supported or opposed capital punishment, leaving no room for determining the intensity of support or for finding out whether supporters had reservations. For example, in more recent polls (both nationwide and regional) when people are asked to decide between the death penalty and imprisonment for life without the possibility of parole, support drops dramatically, with some polls finding death penalty support falling under 50 percent,[23] and others showing Americans almost evenly divided if life without parole is among the sentencing options.[24]

Moreover, modern polling often allows people to respond on a five- or seven-point scale (a Likert Scale), which allows researchers to measure the intensity of a person's views. When this is done, it becomes clear that not all people support capital punishment strongly. Many who claim to support the death penalty are, on closer inspection, quite ambivalent. Intensity of support, and the reasons for that support, are relevant factors omitted in early polls.

Finally, early research only looked at what people in fact thought; no attention was given to what might cause people to change their views about the death penalty.

Peoples' attitudes on a variety of issues change over time, as cultural, economic, or other circumstances change. Are there factors that might cause attitudes about capital punishment to shift? If so, what are they, and what are their effects? Researchers have begun to look not only at the fact of support for capital punishment but also at the reasons for it, the intensity of that support, and the kinds of things that might affect one's views.

The public's attitudes, and our understanding of those viewpoints, are of great consequence to capital punishment's future. "[T]he legal status of the death penalty in the United States depends on popular support, actual and perceived."[25] Elected officials argue that in enacting and enforcing death penalty laws, they are only carrying out the voters' will. As Phoebe Ellsworth and Samuel R. Gross point out:

Popular support may well be necessary to the continued use of the death penalty in this country. If a clear majority comes to reject this form of punishment, we predict that the Supreme Court, if not Congress and the state legislatures will soon follow suit.[26]

Thus, the importance of the public's attitudes, their reservations, the intensity of their feelings, and what motivates those feelings, cannot be overstated. Whether Americans continue to have a death penalty hinges, in part, on these questions.

WHAT DO WE KNOW AND DOES IT MATTER?

Supreme Court Justice Thurgood Marshall argued in 1972 that "American citizens know almost nothing about capital punishment" and if "informed about the death penalty and its liabilities would find the penalty shocking, unjust, and unacceptable."[27] These twin propositions, that Americans know little about the death penalty and that if they were more knowledgeable they would oppose the practice, have come to be known as the Marshall hypothesis. They have spurred a great deal of social science research on attitudes about the death penalty and are the most appropriate starting point in considering American attitudes on the subject.

Just what are the facts concerning capital punishment? Does it deter violent crime? Does it save money and valuable resources? Is it fairly applied in a race-and-class neutral manner? Would it matter if the answer to these questions was "no"? Would people find it "shocking, unjust, and unacceptable"? And if these things do not much matter, what would? Justice Marshall's hypothesis sent social scientists scurrying for answers.

Empirical studies, as we saw in chapter 5, demonstrate that the death penalty not only does not deter violent crime, it may—paradoxically—so brutalize people that both homicide and violent-crime rates are increased. Moreover, it fails to incapacitate effectively since capital murderers rarely kill again; it is racially discriminatory; and it costs far more than life imprisonment.

Does any of this matter? When one reviews the early empirical studies of capital punishment, one finds that traditional criticisms of the death penalty (cost, lack of deterrence, and racial and class bias) have shown limited ability to change attitudes. The desire for vengeance, and endemic discrimination within mainstream America, may simply be too entrenched. Despite the moral gravity of these arguments and their effectiveness with some people, they have not yet served to turn a majority of the body politic against the death penalty. However, the innocence issue—the recognition that Americans are convicting and in some cases executing innocent people—may well have the rhetorical force to effect change. It also strengthens the other anti-death-penalty arguments in powerful ways. The evidence demonstrating the inevitability of executing the innocent is set out in chapter 7; the important point for present purposes revolves around the extent to which the knowledge of this issue changes people's attitudes about capital punishment.

The Marshall Hypothesis—Are We "Know-nothings"?

The first part of the Marshall hypothesis—that Americans know precious little about their society's ultimate punishment—has proven true in virtually every experiment yet conducted. Even criminal justice majors and master's-level criminal justice students appear to know quite little, although the subject is within their area of interest.[28]

This is changing, as the proliferation of college courses covering capital punishment indicates. Moreover, the numbers of books, articles, television documentaries, and the like directed at a lay audience has exploded. So while Americans may still know little about how, why, and who they put to death, interest in and knowledge about the subject rising and may be part of the reason for the recent drop in death penalty support. It also may be that this increased media interest in part *reflects* changed attitudes, particularly by the educated elite. In any event, change is evident: no longer is there an overwhelming pro-death-penalty sentiment across the United States. Other voices are being heard and are having an effect.

Early Tests of the Marshall Hypothesis

In 1976, just four years after Justice Marshall's concurring opinion in *Furman*, Austin Sarat and Neil Vidmar conducted the first reported, and most famous, test of the Marshall Hypothesis.[29] Their general methodology became a model for all else that followed, with other researchers attempting to improve on their design and to test for more variables. Sarat and Vidmar set up a classical experiment, using 181 randomly selected residents of Amherst, Massachusetts. First, participants were given a questionnaire to ascertain their level of knowledge and attitudes about the death penalty. Then they were divided into four groups; participants in each group were assigned an essay to read. One of the essays was a control essay, which did not discuss the death penalty; the other essays provided factual evidence about capital punishment. The first covered what was then known about deterrence, the second articulated a variety of criticisms about the death penalty, and the third combined information from the first two. While the essays stimulated a substantial and statistically significant reduction in death penalty support, they did not result in the majority coming to oppose capital punishment.

Many more studies have been done, all improving on one or more aspects of the Sarat and Vidmar design. Some provided far more information, even to the point of conducting entire classes on the subject. Robert Bohm, along with various colleagues, has been the undisputed leader in this regard.[30]

These studies provide partial support for Justice Marshall's hypothesis, albeit far less than what one suspects Marshall would have hoped. While support for capital punishment is lessened, only two of these studies resulted in an absolute majority opposing capital punishment.[31] Moreover, follow-up studies by Robert Bohm and colleagues suggest that the change is temporary, with pro-death-penalty attitudes rebounding to near pretest levels over time.[32]

Many reasons have been suggested for why solid, factual information fails to have a larger effect and why there is a rebound with time. Bohm, for example suggests that death penalty opinions are based more on emotion, and that facts and reason give way to emotion. Other forces, however, may also be at work. Bohm conducted his studies in the Deep South, where strong support for the death penalty is prevalent. In that region, abolitionist attitudes swim against a powerful current, and it is not surprising that his students would revert to their former positions. But as attitudes moderate even in that region, the knowledge of the death penalty's deficiencies may yet prove useful. Thus, Bohm's courses may have had a more significant impact than his follow-up studies could measure.

Moreover, we do not know just how strongly these former students hewed to a pro-death-penalty line. It may be that they reverted to supporting the death penalty, but did so with reservations not held before the class. A reduction in the intensity of one's beliefs is very important. As with most matters of debate, the strong partisans frame the discussion. People with sufficient knowledge about the death penalty to have reservations may leave the partisanship to others, thus changing the terms of the debate by reducing the numbers who engage in the retentionist side.

More importantly, most of the early research on this subject came before the most recent revelations of so many innocent people wrongly convicted and sent to death rows across the nation. At the point most of these studies were conducted, the prospect of convicting and executing an innocent person must have seemed a rare and improbable occurrence. This has changed.

None of this detracts from the importance of other arguments against capital punishment, but it may be that these issues are more persuasive among those who already have strong doubts. There is good reason to think that wrongful convictions and wrongful executions have greater impact on death penalty retentionists who harbor retributive notions of justice that are relatively resistant to other empirical arguments.

INNOCENCE: VIEWS ARE CHANGING

There have always been those who doubt that modern justice systems convict the innocent. For them, efficient prosecution of crime outweighs their (perceived) slight risk of miscarriages of justice. Judge Learned Hand, who was surely one of the most celebrated judges never to have served on the United States Supreme Court, expressed this skepticism more clearly than most:

> Our dangers do not lie in too little tenderness to the accused. Our procedure has been always haunted by the ghost of the innocent man convicted. It is an unreal dream. What we need to fear is the archaic formalism and the watery sentiment that obstructs, delays, and defeats the prosecution of crime.[33]

As it did for Learned Hand, the innocent person who is nonetheless convicted (and in capital cases, sentenced to death) has, until recently, seemed a mere abstraction to most Americans. Without names, faces, and stories, this nightmare appeared rare and imaginary. Learned Hand's denial of "watery sentiment" applied doubly to heinous murderers whose (in his view, doubtless guilty) ghosts were not mourned. While Americans understood the abstract possibility of hanging an innocent person, as with psychologist Piaget's small child whose toy had disappeared, what was not seen, did not exist.

Of course, not everyone saw it that way. As we will see in chapter 7, doubts about the guilt of those who are executed go back centuries. The Marquis de Lafayette opposed capital punishment on the ground that innocent people would inevitably be executed. Abolitionists were, however, in the minority. One reason is that in many of the older highly publicized cases there was and is no way to conclusively establish guilt or innocence (for instance, reasonable people continue to disagree about the Joe Hill and Sacco-Vanzetti cases).[34] Without clear-cut evidence that most, if not all, reasonable people can agree on, issues remain abstract and thus disputable.

In the 1960s and 1970s, arguments for deterrence provided the primary support for the death penalty.[35] With rising crime, opinions in the 1980s shifted and, by the 1990s, the logic of retributivism, the notion of "just deserts," had triumphed. This hardening public attitude increased social acceptance of retributive justifications of punishment.[36] Retributivism turns on the issue of guilt or innocence; it assumes that the right person is being punished. So it is not surprising that the shift toward retributive justifications for the death penalty would slowly yield to evidence that Americans execute innocent people. Opinions change slowly, and only when new evidence is fully appreciated. By 1990, the evidence that Americans execute innocent people was only then beginning to emerge.

Even as late as 1991, only 11 percent of abolitionists opposed capital punishment on the grounds that people might be wrongfully convicted. Even though most thoughtful people knew that wrongful convictions undermined capital punishment, the issue had not yet gained traction. From that historical perspective, the change is remarkable. By 2003, fully 25 percent of abolitionists opposed the death penalty because of wrongful convictions.[37]

WHAT HAS CHANGED

Two things have changed the face of the debate. First, in 1987, Michael Radelet and Hugo Adam Bedau published their groundbreaking, scholarly work exposing numerous cases of wrongful convictions and of those who were executed but innocent.[38] Retentionists have pecked away at the margins of this work,[39] but have never shaken the central theme, that innocent people were convicted and sometimes executed throughout the twentieth century. Most scholars now accept this central thesis. Even though one might reasonably question one or more of their cases, they are certainly right in the bulk of their research. Their work gave names, faces, and stories to people who were grievously wronged by the system. It also gave new life to the innocence issue.

Second, the modern post-*Furman* capital punishment system was to have righted mistakes of the earlier criminal justice system. The new-and-improved death penalty machine was supposed to be, if not infallible, as fail-safe as humans could make it.

We now know that, in the modern era alone (between 1976 and February 2006), 123 people have been convicted and sentenced to death only to be later exonerated.[40] Some of these exonerations resulted from improved DNA and other scientific testing. Some prisoners, like Gary Gauger, whose story is related in chapter 7, were exonerated and freed after the true murderers were caught. What is different is that Americans now know the names, faces, and stories of dozens of innocent people who suffered for years on death row, and Americans now suspect that killing of innocent people in the modern capital punishment system is as inevitable as it always was. Three-fourths of the American public thinks that an innocent person has been executed within the last five years.[41] Some of these people continue to support the death penalty; but, as we will see, it is likely that the intensity of that support is lessened by the knowledge that the United States executes innocent people.

The recent preeminence of the innocence issue reflects more than public opinion polls. Political and legal institutions change more slowly than public opinion, but even these slow-moving institutions are beginning to reflect this changed climate. Illinois saw 13 exonerations for 12 executions before Governor Ryan decided the system was broken and declared a moratorium on executions. Before leaving office, he pardoned 4 more because of doubts about their guilt, and then commuted or pardoned the sentences of all 167 remaining death-row inmates, thus ending the death penalty in Illinois for the foreseeable future. Governor Ryan had good reason to react to the wrongful convictions on Illinois' death row. Thirteen men (including Gary Gauger) had been close to execution before they were exonerated. Other Illinois cases were equally or more frightening.

In Illinois, Anthony Porter came within forty-eight hours of execution in Illinois' death chamber. Only a last-minute stay by the courts kept him alive. Ironically, his innocence had nothing to do with the grounds for the stay—his low IQ and the question of whether he was mentally fit to be put to death bought him valuable time in the courts. In fact, the Illinois Supreme Court in an earlier opinion, which it surely now wishes it had never written, had called the evidence against Porter "overwhelming."[42] Time, not the criminal justice system, which failed to catch its own mistake, saved Anthony Porter.

It was an amazing group of undergraduate Northwestern journalism students (supervised by Professor David Protess) who reinvestigated the case. Through their efforts, the state's main witness recanted, and then, most improbably of all, the students got the real killer to confess on videotape.[43]

Porter, who had spent sixteen years on death row, lived only because his IQ was low enough for the courts to take more time, and because, in that additional time, undergraduate students doggedly pursued the truth and uncovered police wrongdoing. Before his release, Porter said, "The first thing I want to do is hug my mother and hug my children, and let them know I'm back and I love them very much."[44] This is the kind of story that gets attention, and newspapers across the country ran hundreds of stories mentioning the case.[45] As the *Chicago Tribune*, put it, in its award-winning series on capital punishment,

> The growing list of innocent men who have been sentenced to die in Illinois has attracted attention worldwide and become a rallying cry for opponents of capital punishment.[46]

Stories like these, which "make real" the innocent who suffer on the nation's death rows, are one important reason why attitudes are changing.

Porter's case is not unique. As Illinois Supreme Court Justice Moses Harrison II has written,

The system is not working. Innocent people are being sentenced to death. If these men dodged the executioner, it was only because of luck and the dedication of the attorneys, reporters, family members and volunteers who labored to win their release. They survived despite the criminal justice system, not because of it . . . One must wonder how many others have not been so fortunate.[47]

Case after case demonstrates that the difference between living and dying is blind luck, not institutional competency. Indeed, in many cases elected officials (who, after all, frequently seek reelection and higher office) fought hard to keep their mistakes buried. Governor Ryan was one of the first major politicians to see the potency of the innocence question. His pardoning of some who were plainly innocent, and commuting the sentences of all others on Illinois' death row, has spurred renewed interest in wrongful capital convictions.

Maryland's governor later imposed a moratorium on executions, which has since expired, and at the beginning of 2006 New Jersey instituted a moratorium in order to study the issue. At this writing, California is also contemplating a moratorium on executions. Politicians plainly sense the changing mood and are reflecting that change.

Ironically, Illinois, with eighteen death-row exonerations, is not the nation's leader—Florida has had twenty-one, and Texas and Louisiana have each had eight. Most states with capital punishment have had at least one death-row error. The innocence question affects every state's capital punishment regime. The issue is not likely to go away. According to the Death Penalty Information Center, there was an average of nearly three exonerations a year from 1973 to 1998.[48] From 1998 to 2003, the number doubled to six exonerations a year, and innocent people on the nation's death rows continue to surface.

The rise of Innocence Projects at law schools around the nation, moratoria movements across the country (including the call for a moratorium by America's largest group of lawyers, the American Bar Association), the increased scrutiny on laboratories doing DNA work—all suggest that the innocence issue has gained traction far stronger than other death penalty issues.

Even judges are affected. Recently retired Supreme Court Justice Sandra Day O'Connor has acknowledged that the American criminal justice system may well be executing innocent people. Moreover, the U.S. Supreme Court may be becoming more sensitive to the issue; in June 2005, it agreed for the third time in just over a decade to consider the circumstances under which a claim of innocence suffices to merit a court hearing.[49] Then, in a surprise to many observers, in 2006, it held that the petitioner, Paul Gregory House, had "made the stringent" showing required in order to obtain relief in the courts.[50] Although this opinion opens the door a mere hair's breadth to raise a claim of actual innocence, that it expands the possibility of relief at all is a change from decades-long rulings constricting the grounds upon which death-row inmates could appeal. The courts are also feeling the pulse of public opinion.

Nonetheless, such evidence is anecdotal. It strongly suggests a broad shift in attitudes and provides reasons why such a shift may be occurring, but it does not prove the point. Stories (no matter how numerous and compelling) should be backed up with systematic research. In 1998, Radelet and Bedau called for more research on the innocence issue:

> As things stand now, we have little or no knowledge about the effect of information about wrongful convictions of capital defendants on the public's support for the death penalty. Here as elsewhere, the Marshall Hypothesis . . . remains untested in recent years. In the decade since our research on miscarriages of justice in capital cases was first published, we have some vivid anecdotal evidence from various conversations and courtroom testimony showing that jurors in capital trials who learn about our work find themselves rethinking their support for the death penalty. However, more systematic research is needed before we can gauge the effect of such knowledge on various constituencies."[51]

EXPERIMENTAL RESEARCH ON INNOCENCE AND ATTITUDES

A few researchers have taken up the call. While the research to date is hardly conclusive, it does unambiguously support the notion that the innocence argument has the potential to recast and reinvigorate the death penalty debate. This research indicates that innocence is the death penalty's Achilles heel precisely because it affects the entire range of retributivist positions, undermining the most adamant, as well as the most tenuous, of death penalty supporters. It reframes the debate by moving, if ever so slightly, the hard rock anchoring the right end of the attitudinal scale; and it gives abolitionists a way to reach beyond those already persuaded.[52]

The first published social science research that explicitly looked at wrongful convictions of capital defendants used college students in a classical experiment.[53] The reason professors use college students is simple—they are available and inexpensive to test. College students will usually participate in large numbers, even though they should be (and in this case were) told that they do not have to participate and that their grade will not be dependent on their cooperation. The downside is that college students are not necessarily representative of the public at large, and the results from such studies must be viewed with caution. Unlike a thoroughly random sample of the country as a whole, college students may be different in some ways that bias the results. Nonetheless, a great many of these experiments are performed, and when combined with other evidence and other studies, their results may be persuasive, even if not conclusive.

This first study, by Clarke, Lambert, and Whitt, used 730 college and graduate students ranging from first year to master's level, who were first tested on their general attitudes and knowledge about the death penalty.[54] Three essays were then randomly assigned, thus dividing the students into three groups. One group received a non-death-penalty control essay on the general theories of punishment; another got a factual essay outlining the most recent information on deterrence; and the last group read the most recent information on innocence.

The results surprised even the researchers doing the experiment. The control essay, as was predicted, did nothing whatsoever—that much was expected. The deterrence essay resulted in a small but statistically insignificant change, very slightly reducing support for the death penalty. The innocence essay, however, resulted in a small, but statistically significant change at every point in the scale. Even strong retentionists—with powerfully held retributive views— changed some, and those with weakly held views changed even more.

Most students reading the innocence essay dropped a response category in their support for capital punishment. The student who "somewhat favored" the death penalty before reading the innocence essay was likely to change his or her support for capital punishment to "uncertain" after reading the essay. Likewise, a student who "strongly favored" the death penalty before reading the innocence essay would likely change his or her support to "somewhat favoring" the death penalty. In contrast to the unchanged opinions of the control group, the drop in support for the death penalty in students reading the innocence essay spanned the entire range of students tested.

Perhaps the most important aspect of these findings is that a simple essay, read in ten minutes, changed attitudes along the entirety of the scale. This suggests that with more time to assimilate the information, and more intensive coverage of that information, much larger changes could occur among all groups, including adamant retributivists with strongly held views. If this is true, then this is the kind of understanding about attitudes concerning the death penalty, and the changing of these attitudes, that could make a meaningful difference in the modern capital punishment debate.

This small across-the-board attitudinal change also demonstrates the incremental nature of using social facts to change strongly held views. This is particularly true when the issues are highly charged politically, as is the case with the death penalty. Facts do matter, even to a retributivist, when the facts undercut the basic assumptions of one's theory. This preliminary research suggests that the fact of innocence may play this role.[55]

This central finding—that the innocence issue reduces death penalty support for both strong and weak supporters—is inferentially supported by poll data. Not only is support for the death penalty declining, but also the numbers of those who support capital punishment weakly or with reservations are going up.[56] Thus, as discussed below, declining support for capital punishment comes not just from people whose commitment was weak or ambivalent to begin with.

Gross and Ellsworth point out that declining crime rates are unlikely to be the sole cause of this decline in support for the death penalty. "If people had been ambivalent about the death penalty all along . . . the decrease in crime might be enough to move them towards opposition."[57] But that would not affect those with hardened retentionist beliefs. Thus, if dropping crime rates were the sole cause for the decline in death penalty support, the numbers would have dropped but the intensity of those supporting capital punishment would have remained constant. That, however, is not what has happened. If anything, support with reservations is increasing. Intensity of support is dropping as well as the overall support itself.[58]

From this, Gross and Ellsworth infer that dropping rates of violent crime and homicides—whatever role they may play—cannot be the whole story. Since earlier support for capital punishment had been enthusiastic, and since there is an overall drop in support combined with an increase in weak or ambivalent support, one can surmise from the Gross and Ellsworth research that some factor (such as the innocence issue), rather than dropping crime rates, is responsible. Thus Gross and Ellsworth provide additional support for the proposition that the innocence issue, by moving attitudes at all levels, combines with the other circumstances to recast the entire debate.

We discuss the moral implications of this research more fully in chapter 8, but the implications for abolitionists should be plain: while all of the empirically verifiable issues (deterrence, incapacitation, racism, and costs) are important, innocence is the one issue capable of reaching the committed death penalty advocates who base their positions on a conception of just deserts, untethered to utilitarian concerns. Even the most committed retributivist must blink at an eye-for-an-eye system that repeatedly strikes the wrong person's eye.

Some interesting recent research on the innocence issue makes sophisticated use of modern polls to tease out correlations between support for the death penalty and the innocence issue. These studies, done by James D. Unnever of Radford University and Francis T. Cullen of the University of Cincinnati, tend to support the notion that the innocence issue markedly reduces support for the death penalty.[59] They found that those who believe that innocent people have been executed are less likely to support capital punishment. Moreover, both innocence and unfairness of application were correlated with reduced support for capital punishment. As the authors point out, one can connect the two. A system that regularly punishes the innocent may be viewed as unfair; and innocence is not the only manifestation of unfairness. Racism and class discrimination, for example, are other types of unfairness found in the American capital punishment system.

The authors carefully test the interaction between innocence and unfairness of application and find, not surprisingly, that "the relationship between believing that an innocent person had been executed and support for capital punishment was more substantial when Americans thought the death penalty is applied unfairly than fairly."[60] This research gives innocence newfound consequence. Innocence, as we have been arguing, does not supplant or overshadow other manifestations of unfair administration—it enhances them. The strongest moral position includes innocence and unfairness of application in its larger and more expansive sense.

Unnever and Cullen also found that the race of the respondent was the second-most-important factor in belief in the death penalty, with white people being far more strongly supportive of capital punishment and far less likely to be affected by the information that innocent people are being sentenced and executed with distressing frequency. This has led to some pessimism.[61] If death penalty support is tied to white racism—however subtle—then ending capital punishment may be more difficult than was previously thought.

While race is "the second-most robust predictor of supporting the death penalty,"[62] Unnever and Cullen's research shows that information about innocence and unfairness prompts changes among all groups. Moreover,

> over one-fourth (29%) of the racial divide in support for capital punishment can be attributed to differences in the degree to which African Americans and whites believe that innocent people have been executed and the death penalty is applied unfairly.[63]

Austin Sarat responds to the pessimists by pointing out that abolitionists are making progress among all sorts of groups and that "[o]ur national conversa-

tion about the death penalty is very different than it was 10 or 20 years ago."[64]
He goes on to argue,

> Today's new abolitionists face an important challenge, namely, to ensure
> that their rhetoric does not simply fuel reform, keeping the death penalty
> alive by rationalizing it, streamlining it, and helping prevent its most egre-
> gious miscarriages of justice . . . Unnever and Cullen's analysis suggests
> that [abolitionists] *are making progress in confronting that challenge* even as it
> highlights the continuing need to "show the public that the prospect of in-
> nocents being arrested, placed on death row, and executed is not prevented
> by fine-tuning the punishment process but rather is systematic and inevit-
> able."[65] (Emphasis added.)

The pessimists make an important point about deeply embedded white racism,
but they fail to see the progress that has been made even among the staunchest
death penalty supporters. The finding that innocence and unfairness problems
reduce African American support three times more than it reduces white support is indeed cause for concern,[66] as is the fact that racism is a component in
death penalty support. Abolition, however, does not depend upon convincing
everyone; that is unlikely ever to happen. What is necessary is for the intensity
of support to drop, as well as the overall level of support. And that is, in fact,
what seems to be happening. This trend toward lowered support for the capital punishment system seems likely to continue so long as Americans continue
to convict, sentence, and execute innocent people. That reduction in support
will not end anytime soon. The fallibility of human nature guarantees that mistakes will continue to undermine the perception that we have a fair system that
targets only the guilty without racial or class bias.

Correlational research, such as Unnever and Cullen's, has advantages over
small-scale experiments. It typically uses much larger samples; those samples
are completely random, thus allowing for more precise estimates of probability.
Furthermore, because of sample size, it can often break out demographic differences by race, gender, age, education, and the like. Analysis of poll data from already conducted polls is less expensive and possibly less fraught with error.

All correlations, no matter how strong, have one significant flaw: one cannot determine causation from a mere correlation. With a classic experiment,
one simply designs the experiment so that all variables stay constant. One then
applies a treatment (or intervention) to one randomly assigned group and not
to a control group, to see if there is any change. One cannot do this with correlations. If A is statistically related to B, we still do not know what the relationship is. A could cause B, or B could cause A, or something else might cause

both, or the relationship may even be entirely spurious. Correlational studies, however, have great potential to confirm other evidence. Indeed, that may be one of their greatest uses. When experimental and anecdotal evidence both point in one direction, then analysis of polling data confirming a strong correlation can support, and to some degree confirm, that evidence.

This is what Unnever and Cullen's research has accomplished: it has provided additional evidence that the innocence issue really does have renewed power to influence the death penalty debate.

CONCLUSION

The issue of innocence has breathed new life into an old topic. As Gross and Ellsworth point out, death penalty support is vulnerable in part because it has been unquestioned for so long:

> Unaccustomed for so long to defending their attitudes, or even to thinking much about them, supporters of the death penalty may have become more vulnerable to new information that challenges their beliefs—especially in a period of decreasing crime.[67]

There is little question but that something is different. The death penalty debate is no longer one-sided. The innocence issue is not the only reason for this, nor will it be the only issue in the future. It has, however, taken on increased significance and forced people to reexamine long-held beliefs. That is unlikely to change. The knowledge of capital punishment's manifest deficiencies is gradually seeping into public consciousness, and the expansion of this knowledge shows no sign of abating. Books, articles, documentaries, and college courses on this issue are all increasing, and public interest in it continues to be strong. Research demonstrates that knowledge does make a difference in the death penalty debate. This expansion of public awareness can only result in increased debate.

Moreover, this new awareness puts greater pressure on retentionists to explain why life imprisonment without the possibility of parole does not satisfy retributivist goals. After all, we do not rape the rapist, nor burgle the burglar; why kill the killer, when we know that in some instances we will inevitably get it wrong?

Finally, increased awareness of the empirical reality of capital punishment is only one part (albeit an important part) of the issue. This system's cost, racism, systemic unfairness, and lack of deterrence are also part of the growing awareness that the death penalty fails its essential purpose. This awareness combines with the international pressures recounted in part 1 to make for a predictably lively debate.

7 : Executing the Innocent

If statistics are any indication, the system may well be allowing some innocent defendants to be executed.
—Retired U.S. Supreme Court Justice Sandra Day O'Connor[1]

FROM THE BEGINNING

State execution of innocent people spans the millennia; Socrates and Christ present two long-past miscarriages of justice. The literary equivalent, Sophocles's *Antigone*—a young woman executed for elevating God's law over man's—illustrates this ultimate assertion of state power. Throughout the centuries judges and magistrates have compounded the problem.

The British (whose courts begat America's own common-law system) were long aware that judges and juries at times committed this gravest of errors. Eminent British legal commentators of the seventeenth and eighteenth Centuries, such as Coke, Hawles, Hale, and Blackstone, called attention to cases of persons wrongly executed.[2] For example, in 1611, a man was executed for murdering his niece. The only problem was that she was not dead. No body had been found, and the conviction was based on circumstantial evidence. She later turned up, saying that her uncle had beaten her and she had run away.[3] In another celebrated case, of 1660, a mother, father, and son were all executed as a result of the young boy's delusional confession to a murder (later retracted when he came somewhat to his senses), which incriminated his parents as well. The victim turned up two years later with a tale of abduction, forced service on a ship, enslavement in Turkey, and, finally, escape by way of Lisbon.[4]

In 1762, Jean Calas, of Toulouse, a Protestant Huguenot in Catholic France, was tortured, broken on the wheel, strangled, and burned, all the while protesting his innocence in the alleged murder of his son.[5] Voltaire took an interest in the case and convincingly demonstrated that Calas was innocent. Voltaire's "Treatise on Toleration" speaks through the centuries to the dismay any thoughtful person must feel at such abuse of state power:

> The murder of Calas, which was perpetrated with the sword of justice at Toulouse on March 9, 1762, is one of the most singular events that deserve the attention of our own and of later ages . . . [W]hen an innocent father is given into the hands of error, of passion, or of fanaticism; when the accused has no defense but his virtue; when those who dispose of his life run

no risk but that of making a mistake; when they can slay with impunity by a legal decree—then the voice of the general public is heard, and each fears for himself. They see that no man's life is safe before a court that has been set up to guard the welfare of citizens, and every voice is raised in a demand of vengeance.[6]

In 1775, Jeremy Bentham offered the Calas case as proof of the "irremissibility" of the death penalty and called for English abolition. Nearly two centuries would pass before the United Kingdom abolished capital punishment (in 1965), after it was found that, as late as 1950, one Timothy John Evans had been wrongfully hanged. This most recent miscarriage surprised many— including, presumably, an earlier home secretary, Gwilym Lloyd George, first Viscount of Tenby, who had previously asserted that there were no such modern executions of the innocent.[7]

Postrevolutionary America was not immune. Stuart Banner points out that nineteenth-century abolitionists argued that "innocent people were often executed by mistake,"[8] and "the era saw the first nationally known American cases"[9] of wrongful executions and near misses. In 1819, two brothers were spared the noose when their supposed victim "turned up at the hanging."[10] In 1835, Alabama hanged a man for murder; the real murderer confessed on his deathbed a few months later.[11]

The execution of an innocent man in Windsor, Canada, so aroused Michiganders across the Detroit River that it played a role in Michigan becoming, in 1847, the first jurisdiction in the United States to abandon the death penalty. As Eugene Wanger puts it, "There were at least two possible suspects [for the rape of a nine-year old girl], but Fitzpatrick was an Irishman and he was elected . . . Later, on his deathbed, the actual rapist confessed to the crime."[12] Moreover, innocence played a significant role in the abolition of the death penalty in other states, as well as in Canada.[13]

THE MODERN PROBLEM: EXECUTING THE INNOCENT
Innocence is a far more complex problem than might first appear to be the case. For capital defense lawyers, "innocence" does not merely refer to a situation where the state has convicted the wrong person; it can also refer to cases where the defendant has committed some crime, but, for various reasons, might well have been spared execution had the appropriate evidence been timely submitted to the trial court. It can refer as well to cases where the "right" person was before the court, but was wrongfully convicted of a capital crime. Examples include cases where evidence of self-defense or insanity is over-

looked by less-than-competent counsel, and cases where evidence is omitted that would have, if believed, compelled a guilty verdict on a lesser offense (for example, manslaughter rather than capital murder).

The death penalty also creates other innocence problems. For example, there are those who, although innocent of any crime, accept life imprisonment as a plea bargain to avoid death. Indeed, it may be that prosecutors plea-bargain their weakest cases, thus accentuating the problem of sentencing innocent people to life in prison. This situation, like that of the innocent person who is executed, leaves the guilty person in society.

The death penalty leads to arbitrary outcomes that the retributivist should find abhorrent, such as when, in the case of two defendants, the first to confess gets life as part of a plea bargain, and the one who exercises his right to silence is given a death sentence, though he is the less culpable of the two. There are, thus, many ways in which a crime may be erroneously, or ill advisedly, graded as a capital crime. In each of these cases, a plausible argument may be made that the person was, in some sense, "innocent."

Nonetheless, however important these issues may be, except where the context makes it clear that we refer to *innocence of the death penalty* in this broader sense, references in this chapter to *actual innocence* will indicate cases where the state has convicted the wrong person—where the state has gotten it completely and utterly wrong. This is not to understate the importance of an execution going forward where the court has gotten vital facts wrong, or a person has been imprisoned wrongly; but those circumstances raise both moral and factual complexities beyond the scope of this book.[14]

We begin by reviewing cases of actual innocence where the person was ultimately exonerated, and the reasons why courts so often get it wrong in capital cases. This, in turn, sets the stage for demonstrating why the execution of the innocent is an inevitable, systemic feature of state execution. Finally, we turn to cases where the state appears to have executed an innocent person— where the state got it utterly wrong.

AMERICAN CAPITAL PUNISHMENT PRIOR TO 1976
Wrongful executions continued into the twentieth century. Exhaustive research on the subject by Hugo Adam Bedau and Michael Radelet uncovered 350 wrongful convictions in potentially capital cases and 23 executions of the innocent between 1900 and the modern capital punishment era.[15] Despite vigorous critique from Stephen J. Markman and Paul G. Cassell, who were then officials in the Reagan administration's Justice Department,[16] Bedau and Radelet's methods have largely survived, and most scholars find their later

book with Constance Putnam to be the best and most comprehensive study ever done on the subject.[17] While some may quibble with their inclusion of some borderline cases, most reasonable observers will concede that America executed the innocent, at least in some number, prior to *Furman v. Georgia*'s four-year hiatus.

Moreover, their critics' primary claim was that, given the safeguards put in place in the modern era, the problem of innocence is primarily of historical interest. For them, the "greater care taken" by the courts has resulted in "very few 'miscarriages of justice' . . . in the decade after the Supreme Court upheld the constitutionality of the death penalty."[18]

As we will see, contrary to such critiques, the problem of placing innocent people on modern U.S. death rows has proven a more pervasive problem than even Radelet and Bedau, in 1987, might have suspected. History has plainly demonstrated that the critics were wrong. Markman and Cassell's assertion that "there is, in short, no persuasive evidence that any innocent person has been put to death in more than twenty-five years" can decisively be said to be false.[19] In short, the United States executed innocent people during the entire twentieth century, and it continues to do so.

THE MODERN ERA—EXONERATIONS

On January 17, 1977, a Utah firing squad ended Gary Gilmore's life. Thus began capital punishment's modern incarnation. The states have since executed more than 1,000 persons and the federal government has executed 3 more. By June 2006 there were 123 exonerations out of a total death row hovering at about 3500[20] (there had been approximately 6000 people sentenced to death during that period,[21] but with reversals on appeal and other factors, not all remained on death row). Bruce Shapiro, writing in *The Nation*, calls these death penalty miscarriages "a staggering indicator of the unreliability of the criminal justice system."[22] The ultimate miscarriage of an untrustworthy system, however, is not the innocent suffering for years or even decades on death row, as disturbing as that is; it is the guiltless person deliberately slain by the state in the name of justice, after years of death-row suffering. We continue to discover death sentenced yet innocent people. If the United States added no one else to death row, the discovery of innocent people would continue for years to come. As America adds the guilty to its death rows, it also adds innocents, some of whom will be executed and some exonerated.

Close analysis of the judicial system by legal scholar Samuel R. Gross demonstrates that the problem of executing the innocent is systemic, a by-product of the peculiar nature of capital punishment rather than something that can be corrected by tweaking legal procedures.[23] Professor Gross convincingly argues that "the nature of capital cases multiplies the likelihood of error."[24] One factor that increases the incidence of error is the infamy of many death penalty cases. Sensational homicides are heavily publicized and can be easily affected by the tides of public opinion, especially in situations where no potential juror could have avoided receiving highly charged information about the details of a given case. Other factors, however, stem solely from "the demand for the death penalty itself."[25] The fact that a person's life is on the line in a given case changes the dynamic from the start since

> the death penalty itself undermines the accuracy of our system of adjudication, [and] "tends to distort the course of the criminal law." As Justice Frankfurter put it: "When life is at hazard in a trial, it sensationalizes the whole thing almost unwittingly. The effect . . . is very bad." If true, abolishing capital punishment would reduce the number of erroneous convictions of all sorts in those cases in which we now seek the death penalty, and not merely limit the harm of those errors that do occur.[26] (Emphasis added.)

Juries convinced beyond a reasonable doubt sentenced each of the exonerated persons to death. Most were released despite a criminal justice system that fought against their release even after it was clear that they likely did not commit the crime for which they were sentenced to die: often, prisoners are held on death row even after their innocence has been amply demonstrated.

Some people argue that exonerations show that the system works, that the system discovers and corrects its worst errors. Nothing could be farther from the truth; exonerations typically happen despite the legal process, not because of it, and are often dependant on sheer luck. Judges, police, and prosecutors are loath to admit error in these most politically sensitive of cases. Many are emotionally committed to believing that they have gotten it right, even when the evidence is strongly to the contrary. The problem is endemic to the adversarial process, which must presume guilt following a conviction and in which the role of the prosecutor on appeal is to preserve finality. What America has is a system with many police, prosecutors, and judges, some well meaning and some not, who tend to fight each claim of error instead of admitting error and trying to find the truth.

Earl Washington's death sentence in Virginia for rape and murder provides a case in point.[27] Evidence from crime scene specimens were subjected to DNA testing long after Washington's conviction had become final. These relatively early DNA tests tended to exclude Washington—a black, mentally disabled man, convicted of raping and killing a white woman—but were not absolutely conclusive. (The flawed DNA testing in this case is discussed at greater length in chapter 9.) Nonetheless, if the secretions were not his, then he could not have raped the victim. Because there was only one assailant, he also could not have murdered the victim. Because this evidence came too late, and was thus defaulted, he lacked an effective legal mechanism and could not be released by a court under Virginia law.[28] This left executive clemency as the only way in which his execution could be avoided. Because the then relatively new forensic test was not as accurate as it now is, and was not conclusive proof of Washington's innocence, Governor Douglas Wilder was forced to weigh the political risks; in 1994, he commuted Washington's sentence to life in prison. In 2000, newer testing exonerated Washington, who was finally released. In 2004, additional testing showed that another man was the attacker.

Finally, in 2006, a civil jury found that the police officer in charge of the original investigation had fabricated Washington's supposed confession.[29] Washington's story demonstrates two problems with capital cases. First, police officers are more likely to use a false or otherwise suspect confession in cases where the stakes are so high. The pressure to "solve" a capital case leads to shortcuts, which means more innocent as well as guilty being convicted. Second, Washington, who has an IQ of 69, was the kind of person who could be manipulated into a false confession. People with mental disabilities tend to be more easily manipulable than others. This combination of high pressure and manipulability of the suspect leads to far too many false confessions in capital cases. As Washington's attorney said, this case is "obviously the most powerful proof imaginable that false confessions can put innocent people on death row. Frankly, it's a great relief because many of us have been fighting for years for Earl's innocence and vindication."[30]

Partly as a result of Washington's case, Virginia modified its procedural default rule in 2001 to allow for DNA or "biological" evidence.[31] Other evidence of innocence, however, will not suffice, as the rule only applies to biological evidence demonstrating innocence. Since DNA was the basis of only 12 percent of death penalty exonerations identified by the Death Penalty Information Center,[32] this leaves most cases of innocence untouched by the new Virginia rule—i.e., most provably innocent people in prison or on death row.

Gary Gauger's case provides another instructive example. An Illinois jury convicted Gauger of killing his own parents. No evidence connected Gauger to the murders beyond an ambiguous statement, taken under extreme duress, that investigators interpreted as a "confession," and the testimony of a jailhouse snitch (who was later found to have perjured himself). This was apparently enough for the judge and jury, who sentenced Gauger to death. Months later, Larry Marshall's appearance as counsel on appeal caused the trial judge to reduce the sentence to life in prison. (Marshall, now at Stanford, was the hugely successful lawyer for Northwestern University's Innocence Project.) Later, an entirely unconnected FBI investigation showed that the actual murderers were members of a Milwaukee motorcycle gang. Nonetheless, Gauger spent another three years behind bars for a crime that everyone but the prosecutor acknowledged had been committed by others. That same prosecutor continued to maintain, contrary to all of the available evidence, that Gauger must have had something to do with his parents' murder. Gauger had no criminal record before this and never knew any of the murderers.[33]

Prosecutors are elected officials; many may believe it is in their interest to bury errors, such as those in the cases of Earl Washington and Gary Gauger. This does not mean that they necessarily act in bad faith. Most police and prosecutors genuinely believe that they got it right, even when the evidence points in the opposite direction. As in Gauger's case, Earl Washington's prosecutor continued to maintain that he was guilty for years after it was apparent that he was innocent.[34] (Washington's case was unusual because the state, during the civil litigation, finally stipulated that Washington was innocent.) Human beings often find it difficult to admit errors of this magnitude. Why should police, prosecutors, and judges be any different? As the *Washington Post* pointed out,

> In all this time, Virginia put its efforts to keeping Earl Washington in jail. This was not just stupid, it was downright criminal . . . The reality, though, is that this sort of thing happens more than you might think. Sometimes good people get overwhelmed, overworked, tired, lazy, beat, burned out. They've heard it all before—all this talk about innocence. What they forget is that sometimes it's true . . .
>
> [Washington's] investigators and prosecutors are hardly the first to casually dismiss exculpatory evidence or to be so convinced of their man's guilt that they ignored facts that did not conform to their beliefs. This happens all the time. This will continue to happen all the time.[35]

Moreover, suppose prosecutors do agree to free someone. If that person goes out and commits a crime, that prosecutor will be held responsible—at least in the eyes of the public. From this point of view, it is usually safer to leave someone behind bars or on death row, notwithstanding strong evidence of innocence. Add jaded skepticism to a strong interest in preserving their careers, and it is easy to see why most officials fight to the end even well-founded claims of innocence.

For death-row inmates, this means that the system will almost always work against claims of innocence, and that if innocence is discovered, it will be because of blind luck and the work of mostly unpaid volunteers. Those who are exonerated are very, very lucky. As one newspaper stated,

> Sometimes, sheer luck can free an innocent man. One Texas inmate serving a rape sentence was released after DNA exonerated him; shortly afterward, the county disposed of evidence kits in 50 other rape convictions . . .
>
> But obstacles remain even when evidence exists.
>
> Bennett Gershman, a former prosecutor who now is a law professor at Pace University School of Law in New York, has a theory on prosecutors' reluctance to reopen cases.
>
> "They worked hard to get a guilty verdict," he says. "They've got a victim who has been traumatized by the defendant's crime. I don't think a prosecutor is going to say, 'Hey, this guy might be innocent, and I'm going to go out of my way to prove it.'"[36]

Sometimes, however, police and prosecutors do act corruptly. A groundbreaking *Chicago Tribune* exposé analyzed "thousands of court records, appellate rulings and lawyer disciplinary records from across the United States" and concluded,

> With impunity, prosecutors across the country have violated their oaths and the law, committing the worst kinds of deception in the most serious of cases.
>
> They have prosecuted black men, hiding evidence the real killers were white. They have prosecuted a wife, hiding evidence her husband committed suicide. They have prosecuted parents, hiding evidence their daughter was killed by wild dogs.
>
> They do it to win. They do it because they won't get punished. They have done it to defendants who came within hours of being executed, only to be exonerated.[37]

Walter McMillian, a black man dating a white woman in Alabama, provides an instructive example. Police framed him for a brutal murder. Only luck, and brilliant lawyering by Bryan Stevenson, executive director of the Equal Justice Initiative of Alabama, exposed the fraud and thereby secured McMillian's release.[38]

The story is simple—the police leaned on a snitch in order to frame McMillian. Years after the conviction, a court ordered law enforcement officers to turn over a taped interview that the police had conducted with their jailhouse informant. The officers, however, neglected to erase the flip side of the tape before turning it over to counsel. There, on the back side, Stevenson discovered that the snitch had initially told law enforcement officers that he did not even know Walter McMillian and had asked why they were asking him to make a story up incriminating a man he had never met. The officers made it clear that, by testifying against McMillian, the jailhouse informant could help his own case. His perjured testimony, at government insistence, put an innocent man on death row. But for the mistake in failing to hide law enforcement complicity in the lie, McMillian would have been executed.[39]

Randall Adams is another instance of an innocent man erroneously convicted and put on death row. A movie maker reinvestigated his case and made the movie *The Thin Blue Line*, which exposed Adams's innocence.

That Randall Adams survived death row at all was entirely fortuitous. His original death sentence was reversed because of constitutional error in the selection of the jury. The Texas Court of Criminal Appeals then ordered a new trial, but in the interim the Governor commuted Adams' sentence to life imprisonment. Adams ultimately sought and received a writ of habeas corpus from the Texas Court of Criminal Appeals granting a new trial. Among other things, that court found that the use of perjured testimony at trial could be imputed to the prosecutor, and that the failure to correct the perjured testimony, the failure to disclose a misidentification, and improper coaching of a witness violated Adams' right to a fair trial. Adams was ultimately exonerated. Had the United States Supreme Court not given him time by its initial reversal on grounds wholly unrelated to his innocence claim, the evidence of his innocence might never have materialized. Indeed, it seems almost a miracle that the prosecutorial and police misconduct that put Randall Adams on death row was ever uncovered.[40]

These stories are neither unique nor isolated. The same patterns concerning exoneration repeat themselves, with chance being the most common theme. Hugo Adam Bedau and Michael Radelet have written,

There is no common or typical route by which an innocent defendant can be vindicated, and vindication, if it ever comes, will not necessarily come in time to benefit the defendant. The criminal justice system is not designed to scrutinize its own decisions for a wide range of factual errors once a conviction has been obtained. Our data show that it is rare for anyone within the system to play the decisive role in correcting error. Even when actors in the system do get involved, they often do so on their own time and without official support or encouragement. Far more commonly, the efforts of persons on the fringe of the system, or even wholly outside it, make the difference. The coincidences involved in exposing so many of the errors and the luck that is so often required suggest that only a fraction of the wrongly convicted are eventually able to clear their names.[41]

The criminal justice system has remained remarkably deaf to the circumstances of the innocent person on death row. Reliance on blind luck to winnow out the innocent undercuts trust that the system catches all, or even many, of its errors; thus, this sheer fortuity in finding the mistakes provides initial evidence for the argument that America is executing innocent people.

THE LOGIC OF THE SITUATION

Scholars have found a number of cases in which it appears that the person executed was probably innocent of the crime. How, however, do we translate *probably innocent* into *innocent* in such cases? There are no retrials for the dead. As with Earl Washington, Gary Gauger, and Randall Adams, officials are not willing to spend scarce resources reinvestigating, and do not seek to show that they killed or nearly killed the wrong person. The difference is luck. Some of the innocent are exonerated; others are executed. It is left to scholars, activists, and newspapers to identify cases where state machinery has misfired to the point of killing an innocent person.

There are many cases where one can persuasively, but not conclusively, argue that innocent people were executed, and we illustrate a few of these stories below. The persuasiveness of the argument goes beyond anecdotes, however; only those irrevocably wedded to the illusion of a flawless criminal justice system can continue to suppose that it does not execute the innocent.

The number of people mistakenly convicted of crimes they did not commit is probably much larger than the number of known exonerations. Even though a significant number of people have been exonerated and released from death row, a study by Liebman, Fagan, West, and Lloyd indicates that "serious and geographically dispersed error pervades the capital punishment machinery."[42] This data implies that there is an increasing likelihood that there are innocent people on death row. This important study combines cases involving actual innocence, and those that involve innocence of the death penalty in the broader sense referred to earlier in this chapter.[43] Its true importance, however, is in the magnitude of the systemic errors that it exposes. This empirical study demonstrates that the "overall error-rate in our capital punishment system was 68%."[44] With an overall error rate this large, the rate at which the system miscarries completely—by executing the innocent—may well be a much larger number than anyone has heretofore supposed. However, one does not have to suppose a large rate of error to see that execution of the innocent is inevitable. Even a much smaller rate than that suggested by the Liebman study, or by the large number of exonerations, is adequate to demonstrate the fallibility of the system.

We thus know that the system has at least some error rate. The justice system cannot possibly be catching all of its errors. This error rate—whatever it is exactly—multiplies as the number of trials or cases increase. Think of it this way. Suppose you flip a coin. The odds of a heads (or tails) are one out of two. And it remains that on every flip of the coin. But the odds of two heads in a row are one out of four; three in a row are one out of eight, and so on. The odds against getting a string of heads multiplies with each attempt.

Even a small error rate, spread out over many, many attempts, approaches inevitability of the error occurring. We cannot imagine a hundred unbiased flips of a coin without a tails (yet even a string like that will happen if we make billions of attempts). Imagine an error rate of only 3 percent spread over one hundred executions. Mathematically, this yields a 95 percent probability that we will execute an innocent person, even using this ultraconservative rate. Since the reinstatement of state execution in 1976, the United States has executed more than 1,000 persons.[45] Given that number, and using an even more conservative 1 percent error rate, the odds are more than 9,999 in 10,000 that all were guilty. Conversely, at least some were almost surely innocent. Compare these modest assumptions of an error rate in actual executions with the much larger error rates suggested both by recent exonerations and by the two-thirds overall error rate of the capital punishment system found in the Liebman study. One can readily see that execution of the innocent is inevitable.

Moreover, the problem is a good deal worse than the above analysis suggests. It assumes a small, constant rate of error spread evenly over all cases. But, as detailed below, there are perhaps a dozen or so cases in which the evidence of innocence is quite strong indeed. In each of these latter cases, there is strong reason to believe that the person that the state executed was, in fact, wholly innocent. Thus we have to assign a much higher probability of innocence to each of these cases. We will assume a skeptic who doubts the strength of these innocence claims; who does recognize that each of these reinvestigated cases makes a plausible case for innocence, but is not willing to say that innocence is probable in any of them. Let's assume, then, a very conservative error rate of only 25 percent. That is, in each of these cases there is a one in four chance that the state made a mistake and killed an innocent person. In that subset of the cases alone, there is only a 3 percent probability that all of those dozen were guilty; and this leaves at least some error rate to be accounted for in all of those cases in which the evidence of innocence is not as strong.

The point here is not that we can accurately estimate the probability of executing the innocent. We cannot. The true error rate in execution of the innocent cannot be known with precision. Nor can we know how that rate of error might vary among types of capital cases. The point is that all death penalty cases, irrespective of other factors—such as the atrociousness of the case, or the racial, ethnic, or socioeconomic characteristics of defendant and victim—carry with them some residual and nontrivial error rate. Given enough executions (there have been over a thousand since Gary Gilmore's in 1977), it is statistically probable to the point of near certainty that America continues to execute innocent people.

As University of Michigan law professor and sociologist Richard Lempert has observed, "[T]reating the statistically predictable as other than inevitable is a form of false consciousness."[46] Those innocent persons all had names and lives, families and loved ones. All had stories prematurely and wrongly ended. To ignore the fact that innocent people are killed in America's execution chambers is more than simply a "form of false consciousness." It is a form of moral obtuseness that allows the stories of innocent people, wrongly executed, to be ignored in the interests of executing the guilty. We pretend that because we do not (at least usually) know the names and stories of the innocent who have been killed, they do not exist.

Second, the conviction that the United States has executed and continues to execute the innocent does not rely solely on mathematical inference, however strong that inference may be. Scholars have identified at least twelve problematic cases (including those of Larry Griffin, Ruben Cantu, Cameron Todd Willingham, and Carlos DeLuna summarized below) in which an executed person's innocence is considered probable.[47] How many probably innocent people does the system have to execute before we conclude that mistakes are inevitable? Given the blind luck that separates those who have been exonerated from those executed, and the frequency with which the system misfires, it defies both reason and common sense to deny that the state is executing innocent people.

Moreover, intense pressure within the capital punishment system increases the likelihood of convicting and ultimately executing the innocent.[48] The existence of the death penalty, as we have seen above, puts added pressure on the system to solve these highly publicized cases. This added pressure, this increase in the stakes, increases the probability of error, which leads to miscarriages of justice and, inevitably, execution of the innocent. Thus, "When life is at hazard in a trial, it sensationalizes the whole thing almost unwittingly."[49] This pressure results in more perjured testimony from jailhouse snitches (Walter McMillian's case is an example).[50] As Samuel Gross and others have pointed out, and as pointed out above, the death penalty places enormous pressure on law enforcement to solve and close these cases. Among other things this leads to more perjury, not only by the police, but also by "witness[es] . . . lying to get favors";[51] these lies may be wholly unrelated to the murder in question, or may be by the real killer, who has every motive to lie. If the lying witness's case is unrelated, then "he'll do much better if it's a big case—which usually means a murder, or better yet, a capital murder."[52]

Such pressure also spawns false confessions (as in Earl Washington's case, above), and, "as with perjury, false confessions are a much more common cause of errors for homicides than for other crimes."[53] Finally, the death penalty results in more pressured lab and scientific analyses (Cameron Todd Willingham's case, below, is an example). Samuel Gross summarizes the problem:

> The basic cause for the comparatively large number of errors in capital cases is a natural and laudable human impulse: We want murderers to be caught and punished. In some cases that impulse drives police and prosecutors to lie and cheat, but more often it simply motivates them to work harder to catch killers and to convict them. It works: More cases are cleared, more murderers are convicted. But harder cases are more likely to produce errors . . . If there were some general method for identifying the errors, we wouldn't have this problem in the first place. But of course, there isn't. Instead, the errors that we do discover advertise the existence of others that we don't. What are the odds that an innocent prisoner will run into a movie producer who is struck by his story? What if the real killer is killed in a car crash, or dies from a drug overdose, or is never arrested, or never confesses?[54]

THE "LEGAL IRRELEVANCE" OF INNOCENCE

Miscarriages in capital cases are far more common than previously thought. Contrary to popular belief, the presence of the death penalty may actually increase the odds of convicting and executing the innocent. We catch only a fraction of the system's errors. The lucky are exonerated; others are executed. While the practicalities of politics, and the pressure that the system places on its participants, play a prominent role, the legal system also bears responsibility.

When states convict an innocent person, the primary way for the federal courts to intervene and change the result is through a postconviction process called habeas corpus. The Supreme Court has been restricting postconviction relief—particularly for death-row inmates—for decades. Its assault on habeas corpus proceeded in four ways.[55]

1. It reduced federal oversight of state procedural default rules. When states refuse even to look at an issue on appeal (or other post-trial proceedings) because the lawyer failed to timely address the issue at the trial, federal courts also duck the issue, thus ensuring that those with poor lawyers lose otherwise legally valid claims.

2. The high court restricted rules governing bad lawyering. This results in unqualified lawyers being appointed to capital cases, which in turn ensures that the best constitutional claims will be missed in all subsequent proceedings.

3. Federal courts now rigidly require that all claims be first presented to state courts before a federal court can hear them. While the rule usually makes sense in allowing the state courts the first crack at an issue, its hypertechnical enforcement by the Supreme Court has resulted in otherwise good claims being forever lost. For example, a poor, but not constitutionally ineffective, trial lawyer fails to discover and introduce available evidence showing that the defendant had a persuasive alibi or strong mitigating evidence. If the evidence is not presented at trial, the defendant will ordinarily be barred from raising the issue later on.

4. The Court enforces a strict retroactivity rule, with only narrow exceptions,[56] which "bars application of any 'new rule' to a case that was final (and therefore only addressable by habeas corpus) at the time of the announcement of the new rule." By its very nature, almost any decision of the United States Supreme Court can be said to state, at least in some sense, a new rule. And any rule thus laid down by the Supreme Court is subject to considerable interpretation. What this means for state supreme courts is that, so long as their interpretations of U.S. Supreme Court precedents are not illogical or in outright defiance, even erroneous interpretations are protected from being questioned by lower federal courts in postconviction review. As Justice Brennnan wrote in dissent in *Butler v. McKellar* (1990),

> State courts essentially are told today that, save for outright "illogical" defiance of a binding precedent precisely on point, their interpretations of federal constitutional guarantees—no matter how cramped and unfaithful to the principles underlying existing precedent—will no longer be subject to oversight through the federal habeas system.[57]

Congress has validated these restrictions by passing the Anti-Terrorist and Effective Death Penalty Act of 1996 (AEDPA),[58] which "sharply restricts the previous right of a prisoner to challenge his or her conviction."[59] These actions, taken cumulatively, increase the already high risk that we execute the innocent. Thus, first the Supreme Court, and then the Congress, has worked to speed up executions, and in the process they have jointly made the law complicit in execution of the innocent.

We turn next to the most pressing of such problems—that of the innocent death row-inmate.

THE INNOCENT DEATH-ROW INMATE

There are thus two possibilities for the unlucky innocent person on death row. (1) He or she may have a good legal defense to the conviction (say, an unconstitutionally coercive confession or eyewitness identification, for example). If that otherwise-good claim has been lost or, as lawyers would put it, defaulted because not properly raised or preserved, then one standard applies. Procedural default was briefly explained in chapter 4 and some understanding of that concept is necessary in order to see why it is so difficult to detect innocent people on death row, and why it is so likely that America does in fact execute innocent people.[60] (2) If there are no such constitutional or legal claims—if one has a free-standing claim of innocence—another legal standard applies.

The Botched Case Problem

In the case where the death-row inmate has a defaulted claim (for example, evidence that the defense lawyer could have found and presented to the trial court but for some reason failed to do so), the situation for that innocent on death row is dire. Although the proof might be very strong, even highly probable evidence of innocence is not enough. According to the Supreme Court, the hurdle for the innocent on death row is to demonstrate that the evidence is so strong that "it is more likely than not that *no* reasonable juror would have found petitioner guilty beyond a reasonable doubt" (emphasis added).[61] Consider what this means. A skeptical federal court must be persuaded *not* that the evidence might have hung the jury, or even that most reasonable people would likely have returned a not-guilty verdict. To show innocence at this point, one must demonstrate that no one in their right mind would have found the petitioner guilty beyond a reasonable doubt. Not many claims of innocence pass that high hurdle.

Free-Standing Innocence—The Case That Went Well

While the case of the innocent person with a defaulted claim is bad, the situation of the innocent person whose trial has gone well—who had a good lawyer who did the job correctly—is worse. In this case, the lawyer raised all the appropriate claims and has no valid claims that the petitioner's constitutional rights were violated. All that such defendants have is a plausible claim that they did not do the crime for which they were convicted or sentenced to death. Put another way, they are not arguing that legal error was committed in the course of the trial and appeals. The only argument is that a grievous mistake was made, that the wrong person was convicted. The question is: is it legally appropriate to execute a person whose trial went well, but who was innocent nonetheless?

The Supreme Court in Herrera v. Collins held that a death-row inmate is not ordinarily entitled to relief where a claim of innocence is based on newly discovered evidence, unless the claim also includes an independent constitutional violation.[62] The Supreme Court found that there is no due process violation in the execution of someone who was arguably innocent. In Herrera, the petitioner was a death-row inmate who possessed no other constitutional claim beyond newly discovered evidence, which, if believed, might well prove his innocence. The court allowed the execution to proceed, but left open the possibility that "in a capital case a truly persuasive demonstration of 'actual innocence' made after trial would render the execution of a defendant unconstitutional."[63] The burden here of requiring "truly persuasive" evidence of actual innocence is both very high and singularly ill defined, considering that Herrera was executed by the state of Texas on May 12, 1993,[64] "despite an affidavit [from a former Texas judge] stating that another man had confessed to the crime," as well as other new evidence that threw doubt on his conviction.[65] Although it cannot be said that the Herrera majority advocates execution of the innocent, the nearly unscalable obstacle that it has placed in the path of innocent death-sentenced prisoners suggests that it tolerates the execution of the innocent.

Thus, neither constitutional error nor actual innocence will ordinarily avail the death-row inmate in a federal habeas corpus proceeding. Moreover, some state courts have adopted the Herrera holding as their own, shutting off state postconviction avenues of relief.[66] This lack of federal oversight increases the probability of executing the innocent.

The Herrera Court justified this extraordinary holding with the observation that "[h]istory shows that the traditional remedy for claims of innocence based on new evidence, discovered too late in the day to file a new trial motion, has been executive clemency."[67] In general, governors have not been inclined to grant clemency to death-row inmates.[68] Whether this reluctance on the part of governors will continue in light of the revelations of innocent people on death row remains to be seen. This takes us back to blind luck. Clemency is not governed by any legal standard; governors can do whatever is politically expedient. The politics of the situation usually counts for more than the evidence, and life and death hang on the politics of the moment. Moreover, governors, who lack the capacity to take and consider evidence, are unlikely to catch all, or even most, of the system's errors.

The Supreme Court in *Herrera v. Collins* has virtually cut off claims of actual innocence that are not tethered to constitutional claims.[69] This amounts to the ultimate catch-22: claims based upon the Constitution are barred by the restrictive procedural rules briefly described above, while evidence of innocence cannot be heard if not tied to a claim of constitutional error. Whichever path death-row inmates are confronted with, they face nearly insurmountable obstacles. The American system of justice, then, increases the probability that innocent people are being executed. While the precise numbers of innocent people executed remains unknowable, the statistical likelihood that innocent people are executed approaches near certainty in the present system of justice.

INNOCENT YET EXECUTED

Larry Griffin

The NAACP Legal Defense and Educational Fund (LDF) sponsored an independent investigation by University of Michigan law professor Samuel Gross into the case of Larry Griffin, who was executed in 1995. Griffin, who maintained his innocence to the end, was convicted and sentenced to death for the 1980 drive-by shooting of a St. Louis drug dealer. A second victim, who survived, was shot in the buttocks. That LDF report points out that there had "been serious doubts" about the case from the beginning,[70] and on Griffin's initial appeal in 1983 a dissenting justice on the Missouri Supreme Court had pointed out that the only prosecution witness "had a seriously flawed background, and his ability to observe and identify the gunman was also subject to question."[71] Griffin's fingerprints were not found among the various fingerprints in the car from which the shots were fired. While there were at least two eyewitnesses to the shooting, neither was called to testify at trial. The only witness to testify was a snitch in the federal witness protection program, whose ability to see what he claimed was questionable and whose testimony in other cases had been discredited.

Thus, there were reasons to doubt Griffin's guilt from the beginning. Now those doubts have, as a result of the LDF's extensive investigation, developed into a full-fledged probability of a miscarriage of justice. The facts are complex, but include a secretly taped statement by a police officer, confirming that the prosecution witness could not have seen what he testified to; and the statement of another victim of the shooting—who never testified at trial—in which he says Griffin (whom he knew) was not even present at the time of the murder. The Legal Defense Fund's investigation also shows that other witnesses could have exonerated Griffin and led the police to the actual murderers.

As Bob Herbert, columnist for the *New York Times*, puts it: "If Larry Griffin were being tried today . . . he would almost certainly be acquitted."[72] Professor Gross has provided the state's attorney with names of those who he believes committed the murder, along with the evidence that implicates them. The state has taken the highly unusual step of reopening the case with a view toward prosecuting the real murderers.

Ruben Cantu

There are many other cases in which there is substantial doubt about whether the state executed the person guilty of the crime, or someone innocent of it. Take, for example, the case of Ruben Cantu, from Texas. No fingerprints, murder weapon, or forensic evidence of any kind tied him to the robbery-murder for which he was convicted, sentenced to death, and executed. His conviction rested on the testimony of the surviving victim (two men were robbed, both were shot, one died).[73]

That surviving victim, Juan Morales, was a fearful nineteen-year-old illegal immigrant, who spoke little English and had been shot nine times. Days after the shooting, he failed to identify Cantu on the first occasion on which he was shown Cantu's photograph. Only months later, after Cantu was involved with a serious altercation with a police officer (who had his own history of misconduct and violence), did the police go back and reshow Cantu's picture to Morales. Still no identification. Then, they hauled Morales into the police station, where, fearing deportation back to Mexico, the victim finally identified Cantu. Morales now tells reporters at the *Houston Chronicle* that he lied about Cantu because of police pressure. The local prosecutor, rather than simply seeking the truth, has indicated that if Morales did lie and thereby sent an innocent man to death, she will seek to prosecute him for it. So now Morales, armed with legal counsel, is—not surprisingly—refusing to speak further.[74]

This post-execution switch by one witness, now no longer cooperating, would not be enough to conclude that Texas executed an innocent man, if that were the only evidence. At most it would merely be one more case casting doubt on the system; it would be far from clear proof. But Morales's changed story—that another man (not Cantu) committed the murder and also shot Morales nine times—is backed up by additional and powerful new evidence.

According to the evidence, there were two perpetrators. One, David Garza, age fifteen at the time, denied being the triggerman, pled guilty to robbery, and received a prison sentence. He refused to implicate Cantu at the time, even to help himself, and now says that a different person was with him and shot both Morales and the murder victim. While Garza may also have credibility problems, he appears to have little incentive to come forward to clear the dead Cantu's name. And both he and the victim agree on one thing—whoever the murderer was, it was not the now-dead Ruben Cantu.

Cantu did have an explanation for his whereabouts at the time of the murder. He was hundreds of miles away in Waco, Texas, stealing cars. His one available alibi witness was made to sound unbelievable. Would the addition of other alibi witnesses, Cantu's partners in stealing cars, have made a difference? They were not available to his lawyer at the time, but at least one confirms that Cantu was in Waco on the night of the murder. This adds up to a police-pressured victim who now says he lied to save himself from deportation, a co-defendant who has always maintained that another person helped him commit the crime, and alibi witnesses who were never heard from.

Now "[t]he jury foreman, presiding judge, defense attorney and a prosecutor familiar with the case all have expressed doubts about the reliability of the original conviction."[75] None of this proves absolutely that Texas executed an innocent person, but short of a successful prosecution of the actual guilty party, these facts should persuade most that the system errs gravely in some cases.

Tragically, this is not the end of the story. Confronted with evidence that the state had executed the wrong person, state officials agreed to investigate. Unfortunately, it now appears that the investigation is a sham. According to the *Houston Chronicle* and the *San Antonio Express News*,[76] recently released tape recordings show district attorney investigators have already made up their minds that the witnesses are "all lying"[77] and the investigation is "going to go forward with the fact that it was justified and everything was correct and that's the way it is."[78] As the article puts it,

> [T]he recorded statements stand in contrast to public assurances that the Bexar County DA's office will fully and fairly examine assertions that Cantu played no part in the 1984 robbery that left one man dead and another bleeding from nearly a dozen wounds.[79]

These revelations, combined with conflict-of-interest allegations involving the DA's office, have led to calls for the DA to give up the case and turn it over to an independent investigative body.[80] In addition, the NAACP Legal Defense Fund has called for disciplinary action to be taken.[81] It remains to be seen how officials in Texas will respond to allegations of what appears to be a cover-up investigation into a wrongful state execution.

Cameron Todd Willingham

The only evidence connecting Cameron Todd Willingham to his son's death came from a fire investigator whose evidence has since been found to have been worthless. There is no reliable evidence that the fire that killed his child was caused by arson. Furthermore, as LDF president Theodore M. Shaw writes,

> A panel of the nation's leading arson experts confirmed that conclusion in March. In a strikingly similar case, Ernest Willis, a white oilfield worker from New Mexico, was convicted on the same sort of evidence and sentenced to death for murder by arson in Pecos County, Tex., in 1987. Willis was exonerated and freed in October 2004, eight months after Willingham was put to death.[82]

If the fire that killed the child was not in fact arson, it is difficult to see both how the case could have gone forward and how there could have been a charge of murder. Willingham was executed not because he committed murder, but because of an earlier domestic assault which focused attention on him and led to the erroneous "scientific" evidence.[83]

Carlos DeLuna

The person most recently discovered to be "probably innocent but executed anyhow" is Carlos DeLuna. According to a *Chicago Tribune* investigation of the case,[84] the real killer was probably one Carlos Hernandez (who looked a lot like DeLuna). Hernandez had bragged repeatedly (before his death in prison) that DeLuna had taken the fall for a murder that he, Hernandez, had committed. Moreover, Hernandez (not DeLuna) had a history of knife attacks similar to those in the murder in question. According to the *Chicago Tribune*, "[T]he case was compromised by shaky eyewitness identification, sloppy police work and a failure to seriously consider Hernandez as a suspect."[85] DeLuna went to his grave protesting his innocence, and even a senior detective who knew both men now says that he "believes that DeLuna was wrongly executed."[86]

CONCLUSION

Ultimately, it comes down to common sense. Humans make mistakes. The higher the stakes are politically, the greater the likelihood of error, fraud, and corruption. Capital cases present some of the highest stakes. Officials push harder in these cases and take more chances. While this means more closed case-files, it also means more innocent people convicted and in some cases executed. It also means that those guilty of these crimes have gone free. Sometimes the mistakes are honest; sometimes they are not.

Given enough executions, the criminal justice system inevitably executes the innocent. Present evidence suggests that this occurs far more often than anyone had heretofore suspected. The question for society is whether capital punishment provides some larger good that outweighs the brute fact of execution of the innocent. Thus, critiques of the system's racism, cost, and lack-of-deterrence remain important in part because they undercut the notion that there is some instrumental benefit to capital punishment. It remains for us to investigate, below, whether there is any moral justification for state execution.

8 : The Moral Potency of the Innocence Argument

[I]f . . . the justice system can never be 100 percent right, then how can it administer punishment that's 100 percent irreversible?
—*Robert Jay Lifton and Greg Mitchell*[1]

WILL INNOCENCE MATTER?

In Windsor, Ontario, in 1829, an innocent man was executed. Across the Detroit River in Michigan, citizens responded with outrage. Partly as a result of this, their state became the first American jurisdiction to abandon the death penalty.

In 1976, Canada abolished the death penalty for all but a handful of military offenses. That same year, the United States, reinstated the death penalty, having only four years earlier declared it unconstitutional as administered.

Concerns about execution of the innocent led Canadians to abolish the death penalty for all offenses. As the 2001 Canadian Supreme Court decision in *United States v. Burns* notes, courts and governments in Canada "have come to acknowledge a number of instances of wrongful conviction for murder despite all of the capital safeguards put in place for the protection of the innocent . . . [I]f capital punishment had been carried out, the result could have been the killing by the government of innocent individuals."[2] Yet a scant eight years earlier, the United States Supreme Court ruled that the actual innocence of a death-row inmate is for the most part irrelevant as a postconviction argument.[3]

Is there any reason to think that state executions of the innocent will undermine support for the death penalty in America, as it did in Canada? For abolitionists, it is hard to be optimistic. The American public has remained largely unmoved by solid empirical evidence demonstrating that the death penalty fails to deter, that its implementation is arbitrary and riddled by race and class bias, and that it is vastly more costly than life imprisonment. Yet it is also hard for abolitionists *not* to be optimistic. The morally troubling nature of these empirically well-established arguments is markedly enhanced by the innocence argument, which has considerably more force now than it has had at any other time in the twenty-five years since executions by the state resumed. While the empirical studies supporting this are preliminary, they are encouraging, as we have seen in chapter 6. Even hard-core retentionists scale down their endorsement of a system of capital punishment when informed of the likelihood that this system has executed, and will continue to execute, the innocent.

More promising yet are a series of recent developments, including the rise of Innocence Projects across America, growing calls for a moratorium, and the increase in seeming defections by retentionists—including the former governor of Illinois, George Ryan, who commuted the sentences of all 167 death-row inmates before leaving office. Said Ryan: "Our capital system is haunted by the demon of error, error in determining guilt, error in determining who among the guilty deserve to die."[4] Like Ryan, many Americans are realizing that innocent people are being executed, that these irrevocable events are actual, not just hypothetical, and that they are being performed by the state in their name.

The issue of innocence has extraordinarily persuasive power in eroding support for capital punishment. Moreover, other abolitionist arguments centered on the death penalty's administration are strengthened by its presence. The unjustness of a criminal justice system in which racial and class discrimination figure in the determination of whom the state executes is massively compounded by the fact that significant numbers of those thus selected are innocent. Increasing public and judicial reliance upon retributivist justifications for the death penalty, combined with retributivism's singular vulnerability on the innocence issue, wholly transforms the death penalty debate. This chapter examines some of these transformations. We allude throughout to the innocence argument. This is the claim that since the American death penalty is resulting in the execution of significant numbers of innocent people, and that since any penalty that does this is morally unacceptable, the death penalty is morally unacceptable. America must abolish it, as Canada has done, as the European Union has done, as the majority of countries in the world have done.

What differentiates the innocence argument from its ancestors is the empirical evidence now available to support the first premise. As chapter 7 demonstrates, the case can now be made that significant numbers of innocent people are being executed. We turn now to why this empirical evidence should make a difference in the debate over state execution. Our contention will be that it effectively undermines the retentionist position, whether utilitarian or retributivist. In other words, both theories, or justifications, of punishment converge on abolition when they are appropriately applied.[5] To the degree that the death penalty debate relies on reasoned, moral argument, then, we hope to advance thereby the case for abolition.

IMPLICATIONS OF THE INNOCENCE ARGUMENT
FOR A UTILITARIAN RETENTIONISM

Retributivism—the theory that justifies punishment on the grounds that the offender deserves it—has become deeply entrenched within the American criminal justice system over the past thirty years, dominating at the level of theory as well as practice. As David Dolinko observes, retributive theory is "the most influential philosophical justification for the institution of criminal punishment in present day America."[6] It has permeated to the practical, shaping rationales for sentencing "despite the gulf that normally exists between theories of punishment and sentencing practice."[7] State courts and legislatures have joined legal scholars and philosophers in recognizing its centrality. What is true for punishment generally is a fortiori the case for capital punishment. A long series of U.S. Supreme Court decisions in death penalty cases has reflected and strengthened the reign of retribution; indeed, in *Spaziano v. Florida* the Court categorically asserts that retribution is "the primary justification of the death penalty" and "is an element of all punishments that society imposes."[8]

Retributivism, as Mirko Bagaric and Kumar Amarasekara note, rose to dominance because it seemed able to avoid or rebut widespread criticisms of the utilitarian theory of punishment, which justifies punishment on the grounds that it prevents or deters further crime and so maximizes social utility. Most notably, it seemed to avoid the charge leveled against utilitarianism that it permits punishment of the innocent: "Punishing the innocent . . . supposedly so troubles our moral consciousness that utilitarianism can therefore be dismissed. The outcome, it is argued, is so horrible that we are forced to say 'there must be a mistake somewhere.'"[9] In support of utilitarianism, Bagaric and Amarasekara maintain that the force of this criticism is lost once we acknowledge that "punishing the innocent is in fact no worse than other activities we condone."[10] Their examples are drawn from contexts of war, but their discussion can be brought to bear directly on capital punishment and the execution of the innocent. Two questions are then worth asking: how vulnerable is utilitarianism to this common criticism (essentially a version of the innocence argument), and how satisfying is Bagaric and Amarsekara's response to it?

The principle of utility tells us that we ought to act in such a way as to maximize utility, i.e., to bring about the greatest happiness on balance for all concerned. It can be applied either directly to acts, or at the level of rules. Rule-utilitarians can certainly mount a plausible argument that a rule prohibiting the execution of the innocent would on balance yield more good consequences than bad.[11] So even if utility would be maximized by executing an innocent person in some specific case, this would violate a rule whose acceptance by society would maximize utility, and would therefore be unjustifiable.

Does this change if we assume the current U.S. situation, in which a social policy allowing for state execution of the guilty is resulting in the execution of substantial numbers of innocent people? Such empirical information will weigh heavily in rule-utilitarian calculations, as will the growing public unease attending this practice. If the lack of evidence that the death penalty deters more effectively than life imprisonment did not previously result in its rejection on rule-utilitarian grounds, these developments certainly should. So it is hard to see how rule-utilitarianism plausibly could, much less would, sanction a social practice (as in the contemporary American death penalty regime), where the state is statistically unable to avoid executing the innocent, and where no demonstrable counterbalancing benefits (such as deterrence) are forthcoming. Faced with clear evidence that the American criminal justice system is regularly and systematically putting the innocent to death, that the public at large is increasingly aware of and responsive to this, and that the procedural mechanisms intended to prevent this have been effectively eroded, a rule-utilitarian would surely condemn the American practice of capital punishment.

These results are not surprising. Rule-utilitarianism was developed in response to theoretical criticisms of act-utilitarianism, and permitting the innocent to be punished was among the most serious of these. So what, then, of act-utilitarianism? This objection to act-utilitarianism is most often raised in the form of a hypothetical case. Such cases are used to test moral theories, to reveal their full implications, and to evaluate them comparatively. When the hypothetical case—classically, of framing an innocent person for a crime in order to stave off massive riots—is raised, it becomes clear that act-utilitarianism could in principle justify punishing the innocent, including executing the innocent. Whether this would be so in practice, in any specific case, and whether such a case is not merely possible but probable, are of course very different matters.

Since these hypothetical cases typically build-in a provision that the public never learns of the innocence of the framed person,[12] the act-utilitarian response is likely to be that this is unrealistic; it is more likely than not that word would spread that an innocent person had been executed, and so utility would not be maximized by executing an innocent person, even in these circumstances. Bagaric and Amarsekara, however, do not respond in this way. Their defense of a utilitarian theory of punishment tries to ease the sting of the innocence objection by noting that hard cases lead to hard decisions. This particular result for act-utilitarianism is not, after all, so unlike other cases (e.g., sending soldiers to die "for the greater good," or sacrificing innocent lives in times of war) where, they contend, "when pressed we do take the utilitarian option, [and feel] . . . that this is the option we should take."[13] Since punishing the innocent is no worse than other activities we condone, they conclude that the force of this criticism is not telling.

What of this response? Bagaric and Amarsekara are addressing punishment in general, not a specific form of punishment, but would substituting "executing" for "punishing" make a difference in their reasoning here? Ultimately, perhaps not; hypothetical cases can always be rehypothesized. And since utilitarian theory turns on an assessment of the likely consequences of a specific act, not on the nature of the act itself, it cannot rule out entirely that, in some possible world somewhere, even the vilest case of slowly torturing an innocent child to death might generate more good consequences than bad over the long run, and so be the morally right thing to do. As philosopher R. A. Duff observes, "The crucial charge is not that a consequentialist will in fact punish the innocent, but that she is ready to contemplate it as an open moral possibility."[14]

Having acknowledged this, we should immediately note two things: (1) there are substantial differences between state executions considered hypothetically—unburdened by the empirical data that weighs down the current practice of capital punishment—and those performed in America in the twenty-first century,[15] and (2) moral theories (as well as theories of punishment) are intended to guide human action, i.e., to be applied to and in the actual world, by real moral agents embedded in nonhypothetical contexts. What happens when we leave the hypothetical and return with the act-utilitarian to the actual world? That world, as we have seen in chapter 7, is one in which (1) the death penalty has not been demonstrated to deter more effectively than life imprisonment, (2) increasing numbers of those currently confined to death row are being found innocent, (3) public unease with judicial execution is mounting as a result, and (4) constitutional safeguards to increase the likelihood that only the guilty are executed have been drastically reduced. As we have seen in chapter 5, it is also one in which (5) race and class biases impact who receives the death penalty, and (6) the death penalty is far more costly than life imprisonment. Situate an act-utilitarian in this context, introduce an actual pending case of judicial execution, and inquire whether it should proceed. The act-utilitarian calculation will be quick and confident: the execution ought not proceed. Social utility would not be maximized by so doing. Some alternative sanction, such as long-term imprisonment, is the only justifiable recourse.[16]

PARSING RETRIBUTIVISM

The rise of retributivist theories of punishment is partly due to the perceived vulnerability of utilitarian theories on matters of innocence, and partly to the conviction that "whatever else justice may be, it does not involve sacrificing some innocents for the sake of others."[17] At the heart of all theories of retributivism is the principle that the guilty—and only the guilty—deserve punishment.[18] One would thus expect the innocence argument to seriously impact the retributivist case for the death penalty. If a practice of capital punishment, justified on retributivist grounds, is in fact resulting in the execution of innocent people, this raises significant problems for retributivism as a normative theory whose purpose is to guide and justify society's practices of punishment. Matters of innocence assume an even greater urgency in light of the contemporary scholarship examined in chapter 7, demonstrating the likelihood that the death penalty actually causes more convictions of innocent persons than would otherwise be the case. In other words, the very system of justice that kills the prisoner increases the odds that the innocent will be executed. We will argue that given the problem of innocence, retributivists must either concede that state execution is unjustifiable or be reduced to incoherence. Two sets of distinctions will be helpful in developing this argument. The first is between pure and mixed retributivist theories of punishment; the second is between thorough going and partial retributivism.

According to *pure retributivist* theories, in justifying the death penalty we should make no reference at all to consequences (to, say, whether death deters more effectively than life imprisonment). Punishment is morally justifiable because offenders deserve it; it is a means of giving them what they deserve.[19] Similarly, a specific form of punishment, such as the death penalty, is justifiable because those who commit the most serious crimes deserve the most serious punishment; it is a means of giving them the kind or amount of punishment they deserve.

By contrast, *mixed retributivist* theories, "hybrid syntheses of retributive and consequentialist elements,"[20] allow consequences to play some role, but not the whole role, in justifying punishment. Mixed retributivism is, in turn, a mixed category, since *justice* and *utility* tend to be invoked differently in different accounts, prompting some to question their theoretical coherency. At least two different strains of mixed retributivism can be usefully identified, one attributable to Cesare Beccaria and the other to H. L. A. Hart. The Beccarian strain resembles moderate nonconsequentialism, invoking principles of justice and of utility simultaneously in justifications of punishment. While Beccaria embraced deterrence, he also prohibited unjust punishment even where utility would be maximized by it, proclaiming that "a useful injustice cannot be tolerated."[21]

More commonly, perhaps, consequentialist considerations are invoked to justify the general aim of punishment as an institution. This was the approach of H. L. A. Hart, who parsed the competing justifications of punishment according to their level of application. In a distinction that remains influential today, Hart separated the justification of punishment as a social institution or practice from its justification in individual cases, or, as he put it, punishment's "General Justifying Aim" from its "Distribution."[22]

Don Scheid has advanced another distinction that will be useful in keeping the lines of our argument clear.[23] *Thoroughgoing retributivism* is any view that adopts retributivist rationales to justify punishment, both in the particular case and as a social practice. By contrast, *partial retributivism* offers retributivist justifications for the punishment of particular individuals, but consequentialist arguments to justify punishment as an institution or social practice. We will frequently use this distinction to contrast retentionists who are thorough-going retributivists with those who are partial retributivists. To anticipate, our argument will be that thoroughgoing retributivist retentionism is untenable in light of the innocence argument, and that efforts to salvage retentionism by moving to partial retributivism and invoking the principle of double effect are fruitless.

IMPLICATIONS OF THE INNOCENCE ARGUMENT
FOR A RETRIBUTIVE RETENTIONISM

While retributivism's vulnerability on the matter of executing the innocent has not been overlooked, it tends to be sidelined in the death penalty debate by other arguments. Hugo Adam Bedau, among others, has noted that the question of the guilt of those punished and the fairness of the procedures used to determine their guilt "does, or ought to, play a role" in undermining retributivist support for capital punishment, since "the retributivist is interested only in the accused getting what he deserves and that entails being at least as interested in the innocent being fairly acquitted as in the guilty being fairly convicted."[24] Yet one of the few people to treat this issue in a sustained manner, Richard Lempert, did so twenty years ago, well before the potent mix of recent developments that inform the innocence argument of today (i.e., the rise in exonerations, the statistical data regarding the frequency of erroneous convictions, the massive erosion in due process constitutional safeguards, etc.). He contended that retributivism is "haunted by the executions of the innocent which inevitably occur if the death penalty is allowed,"[25] because "however good a just punishment system and however much such a system demands the death penalty, the philosophy of retributivism apparently forbids the sacrifice of innocent lives as a condition for the maintenance of such a system."[26] Lempert relied on statistical inference to make the empirical case, arguing,

> If the retributivist's principles do not allow the intentional taking of the innocent life as a means to greater justice . . . they will not justify a system

that makes such things inevitable. Those who think that modern retributivist philosophies allow this confuse the comforts of ignorance with justification in principle. Statistical thinking is not only thoughtful, it is, in its own way, precise.[27]

If the statistical point Lempert made was compelling then, it is even more so today, particularly when one considers the significance of the error rates discussed in the preceding chapter. As we saw there, even using the ultraconservative rate, there is an overwhelming probability of executing an innocent person. These probabilities are even more unsettling given that America has executed over a thousand people since 1977. Moreover, not only are the probabilities overwhelming that the United States will execute innocent persons, it is virtually certain that it has already done so.[28] What Stephen Nathanson observes regarding race and the death penalty is also true here, regarding innocence: "[A]lthough no one decides that [it] will be a factor, we may predict that it will be a factor, and this knowledge must be considered in evaluating policies and institutions."[29]

How concerned should retributivists be about such innocent but unknown "statistical" lives, and their execution—past or pending—by the state? Can they coherently remain retentionists in the face of them? Before taking these questions up, we should consider an important rhetorical point. In his reflections on the law of torts, Guido Calabresi stated that "in the temple of truth all lives are real, whether originally described in statistical terms or not."[30] Yet, he continues, the public's attitudes toward the lives of clearly identified, actual individuals and toward those described only in statistical terms do differ. Society is, for example, willing to expend massive resources to save the lives of the former, but not to enact safety precautions that would have a comparable impact on the latter.[31]

A similar tendency to discount the significance of innocent "statistical" lives has been operative in the death penalty debate. Abolitionists have not been unresponsive to this. Accounts of actual, innocent individuals wrongfully convicted and sentenced to death by a system gone awry have proliferated in recent years. They are invaluable as concrete instances of the fatal unfairness of the actual administration of the death penalty, often undermining support for capital punishment.[32] Part of their value also derives from a point they help us make regarding the logic of the death penalty debate. Such stories draw attention to the fact that when one considers the policy or practice of capital punishment, it is the morality of an *entire system* that is being evaluated—one that has, in these cases and others, regularly "got it wrong."

The debate over the death penalty, however, has also tended to focus on individual cases like that of Timothy McVeigh and Ted Bundy, where culpable wrongdoing seems plainest and the crimes committed are heinous beyond measure. Abolitionists are then encouraged to focus their arguments on these so-called poster children for capital punishment. Patricia Williams writes, regarding the McVeigh case,

> It was incredible to see anti-death-penalty commentators apologizing constantly, always having to blither "of course no one condones his actions"— as though arguing for life imprisonment made one the squishiest, most bleeding-heart of moral equivocators. As a New York Times commentary observed, "Experts said it was the wrong case to debate—many people who do not approve of the death penalty wanted Mr. McVeigh to die."[33]

Williams goes on to endorse this focusing of the debate on the unjustifiability of executing even the undoubtedly guilty, contending that it is precisely cases like McVeigh's that should be foremost. "It is," she states,

> precisely the dimension of his evil that presses us to consider most seriously the limits of state force. The question is whether we want to license our government to kill, rather than just restrain by imprisoning, the very worst among us . . . [T]he debate we must have is . . . about the limits of state force, not about devising the perfect mirror of each victim's suffering.[34]

Her observations regarding the limits of state force return us to the issues raised in chapter 2. Does the state, by virtue of its sovereignty, have the right to deprive those within its jurisdiction of their most fundamental human rights, including the right to life? Should those in a democratic state grant it that right?

We have seen that based on a Hobbesian understanding of sovereignty as absolute, it has both the legal and moral right to do so. We also saw that there are good reasons for regarding that view of sovereignty as untenable. Part of what is involved is construing sovereignty as interdependence—recognizing that there are, indeed, moral and legal limits on the power of the state, and that among the state's foremost sovereign responsibilities is respecting and protecting the rights of those with whose care it is entrusted, including those it punishes. If the members of a democracy are unwilling to grant the state the power to torture in their name and in the name of justice,[35] they should also be unwilling to grant it the power to execute, for the very same reasons. If the state cannot justifiably torture a McVeigh or a Bundy, it cannot justifiably kill him. Further, the death penalty still would not be justifiable, even if we were to grant, for the sake of argument, that executing those guilty of the most heinous crimes was the only way to "give them what they deserve." The reason, to paraphrase a similar point by Nathanson,[36] is that governments have other responsibilities as well, such as the protection of innocent life; executing a McVeigh or a Bundy to give them what they deserve may well conflict with those other responsibilities. Indeed, given the empirical argument of chapter 7, it clearly would.

While it is important for abolitionists to make arguments against the use of the death penalty in specific cases, including those in which guilt seems least in doubt, it is also crucial to bear in mind the following point about both the rhetoric and the logic of the death penalty debate. If the use of state power to execute is abusive when inflicted at the individual level, it is all the more so when one considers its status as a legitimate *social institution* sanctioning the regular performance of executions in the name of justice, by a state riddled with class, racial, and ethnic biases. The retributivists' focus on such "poster children" can amount to a red herring, distracting attention from the crucial fact that when the morality of the death penalty is being addressed, it is the morality of the *system as a whole*—with all its shortcomings—that is at issue. When the state claims the right to execute, it is claiming the right to formulate, institutionalize, and carry out a policy, to engage in an ongoing practice. As one commentator puts it: "It is not possible to be in favor of the death penalty á la carte. The state either claims the right to impose this doom or it does not."[37] Whatever a retributivist might say about individual cases does not justify the social policy that permits the state to execute. As John Rawls has stressed, "We must distinguish questions about the justification of actions within a practice from questions about the justification of the practice itself."[38] Winnowing the death penalty down to only the most heinous offenders about whose guilt we are most confident still will not resolve the problem of innocence. That problem is, and would remain, a systemic one.

Thoroughgoing retributivism cannot justify a system of capital punishment by focusing on individual cases of allegedly justifiable executions. Even if a retentionist is convinced that it is morally permissible to execute in some specific case like McVeigh's, that does not establish the morally permissibility of state execution.[39] To make that argument, the empirical data concerning the actual practice of that system must be addressed. This includes the whole, sorry record in capital trials of coerced confessions,[40] of compromised testimony by jailhouse snitches,[41] of drunk, sleeping, or inept defense lawyers in capital trials,[42] of class and racial bias,[43] and so on. Such factors drive up the error rate, and the presence on death row of innocent, if unknown, persons.

They are in turn exacerbated by Supreme Court decisions that, in the name of efficiency, have eviscerated federal habeas corpus rules protecting the innocent from execution.[44] The evidence that America has executed and will continue to execute innocent people is substantial, and it must be weighed in assessing the moral acceptability of capital punishment as a social practice. When it is, when retributive retentionists attempt to support a social practice that executes the innocent with statistical certainty, a thoroughgoing retributivism is rendered untenable and unjust by its own criterion, for the actual system of capital punishment manifestly and massively violates the constraint that only the guilty must be punished.[45] In order to morally justify a social practice such as punishment, we must establish "that we may institute or engage in that practice without behaving immorally."[46] This is all the more urgent when the form of punishment at issue is execution. As George Wright observes, "[T]he basic problem with capital punishment" is one of "extinction. A unique, irreplaceable locus of immense mystery and value, in the form of a particular consciousness, self-consciousness, and active free will, is simply annihilated."[47]

It is this result, and the attendant disparity between justifying a specific case and justifying the practice within which it is embedded, that might move someone to abandon thoroughgoing for partial retributivism, allowing consequentialist considerations to come into play. This has the seeming advantage of preserving a retributivist-grounded retentionism. Burton Leiser, for example, contends that death penalty proponents

> must be prepared to live with the fact that the policy they advocate may result in the state's executing persons who will later be found to have committed no crime. . . . If, despite all precautions, an inadvertent error is made that is the price that must be paid for the sake of the greater benefit that it is hoped the death penalty will confer upon society as a whole.[48]

A partial retributivism, then, might acknowledge the empirical evidence regarding execution of the innocent under the current capital punishment regime, but go on to claim that this is morally acceptable on consequentialist grounds, in the interests of punishing the guilty.

Yet this move from thoroughgoing to partial retributivism comes at what, for many, should be an unacceptably high price. What retributivism takes issue with in utilitarianism is the latter's ability to rule out a moral justification for sacrificing the welfare of some innocents for the sake of others. Retributivism is not a viable alternative to utilitarianism if such a trade-off in innocent life is made at the level of social practice in order to justify an institution of state execution that death penalty proponents deem of great benefit to society.

Indeed, the situation is actually a good bit worse. At least utilitarians leave it open as a moral possibility that the innocent may be executed *for the sake of other innocent lives.* The partial retributivist here is willing to condone (as a statistical "inevitability," not just a hypothetical possibility) executing the innocent for something ostensibly of much less value than other (innocent) human lives. For what, exactly, is unclear; presumably for whatever benefit accrues to a society from giving the guilty their just deserts.[49] For Igor Primoratz, it has to do with not "privileging" murderers over other offenders, and avoiding "a situation in which proportionate penalties would be meted out for all offenses, *except* for murder . . . In all other cases justice would be done in full . . ."[50] This essentially renders irrelevant the lives of the innocent people whose execution is allowed.

Leiser, for his part, attempts to shore up the retributivist position by noting that "we have many policies which we *know* will result in the loss of innumerable innocent persons."[51] His example is our tolerance for the ownership and use of cars, which results in massive numbers of accidental deaths on the highway. However, as Richard Wasserstrom notes in another context, "the highway does not, typically, cause the death of the innocent passenger; the careless driver or the defective tire does."[52] The situation is different in the case of the death penalty, where the death of the innocent is caused and carried out by a system of punishment mandated by the state in the name of justice, a system in which safeguards to protect the innocent and prevent errors have been eroded in the name of efficiency.

The retributivist might persist, pointing to other policies and practices mandated by the state, such as requiring certain vaccinations with a statistically predictable mortality rate, which the abolitionist would have to regard as unjustifiable for the same reason.[53] Yet this response neglects relevant disanalogies. There is a significant difference between practices, or policies, of state vaccination and of capital punishment. The former, unlike the latter, is able to appeal (indeed, *must* appeal) to probable benefits that will result from the practice;[54] the death of innocents results from a social policy that *aims to prevent* (and presumably succeeds in preventing) *death and illness* in the majority of the population. A compelling consequentialist argument can be made that these likely benefits justify its implementation, especially in the absence of a less lethal alternative. Nothing comparable can be claimed of the practice of capital punishment; as we have seen, it cannot be justified on grounds of social utility. This line of reasoning, in any event, is not open to the retributivist, who must attempt to justify it on the grounds that it punishes those who deserve or merit it, and that it does so in a way not adequately met by nonlethal alternatives. Capital punishment, in contrast to state vaccination, is a practice in which the death of innocents results from a social policy that *aims to inflict death* on those individuals it determines deserve or merit it. As Bedau notes, "[T]here is no analogy between a morally defensible practice in which lethal accidents do occur that take statistical lives and a morally dubious practice in which lethal events are designed for particular individuals in the mistaken belief that they deserve it."[55] These disanalogies are significant enough to say that the practice of state execution is morally problematic to a degree and in a manner in which the practice of state vaccination is not.

Attempting to move to a partial retributivism (like the above) in order to justify the current practice of capital punishment fails. And with it, any attempt to justify state execution on retributivist grounds fails as well. If the principle of retributive justice employed is Kantian, then allowing a practice in which the innocent are executed so that the guilty may be punished fails utterly to respect the innocent as rational, autonomous beings, and reduces them to a pure instrumentality, a mere means to other societal ends. If the retributivist argument is based on paying the offender back for wrongdoing, executing innocent people is wholly unmerited; we not only have not accorded them their just deserts, we have visited an injustice upon them for which no restitution whatsoever can be made. If the retributivist is a social contractarian, no greater and more irreparable breach of the social contract is conceivable than one where the state executes the innocent to ensure that the guilty not benefit unfairly from breaching the social contract.

The moral to be drawn from the fact that a system of state punishment is necessarily imperfect, and mistakes are inevitable, is that the form of punishment imposed be such that mistakes are not final and restitution can be made. Precisely because retributive theories of punishment are so committed to the view that justice does not allow us to punish the innocent for the greater good, they cannot justify allowing an imperfect system to impose perfectly final and irrevocable sanctions like the death penalty.

THE RETRIBUTIVIST'S REBUTTAL: APPEALING TO DOUBLE EFFECT

To summarize the argument thus far, the problem with basing retentionism on retributivism is twofold. If the retributivism is thoroughgoing, then, given the innocence argument, incoherence ensues, since retributivism fails to satisfy its own cardinal principle that only the guilty should be punished. If the retentionist moves to partial retributivism to avoid this result, then the same criticisms that retributivism makes of utilitarianism turn back on it.[56] But retributivists have a rebuttal, which relies upon the principle of double effect, according to which it may be morally permissible to perform an action otherwise morally impermissible, provided that the resulting harms were foreseen but not intended.[57] The retributivist might acknowledge that the American system of capital punishment is executing significant numbers of innocent people, but contend that this is a merely foreseen, not intended, aspect of the system, occurring despite the existence of safeguards to prevent it. No actual system, the retributivist might conclude, can be perfect, and it is unreasonable for the critic to insist that it be so.

Appeals to this principle are evident in many scholarly as well as popular responses to state execution. Michael Moore uses this strategy to dismiss concern about the execution of innocent statistical lives:

> The probable punishment of the innocent by any real-world punishment scheme is not much of a worry . . . We rightly set up many social institutions where we know that some percentage of individuals affected by them will be hurt or even killed . . . [This] is not to be equated with either our intending that they be so harmed, or knowing that some identified individual will suffer that harm.[58]

"Moral norms bind us absolutely," he adds, "only with respect to evils we either intend or . . . knowingly visit on specified individuals."[59] So this retributivist rebuttal to the innocence argument acknowledges that the American system of capital punishment is executing significant numbers of innocent people but contends, that since this is merely foreseen, not intended, it is morally unproblematic (in Moore's terms, "not much of a worry"). Because appeals to double effect are so common, and do such heavy lifting in the death penalty debate, we should attend to them. Drawing on the work of Alison McIntyre, we will consider a series of responses.[60]

1. The first is simply to dismiss this appeal *because* it invokes the principle of double effect, which many have argued is suspect "as a *decision procedure* for deliberating about morally right action" (Emphasis in original).[61] Since it lends itself to serious misuse, it is unsuitable as a practical maxim. Nicholas Barlow, for instance, maintains that this principle "becomes an empty doctrine since one can justify any action at all, given enough time to work out an excuse."[62] A recent example of this is Timothy McVeigh's justification of the Oklahoma City bombing:

> Even war criminals usually go to the trouble of claiming some moral justification for their crimes, some moral equivalence with their enemies. Timothy McVeigh argued that the arrogance of the Federal Government . . . was so vast and so dangerous that he needed to

blow up a building, start a revolution. "I did it for the larger good," he claimed, and if innocent people had to die, well, that's what happens in war. He called the 19 dead children "collateral damage" . . .[63]

This is in essence an invocation of the principle of double effect to justify the "collateral damage" caused by the current system of state execution, and might itself be regarded as an instance of such misuse. Indeed, there are some who regard recourse to this principle as generally suspect and dangerous, and as encouraging "a hypocritical attitude towards moral problems."[64]

While the fact that a principle is prone to abuse doesn't invalidate it, it ought to incline us to be extremely wary when it is used. All the more so when it is one that is appealed to, as double effect is, to help resolve cases that are particularly problematic morally. This response to the retributivist's rebuttal is not entirely satisfying, however. Among other things, it is unlikely to convince many of those who make this rebuttal, and who do find something persuasive about the principle of double effect. So we should look elsewhere as well.

2. A second response argues that the retributivist's rebuttal violates one of the standard constraints on appeals to the principle of double effect, which is that a harmful effect is not morally permissible if the good effect can be obtained without the bad. As Alison McIntyre puts it, "[I]f some other equally feasible course of action would realize the good result with less harmful side effects, then that should be pursued instead."[65] To see how the retributivist's rebuttal fails to do this, consider the following dilemma.

Americans must choose between two actions. Either they will embrace or they will reject the current system of capital punishment as a means of punishing those guilty of particularly heinous crimes. If the system is embraced, innocent people will certainly continue to be executed. If it is rejected, not only will these innocent people be spared execution, but those guilty of such crimes will not go unpunished. Their penalty, perhaps, will be life imprisonment. While it is true that, given the fallibility of the criminal justice system, innocent people may well be imprisoned, at least it will remain possible to rectify such miscarriages of justice and to make restitution of some sort to them. Death rules this out.

The retributivist's rebuttal thus violates an important constraint on the principle of double effect, since the good effect (ensuring that the guilty receive their just deserts) can be obtained without enduring the bad effect (executing the innocent). The bad effect can and should be avoided, particularly in light of its gravity, finality, and irrevocability.

3. A third response to the retributivist's rebuttal to the innocence argument is that it dismisses our responsibility for foreseen harms. Consider the following two societies.[66]

Society A: In this society, three innocent people are knowingly selected and sacrificed in order to enable the judicial execution of ninety-seven others who are guilty of heinous crimes and held to deserve death.[67] There is no doubt about the innocence of these three, their identity is known, and their deaths are fully intended. Most retributivists would not hesitate to condemn this; the three innocent people have done nothing to merit such treatment. Although known to be innocent, they are sacrificed, reduced to a mere means to enable the ends of executing the ninety-seven who are guilty.

Society B: The situation here seems initially quite different, since this society has worked hard to develop a system that separates the innocent from the guilty, and it selects people for execution with no error, insofar as the society is able to determine this. Retributive retentionists would likely find such a system morally acceptable and contend that it would be morally permissible to execute those found guilty of heinous crimes. As time passes, however, evidence mounts that the safeguards established to protect the innocent are no longer effective, and innocent people are indeed being executed. As members of the society learn this, they also learn more about the human factors that make error inevitable. The error rate is, let us assume, 3 percent. So they now know that their criminal justice system, devised to retributively punish the guilty, is also executing the innocent. The identities of the latter are unknown and their deaths are foreseen, but not intended.

The retributivist reasons that, unlike those in Society A, Americans do not intend the execution of the innocent as a means to securing the good ends of giving capital offenders what they deserve. They are in a situation similar to those in Society B, where the execution of the innocent is a harmful side effect for which, since it is merely foreseen, they are not responsible. The problem with this reasoning is that it mistakes one distinction—between intending a harmful effect as a means and foreseeing it as a side effect—for a different distinction—between actions for which we can and cannot be held responsible. For any action we may take, there are irrelevant consequences that may legitimately be "screened off," and there are consequences that constitute reasons for not taking such action.[68] By allowing state execution, for example, Americans are also making more work for the courts—but this is insignificant to a decision about the moral justifiability of capital punishment. Another consequence of allowing capital punishment is that the innocent will be executed—and this is significant to moral decision making; it counts as a reason against allowing capital punishment. It may be true that the members of Society B do not intend for the innocent to be executed, but (unlike increasing the courts' workload) it is a significant effect that provides them with a reason for not allowing their state to execute. It cannot justifiably be screened off as something to which retributivists need not attend or for which they are not responsible.

As Alison McIntyre would put it, the retributivist's rebuttal misinterprets the principle of double effect as according to all side effects "the special status of side effects which may be screened off."[69] The fact that the harmful side effect of executing the innocent is merely foreseen (and not intended), does not justify ignoring such consequences, or treating them as irrelevant. Nor does it absolve Americans of responsibility for them. They must be weighed in the retributivist's deliberations about capital punishment. And pace Moore, they are not only a "bit of a worry," but a considerable one.

For Moore, of course, the fact that in Society A the identity of the innocent is known is relevant; they are "identified," "specified individuals," and it is impermissible to execute them. But how is the moral situation in Society B significantly different? Members of Society B may be uncertain which three innocent people will be executed, but they are not at all uncertain that three people will be executed; they know the error rate is 3 percent. The innocent will be executed in both cases. Knowing who they are may make it more difficult in various ways for members of Society A to carry out executions, but death is as knowingly and surely being visited upon three members of Society B. So, too, in American society today. The statistical probabilities that the American criminal justice system is executing and will continue to execute significant numbers of the innocent cannot be ignored. As Richard Lempert notes in the quote that opens this chapter, "[T]reating the statistically predictable as other than inevitable is a form of false consciousness." We know that such executions are not merely possible, or slightly probable. Call them massively probable; thus, this knowledge is as close as one comes in the empirical world to certainty. Such knowledge about the consequences of the death penalty makes a difference, and should make a difference, in deliberations about the morality of this social practice, whether we are thinking about the members of Society B or of American society. As knowledge of the consequences of the death penalty becomes widespread, we are inclined to say that the situation in either of these latter two societies is no different, morally speaking, from that in Society A. This is why it is important to disseminate such information in American society today, and why the work of the Innocence Projects on the death penalty is so morally significant.[70]

We have focused closely in this chapter on the arguments that death penalty proponents might make to respond to the growing empirical evidence that has come to light over the past few decades and made the innocence argument such a potent force in undermining state execution. That the American criminal justice system is and has been executing innocent people, and that it will continue to do so as long as the death penalty is implemented by imperfect beings, challenges the moral legitimacy of capital punishment directly and effectively. Some scholars suggest that little can change the debate's footing; that death penalty support turns on emotions that are well-nigh immune to argument.[71] While this may be true, we appeal here to those who remain open to reasoned argument, and we believe that their numbers are greater than the pessimists postulate.

The now-nearly-trite phrase "death is different" captures the pivotal role that matters of innocence play in this debate and underscores just how much innocence matters. Death is different because it does not permit us to revoke unjustly inflicted punishment, because it rules out all possibility of offering the unjustly punished proper restitution and all opportunity of making our admittedly imperfect amends; because, as the secretary-general of the Council of Europe recently stated, "[I]t transforms judicial errors into irreparable tragedies."[72] For the average person, as well as the philosopher, death's irrevocability makes the problem of innocence more compelling than if the same innocent person were confined in prison. So long as the wrongfully convicted person lives, the error can be rectified—if only partially and belatedly. But the state cannot correct error, or make restitution, posthumously. As the Canadian Supreme Court justices commented in the Burns decision, regarding erroneous convictions in Canada:

In all of these cases, had capital punishment been imposed, there would have been no one to whom an apology and compensation could be paid in respect of the miscarriage of justice . . . and no way in which Canadian society with the benefit of hindsight could have justified to itself the deprivation of human life in violation of the principles of fundamental justice . . .[73]

Fortunately, because of the abolition of the death penalty, meaningful remedies for wrongful conviction are still possible in this country.[74]

9 : The Imperfectability of the System

We now know, in a way almost unthinkable even a decade ago, that our system of criminal justice, for all its protections, is sufficiently fallible that innocent people are convicted of capital crimes with some frequency.
—Justice Jed S. Rakoff[1]

MORATORIA AND REFORM: CAN THE SYSTEM BE FIXED?

The previous chapter considered various implications of the innocence argument for utilitarian and retributivist reasoning regarding state execution. One obvious response retentionists can make to the arguments developed there is that the problem lies with the imperfections not of retributivist theory, but of the current system of capital punishment; that system needs to be improved so that the force of the innocence argument is nullified. The innocence argument has already had substantial impact on the American death penalty system, notably in the growing number of reforms introduced, as well as in calls for a moratorium on capital punishment within certain state jurisdictions. Our question in this chapter is whether efforts to reform the administration of the death penalty and, most notably, the move to a moratorium until such reforms can be addressed, appropriately and adequately responds to the issues raised by the innocence argument.

Shortly after George Ryan's inauguration as governor of Illinois, a group of Northwestern University journalism students approached him regarding the case of death-row inmate Anthony Porter. They presented the governor with a videotaped confession by the real criminal, which freed Porter after eighteen years. Said Ryan: "I was completely caught off-guard . . . That mentally retarded man came within two days of execution, and but for those students Anthony Porter would have been dead and buried. I felt jolted into re-examining everything I believed in."[2] This reexamination—conducted in light of a study revealing that nearly half of all capital convictions in Illinois had been reversed on appeal—led Ryan to conclude, "I cannot support a system which, in its administration, has proven so fraught with error, and has come so close to the ultimate nightmare, the state's taking of an innocent life."[3] In 2001, he issued an ultimatum halting indefinitely all executions in the state and setting up a commission to examine the system. The moratorium would remain in place "until I can be sure with moral certainty that no innocent man or woman is facing a lethal injection."[4] It was a certainty that never came. Two years later, Ryan commuted the sentences of all 167 death-row inmates, stating, "The facts that I've seen in reviewing each and every one of these cases questions not only . . . the innocence of people on death row, but [also] the fairness of the death penalty system as a whole."[5]

Another governor, Mitt Romney, proposed administrative reforms to Massachusetts's criminal justice system intended to reinstate a death penalty that is "as infallible, as humanly possible."[6] His bill narrowed the crimes eligible for the death penalty and relied on scientific evidence (together with a series of reviews by scientific experts and the courts) to establish a "no doubt" standard of guilt in order to avoid the "ultimate nightmare" of state execution of the innocent that so troubled Governor Ryan. It required that the jury find "conclusive scientific evidence" establishing guilt with "a high level of scientific certainty."[7] Romney's faith in science and its use in the courtroom appeared to be unqualified: "Just as science can free the innocent, it can also identify the guilty."[8] This, he maintained, "removes the major weakness in death penalty statutes in other states . . . the fear that you may execute someone who is innocent. We remove that possibility."[9] Science would dispel the "demon of error" that Ryan was convinced ineradicably "haunted" Illinois' capital punishment system.[10] The hope was that such reforms would have influence well beyond the borders of Massachusetts:[11] this death penalty bill "is the best in the nation. This is the model, the gold standard, if you're going to consider the ultimate punishment."[12] "It's a model for the nation."[13]

Romney's proposal to "fix the system" in response to the force of the innocence argument received little support from either retentionists or abolitionists, and was defeated in the Massachusetts legislature. It is, however, instructive as a compelling illustration of the difficulty, expense, and ultimate futility of efforts to reform the system in the conviction that error can indeed be eliminated. First, Romney proclaimed that his proposal would eliminate the possibility of executing the innocent: "This legislative standard ensures that the innocent will not be found guilty . . . You will not have false executions under this bill."[14] Yet the death penalty reform commission that he established to advise him repeatedly qualified their claims, stating that the system would be as infallible *as humanly possible*, that it would ensure as much *as humanly possible* that the innocent would not be executed. Clearly the commission believed that the possibility of error cannot be entirely removed. This was stated even more plainly by the Illinois commission, which advised Governor Ryan that "no system, given human nature and frailties, could ever be devised or constructed that would work perfectly and guarantee absolutely that no innocent person is ever again sentenced to death."[15]

Second, even the commission acknowledged that the evidentiary standard it recommended, and the multiple layers of review required, would be expensive. The cost, they thought, would be offset by "the extremely narrow proposed criteria for death eligibility which ensure that, at most, only a small handful of murders" would be eligible each year, and that in any event they "simply must be borne" in the interests of fairness and accuracy.[16] Members of the Massachusetts bar have protested that the "long-term effects on already resource strapped courts would be devastating."[17] Romney himself predicted that only one or two people per year would face the death penalty under his bill, but others suggest it might be as rare as one every fifteen years.[18] The result, according to critics, however, is a "purely symbolic criminal statute,"[19] introducing "an expensive and complicated new bureaucracy that would execute nobody":

> The bill calls for layers and layers of new processes and legal requirements, while restricting death-penalty eligibility so narrowly that it's hard to find any real case to which it would ever apply.[20]

Indeed, Romney conceded as much when he offered an alternative justification for the plan, claiming that the accused would be moved to plead to first-degree murder in exchange for a death penalty waiver, foregoing enough expensive trials to make the new system cost-effective. He neglected to consider, however, that this would cut both ways, prompting not only the guilty but also the innocent to make such a plea.[21] According to one report, District Attorney Bill Keating observed that

> the Supreme Judicial Court has noted that the death penalty could be unconstitutional because it unduly pressures defendants to accept life in prison rather than face the possibility if death. "And now they highlight it as a reason for passing the bill," Keating said.[22]

More important, however, are Romney's faith in scientific certainty and his accompanying assumptions about the role of science in the courtroom, assumptions that are commonplace, if ill-founded. One of these is that scientific evidence can be transformed seamlessly and unproblematically in the courtroom into legal evidence, and even incontrovertible proof: "You may have ballistic evidence that proves a certain gun was the murder weapon. But you need 'people evidence' to say, 'That was the defendant's gun.'"[23] Another is that scientific evidence is somehow insulated from error and manipulation, and that it is not itself subject to challenge and dispute. As one former prosecutor commented, supposing that DNA evidence "is a panacea is just completely and 100 percent wrong":

DNA evidence and scientific evidence is only as good as the human being who is collecting the evidence or who is analyzing the evidence in the laboratory. Anyone who thinks this is a foolproof gold standard bill is being misled gravely.[24]

In fact, one week after Romney introduced his death penalty legislation, Virginia governor Mark Warner released a report that documented "numerous errors in the analysis and interpretation of DNA evidence" in one of his state's capital cases.[25] These included misinterpretation of the results, test contamination, inconsistent results, departures from lab protocols, and unsound conclusions.

Sheila Jasanoff, professor of Science and Technology Studies at Harvard, notes that "[t]he governor's faith in the perfectibility of the death penalty reflects modern societies' conviction that science can deliver failsafe, just legal outcomes where the law, acting on its own, might fall short."[26] The mistaken nature of this faith, she persuasively argues, is due to a series of misconceptions about the nature of science and the law, and of their relationship. Their differing aims, normative commitments, and institutional settings combine to make acutely problematic Romney's conviction that the courts can, by relying on science, establish guilt with certainty and produce the kind of incontrovertible, foolproof evidence that will eliminate the possibility of executing the innocent.

Jasonoff singles out three particularly salient differences.[27] (1) The roles of fact-finding in law and in science differ markedly. This has implications for justice, since facts developed for litigation in order to establish specific causation are not likely to be subject to the processes of peer review, of replication, and of communal scrutiny that characterize scientific activity. (2) The standards of certainty required to establish factual truth in science differ from the standards of certainty litigants must meet to win cases. The legal evidence that will produce reasonable doubt among jurors is not, and ought not to be, held to the same rigorous standards of science. (3) The production and use of knowledge in law and in science are subject to differing ethical constraints. The application of a no-doubt standard, for example, inaccurately suggests that rigorous scientific and legal quality control will themselves suffice to remove jurors' doubts. This is, however, far more a function of the kind of high quality, and expensive, legal representation that most capital defendants never enjoy:

> Forensic science, in other words, cannot rule out doubt on its own, but only as it is represented, and contested, in court, as a component of a larger story. Well-paid lawyers defending wealthy clients tend to be more diligent

in deconstructing the weaknesses in the prosecution's incriminating evidence. Indigent defendants, who cannot afford expensive lawyering, may find their fates decided less by the strength of scientific evidence as assessed by technical experts than by the vigor and ingenuity of the advocacy mobilized in their defense.[28]

The idea that science can be relied upon to establish incontrovertible truth in the courtroom carries with it the illusion that human subjectivity—and so fallibility—is thereby removed from the legal process, that the facts will then speak for themselves rather than require representation, and that they will not be subject to biases or flaws. This is reflected in the contrast Romney's commission drew in its recommendations: the use of "human evidence" should be limited in establishing guilt, while conclusive "scientific evidence" is required in doing so. It is as though scientific evidence was not produced and applied by humans, and thus is not subject to the distorting factors that led the commission to be wary of the use of human evidence; as though both were not potentially impacted in similar ways by their selection and representation as evidence in a trial; as though neither type of evidence were vulnerable to mishandling, tampering, even fabrication.[29] Science, Jasonoff reminds us, is a purposive social activity and product, situated in specific contexts and cultures, and responsive to specific institutional demands.

> Scientific truth-making, in particular, as human beings engage in it, is always a social enterprise . . . As such, even scientific claims are subject to distortion, through imperfections in the very human systems that produced them. In attempting to render justice, the law's objective should be, in part, to restore to view these potential shortcomings, instead of uncritically taking on board a decontextualized image of science that ignores its social and institutional dimensions . . . In a court of law, science cannot hold itself out as simply science, the source of transcendental truths . . .[30]

The association of DNA profiling with infallibility, the readiness to seize on it as a "transcendental truth" that will itself determine jury outcomes in capital cases, is a failure to acknowledge and accept the fact that science is a social product—one subject to error and distortion within the context of its own institutional imperatives, and even more so when it is subjected to the institutional imperatives of an advocacy-intensive and efficiency-driven criminal justice system. This uncritical embrace of decontextualized science and the growing reliance of law on science in the context of state execution are instructive. Faith in the system of capital punishment has been shaken by the wealth of evidence regarding both the tenacious racial and socioeconomic biases that trouble its operation and the extent to which the system erroneously convicts the innocent. With such faith shaken, that system can no longer present itself convincingly as purely neutral, disinterested, and facilitative, or "set itself outside the social order, as if through the application of legal method and rigour, it [were] a thing apart which can in turn reflect upon the world from which it is divorced."[31] Those who (like Romney) would refine the system of state execution in order to restore it must find a way to eliminate bias, error, and discrimination. To do this, they turn to a discredited, positivist view of science as unbiased, value-free, and the source of hard certainties, of transcendental truths; one seen "to take the establishment of the truth away from fallible human beings . . . and lodge it instead in various more or less reliable impersonal agents."[32]

Of course science, including genetic science, has a crucial role to play in the criminal justice system generally and in the capital punishment system in particular. Both sides of the death penalty debate have called upon it to do invaluable work; the Innocence Project, for example, has drawn upon it to exonerate approximately 170 wrongfully convicted persons, 14 of whom were at one time sentenced to death.

> DNA testing has been a major factor in changing the criminal justice system. It has provided scientific proof that our system convicts and sentences innocent people—and that wrongful convictions are not isolated or rare events. Most importantly, DNA testing has opened a window into wrongful convictions so that we may study the causes and propose remedies that may minimize the chances that more innocent people are convicted.[33]

But it will not do to set science up as an infallible god, or to rely on it as a deus ex machina that rescues the current death penalty system from the imperfect human hands that shape and adminster it, turning it into a "foolproof" system that "ensures that the innocent will not be found guilty . . . [that] no single innocent person [will] face the death penalty."[34] For one thing, such biological evidence is available only in a small percentage of cases. For another, the divergent institutional imperatives within which science and the law operate are such that "tendencies to bias and error may not apply symmetrically in cases of inculpation and exoneration."[35] The use of DNA brings the two institutions into collaboration, but the passage from scientific observation to legal evidence is not seamless or transparent. The former is often altered in significant ways by being subsumed within the institutional imperatives that drive the law, such as the pressure to convict.

The superficial parallel between using DNA evidence to establish guilt and using it to establish innocence ignores important contextual differences. When the purpose is to free a presumably innocent, wrongfully convicted prisoner, forensic scientists have every incentive to produce the most reliable and persuasive results within their power. By contrast, when the purpose is to convict the guilty, extraordinary pressures may exist to produce results that will satisfy the prosecutor's and the public's desire for speedy convictions.[36]

A case in point is that of Earl Washington, discussed in chapter 7. An analysis and interpretation of DNA evidence, completed long after his conviction, was determined (by an independent scientific audit conducted by specialists from the American Society of Crime Laboratory Directors) to have been seriously flawed, suffering from unsound conclusions, deviation from lab protocols, inconsistent results, possible text contamination, and pressures from within and without the lab "to produce quick and conclusive reports in the Washington case, even when the evidence was muddled."[37] (Later tests of this DNA evidence would conclusively demonstrate Washington's innocence.) The report called for, among other things, the development of procedures "to insulate the examiners from pressures that may be applied from inside and outside of the laboratory in situations similar to this case."[38] The Virginia Division of Forensic Science had repeatedly refused calls for an outside review of the evidence, even after five leading DNA experts concluded that the lab had erred in Washington's case. "I'm not going to admit error where there is none," the lab's director declared, shortly before then governor of Virginia, Mark Warner, intervened and ordered the outside review.[39]

Where Ryan sought, but did not find, a moral certainty that would exorcise the demon of judicial error, Romney proposed to fix the system to "remove that possibility" by substituting a scientific certainty. It was a quixotic gesture, however; one made in ignorance of the empirical and normative differences that distinguish scientific and legal practices, and of the institutional imperatives in which each operates; one that illustrates both the desire to perfect an imperfectable capital punishment system by those who support it, and the impossibility of doing so. The prospects for using moratoria in order to fix the system do not seem promising. "We are still relying on the vagaries of human nature," Amnesty International's northeast regional director observed, "and there's nothing Governor Romney can do about that."[40]

The American Bar Association (ABA) proposed a moratorium in 1997.[41] It was motivated in part by the willingness of American courts to accept that they are executing the innocent,[42] as shown by decisions like *Herrera v. Collins*, where new evidence demonstrating the actual innocence of someone on death row is set aside in the interests of finality. While taking no position on the death penalty itself, the ABA continues to support a moratorium. Its president, Martha W. Barnett, began her term in 2000 "by calling for a moratorium on executions in the United States until fairness can be assured."[43] And that same year, in the wake of Illinois governor Ryan's decision to impose a moratorium on executions, the ABA sponsored a national conference, "Call to Action: A Moratorium on Executions."[44] Whether one sees the bar or Governor Ryan as leading, pressure toward a moratorium has plainly been gaining steam. By the end of the year 2000, thirty-one cities, including Greensboro (North Carolina), Atlanta, Baltimore, Philadelphia, and San Francisco had passed resolutions urging moratoria on executions.[45]

At the federal level, a variety of proposals have been put forward either to circumscribe the death penalty, as in the Innocence Protection Act, or to abolish it altogether.[46] A series of measures have been advanced by state legislatures attempting to reform various aspects of their states' death penalty systems. These include amending statutes to provide better legal representation in capital cases and to offer jurors a life-without-parole alternative to death sentencing, as well as the initiation of studies to address areas where state death penalty systems need reform. Concerns for innocence contributed to the New Jersey legislature's decision in 2006 to declare a moratorium on executions.[47] Proposals for moratoria are being considered (primarily because of innocence concerns)[48] in at least 14 death penalty states, and some 150 different city councils have called for moratoria.[49]

An ABC poll, reported in May 2, 2001, showed that 51 percent of the American public supported a moratorium on the death penalty. That number rose to 57 percent when people were told that Illinois already had a moratorium on the death penalty.[50] Similarly, a Roper poll conducted between May 23 and 24, 2001, found that 59 percent of the public favored a moratorium in order to "reduce the chances that an innocent person will be put to death."[51] Results of an ABC news poll from 2001 are similar.[52] It is little wonder that there have been renewed calls for a moratorium on the death penalty. "Politicians rarely vote against what they perceive as their constituents' wishes except when weighty contributors are involved."[53] While not all politicians may yet be convinced, there have been significant inroads.[54]

A moratorium may well present itself as a conceptual compromise in the American death penalty debate; it is a position to which opposing parties are drawn for conflicting reasons. Abolitionists are likely to support calls for a moratorium, but are unlikely to be satisfied with them as anything more than a strategic measure—one effective step away from judicial killing, to be followed by its complete elimination. They may well do so with marked reservations, since moratoria, and attendant procedural "adjustments," might delay full abolition. "It is even possible that a moratorium . . . could serve as a means for marshaling support for the continued use of capital punishment rather than its abolition."[55] This seems particularly likely if the general population were to come to believe (erroneously, as we have just argued) that such things as DNA evidence are able to provide the requisite technological "fix," eliminating execution of the innocent.[56] While the enthusiasm with which moratoria are embraced by American abolitionists may differ, given their differing views about how best to abolish the death penalty, it is hard to see how even those most strategically wary of moratoria could fail to support their actual enactment. For that period of time, at least, their state will not be executing, will not be violating the most fundamental human rights of its citizens. Those on death row, whether actually guilty or actually innocent, will be spared for the duration. On any abolitionist assessment, that is a result to be embraced.

Calls for a moratorium have recently been issued by retentionists as well, whose doubts about the present system of capital punishment have been stirred by the innocence argument (among others). For some retentionists, those doubts have grown so acute that they are now questioning the propriety of *any* system of state executions. A moratorium is, for them, a means of moving away from—and withholding their sanction for—a social policy they are not yet prepared to reject entirely. But for others, a moratorium may be best construed as a strategic move of a different sort; an opportunity to acknowledge, address, and redress the problematic aspects of the current practice of state execution. Such retentionists remain fully committed to the death penalty "in principle"; they are intent on fixing the faulty system so that state execution may continue.

A POTENTIALLY FATAL DISTINCTION

This distinction between supporting the death penalty "in principle" and supporting it "in practice" figures prominently in the death penalty debate and is worth a closer look. Frequently, it emerges in philosophical discussions as a retentionist counter to abolitionist arguments.

> [T]his [innocence] argument . . . does not speak out against capital punishment itself, but against the existing procedures for trying capital cases. Miscarriages of justice result in innocent people being sentenced to death

and executed. . . But this does not stem from the intrinsic nature of the institution of capital punishment; it results from deficiencies, limitations, and imperfections of the criminal law procedures in which this punishment is meted out. *Errors of justice do not demonstrate the need to do away with capital punishment; they simply make it incumbent on us to do everything possible to improve even further procedures of meting it out.*[57] (Emphasis added.)

This response by Igor Primoratz to the innocence argument is fairly typical in retentionist philosophical literature.[58]

Such invocations of the in-principle/in-practice distinction have several disturbing features. The first is that they are generally not followed by calls for a moratorium; seemingly content to make a point of logic, they fail to follow through with its implications, either practically or morally. Retentionists who believe that the innocent are being executed under the current system of capital punishment, but that capital punishment nevertheless remains justifiable in principle, if not in practice, should at least be arguing vigorously that a moratorium is morally required until "procedures" have been "improved." Not to do so is to fail to treat the issue with the seriousness it is due, especially for a retributivist. The execution of innocent men and women is among the gravest of injustices, and one of the most extreme abuses of state power. The errors of justice responsible for their execution certainly do demonstrate the need to do away with capital punishment as currently practiced, although retributivists such as Primoratz do not see that as calling into question the "intrinsic nature of the institution of capital punishment."[59]

As for improving "even further procedures of meting it out,"[60] it should be observed that the erosion of such measures, as a result of recent Supreme Court decisions and of the Anti-Terrorism and Effective Death Penalty Act, must first be reversed. And even in the unlikely event of this, it is simply not possible to improve procedures to the point where we can be confident that no innocent people will be executed. Primoratz admits as much, but goes on to argue that this "is actually a demand to give a privileged position to murderers as against all other offenders,"[61] since proportionate penalties would then be meted out for all other offenses, but not for murder.[62] His commitment to the principle that only the guilty deserve to be punished lapses at this point, aided and abetted by a gross underestimation of the incidence of wrongful convictions and executions, as well as of the gravity of executions:

It is a great and tragic miscarriage of justice when an innocent person is mistakenly sentenced to death and executed, but systematically giving murderers advantage over all other offenders would also be a grave injustice. Is the fact that, as long as capital punishment is retained, there is a possibility that over a number of years, or even decades, an injustice of the first kind may be committed, unintentionally and unconsciously, reason enough to abolish it altogether, and thus end up with a system of punishments in which injustices of the second kind are perpetrated daily, consciously, and inevitably?[63]

Even the data available in 1989, when Primoratz's book was published, did not support such a massive underestimation of miscarriages of justice in capital cases.[64]

There is, moreover, something acutely dissatisfying about the washing-of-the-hands that occurs in the passages just quoted. It suggests a glib disregard for the social policy implications of philosophical reasoning. Conjuring some ideal system whose merits one then contemplates in the abstract becomes an ostrichlike maneuver *if that is all it leads to*. And when that is all that it leads to, it is as unsatisfying from a philosophical, as it is from a social policy, perspective. Yet many misuse the in-principle/in-practice distinction in just this manner, failing to appreciate its practical implications—as though simply making such a distinction somehow settles the matter. It may well be this failure that prompts some legal scholars to maintain that retributivism is "a philosophy fit only for an ideal world," suffering from a "fundamental irony":

> Basic principles of moral justice that are believed to justify or even demand the death of those who maliciously kill others are necessarily offended by the attempt to impose a system of state executions in an imperfect world. The emphasis that retributivism places on human beings as ends and not as means, the high value they place on innocent human life, and their insistence that retributivism (unlike revenge) respects the bounds of law combine to form a philosophy from which one cannot derive a policy that trades the wrongful execution of a few for the proper execution of the many. Capital punishment implements such a policy.[65]

Without impugning the valuable guidance that the construction of ideal accounts and their application to "an admittedly imperfect society" can provide,[66] there is a pressing need to develop philosophical arguments capable of guiding human conduct in such imperfect societies. Those are, after all, the ones humans inhabit, and must work with and through in the hopes of improving. Whatever their level of generality, moral theories, theories of punishment, and retributivist theories of capital punishment must be responsive to the actual world if they are to be responsible for prescribing human behavior in it. Reasoning about the death penalty must attend to its context; and in the United States that context is one in which a system of capital punishment is in place, has a demonstrable "track record" as regards wrongful convictions, and has sorely eroded the constitutional safeguards intended to insure that only the guilty are executed. A distinction between justifying capital punishment "in principle" or "in theory" and doing so "in practice" should not be invoked to insulate moral reasoning from the imperfect world in which theories and principles are applied.[67]

The problem is not just that even an ideal, "perfected" system must be administered by imperfect, doubtless imperfectible, humans. It is also that the American death penalty system has already trod this path, with disastrous results. The Supreme Court decision that reinstated the death penalty essentially claimed that the administrative problems that prompted that Court to bring state executions to a halt four years earlier had been satisfactorily addressed. The system, if not completely perfect, was deemed sufficiently so in 1976. Yet since Gregg v. Georgia, that same Court has steadily and systematically gutted the very constitutional safeguards that reduce the likelihood that the innocent are executed—federal habeas corpus rules—effectively replacing due process with procedural efficiency.[68] The result was travesties such as Virginia's twenty-one-day rule, which bars even conclusive evidence of innocence to reverse a sentence of death if more than three weeks have lapsed since the date of sentencing.[69] Even the improved but still imperfect system endorsed by Gregg, it would seem, came at too great a price. Finality is seen to promote efficiency at the expense of justice, and at the cost of executing the innocent.

Some have drawn on the in-principle/in-practice distinction to argue that abolitionists should be content to expose the gap between the retributivist ideal and actual death penalty practice. Donald Beschle contends that it is "unlikely that a direct assault on the [retributive] theories put forward to support the death penalty will effectively refute it."[70] He suggests that abolitionists may be more effective if they adopt a strategy that "points out the empirical reality of the death penalty, and the ways in which it fails to satisfy the demands of the theories used to justify it."[71] Such a strategy "will not undermine the theoretical validity of retributive notions, but instead will undermine the practical ability to act as the theory demands."[72] Faith in capital punishment as a sanction will thereby be shaken.

According to Beschle, Justice Blackmun's own change of heart on the issue is an example of this, and the position Blackmun ultimately takes up is itself an instance of such an approach. In his dissent in Callins v. Collins, Blackmun stated,

The problem is that the inevitability of factual, legal and moral error gives us a system that we know must wrongly kill some defendants, a system that fails to deliver the fair, consistent and reliable sentences of death required by the Constitution . . . It is virtually self-evident to me now that no combination of procedural rules or substantive regulations ever can save the death penalty from its inherent constitutional deficiencies.[73]

Blackmun's position is contrasted with that of Justices Brennan and Marshall, who "reject capital punishment in theory as well as in practice."[74]

On the surface, the Brennan-Marshall approach seems more attractive to abolitionists. It is more "principled"; it refutes death penalty advocates more thoroughly. By disposing of the underlying theory, it assures the end of capital punishment, not merely its reform. The Blackmun approach is seen as conceding too much, as insufficiently grounded in principle; it is somewhat grudgingly endorsed as a second-best approach.[75]

Beschle proposes that abolitionists reverse their comparative assessment of these two lines of argument.

Calls for a moratorium would certainly be part of such a strategy, though Beschle does not raise this issue directly. And if Beschle is correct, the innocence argument we have developed here would fall on the right side, the Blackmun side, of the in-principle/in-practice distinction, rejecting it only in practice. There are, however, two observations that should be made regarding Beschle's discussion.

The first is that it is mistaken to suggest that arguments like Blackmun's, emphasizing the execution of the innocent, are "insufficiently grounded in principle," or are somehow less "principled" than those advanced by Brennan and Marshall.[76] The innocence argument, as we have seen, appeals to moral principle, specifically to the principle that only the guilty should be punished. Utilitarianism's inability to completely rule out scenarios involving the execution of the innocent is regarded by many, and certainly by many retributivists, as a major weakness. Prima facie, one comparative advantage of retributivism is that guilt is a necessary condition for justified punishment. On the innocence argument, it is this (together with the irrevocability of death as a penalty) that causes retentionist arguments that rely on retributivism to ultimately fail.[77] Capital punishment plainly is not being visited only upon the guilty; significant numbers of innocent people are being executed. There is no way to ensure that the innocent will not be executed. And, if the assessment of Blackmun and others is correct, there is no way even to substantially reduce their numbers.[78]

So the innocence argument uses moral principle to reject capital punishment in practice. Beschle's suggestion that there is something less "principled" about this line of argument is in error, and is perhaps due to an equivocation. Most commonly in discussions of the justifiability of the death penalty, "principle" refers to moral principle. But when the term appears in the context of the in-principle/in-practice distinction, it has a different, nonmoral meaning. When capital punishment is ruled out "in principle," it is ruled out in all possible situations or worlds, not just in the actual one. And this leads us to a second observation.

Even were Beschle correct in his assessment of innocence arguments like Blackmun's, the reason he offers is misleading. He suggests that such arguments are insufficiently based in principle, because "[i]nstead of attacking the fundamental theoretical underpinnings of capital punishment," they focus on "the empirical reality of the practice."[79] Such a judgment is an artifact of the in-principle/in-practice distinction itself, or perhaps of a corresponding one (which is often, as here, mixed with the former) between theoretical claims and empirical ones. Since the demise of logical positivism, it has been fairly clear that the distinction between theoretical and empirical claims is not a "bright line" and is, at minimum, highly permeable.[80] As we have argued above, focusing on the empirical reality of the death penalty's application (i.e., on the execution of the innocent) has significant implications for retributivism at the *theoretical* level, given the reasonable assumption that (1) theories of punishment are to be used (applied to the world, rather than merely "held" on paper), and (2) their merit in large part should be a function of their problem-solving abilities.[81]

The innocence argument generates serious problems for retributive theories of (capital) punishment, since it establishes that the necessary condition of retributivism—guilt—is repeatedly violated when retributive theories are set into practice and people are executed. The absolute finality that characterizes this form of punishment makes it impossible to correct, or make restitution for, miscarriages of justice. Such theories are seriously wanting; they cannot provide the guidance they are supposed to or justify the social policies they are intended to. That is the force of claiming that they fail to justify capital punishment in practice. It is worth pointing out that it does not follow from the innocence argument that executing the guilty is morally acceptable. The innocence argument implies only that because of the systemic nature of capital punishment, and the fact that fallible humans administer it—determining who is prosecuted, who is convicted, whose convictions are upheld, and whose appeals are denied—it can never be, as Mitt Romney would have it, "foolproof." It *will* take the lives of the innocent.

At some juncture, invoking the in-principle/in-practice distinction becomes an exercise in irrelevance. If the state is repeatedly executing the innocent, there is little solace in—and less point to—a retentionist mantra that capital punishment remains justifiable in principle but not in its current application.[82] The death penalty that most parties in the debate are addressing is an existing social policy, with a clear track record. If it is morally unjustifiable, it must stop. Americans, who grant the state such ultimate power, must stop it.

But what, then, of a moratorium, and the prospect that a faulty system, once fixed, could be reinstated? What bearing could an innocence argument have on such a chain of events? To see this, we must consider one other way in which the in-principle/in-practice distinction is invoked in the death penalty debate.

WHEN MISTAKES ARE FATAL

> Our capital system is haunted by the demon of error: error in determining guilt and error in determining who among the guilty deserves to die . . . [W]hat effect was race having? What effect was poverty having? . . . Because of all these reasons today, I am commuting the sentences of all death row inmates . . .
> —former Illinois Governor George Ryan[83]

Douglas Blount contends that mistakes-are-fatal arguments against capital punishment have a limited scope.[84] Such arguments can, he acknowledges, "constitute an impressive reason for refraining from an action," provided that there is "a significant chance that performing that action will result in the person's death."[85] But to demonstrate this in the case of the current American system of capital punishment would only impugn that particular system. "To show that capital punishment per se ought to be eschewed," one needs to show that the risk of error "is significant under any capital punishment program."[86] But this cannot be done, since there are an infinite number of possible programs that would need to be assessed in this way. Hence, "if one does oppose capital punishment, it should be on the basis of something other than a mistakes-are-fatal argument."[87]

When mistakes made by a social practice are, and have been, *fatal*, surely the burden of proof is not on someone opposed to the practice to demonstrate that there is no possible world in which they could be other than fatal. Here again, in the current debate over the death penalty, what is most pressingly at issue is not the state of capital punishment in all possible worlds, but in this one. And in this one, a mistakes-are-fatal argument based on innocence may well be the most compelling of all objections to capital punishment as currently practiced. If it demonstrates that the current system is morally unjustifiable, then that system, at the very least, must be suspended. This signal event will not rule out executions in all possible worlds. But the onus will then be on those who would have it resume to shore up safeguards and "improve" procedures so that only the guilty will be executed. The history here is far from encouraging. Such efforts were made thirty years ago, and their failure has been complete.

> In 1972, when the Supreme Court ruled in *Furman v. Georgia* that the death penalty as then applied was arbitrary and capricious and therefore unconstitutional, a majority of the Justices expected that the adoption of narrowly crafted sentencing procedures would protect against innocent persons being sentenced to death. Yet the promise of *Furman* has not been fulfilled: It is now irrefutable that innocent persons are still being sentenced to death, and the chances are high that innocent persons have been or will be executed . . .[88]

For (the comparatively small number of) those who support retentionism on utilitarian grounds, providing the system with its requisite "fix" would come at improbably great cost. Given the current lack of proof that the death penalty is a greater deterrent than its (far less expensive) alternative, together with the need to introduce substantive (and expensive) due process safeguards, calculation of the utility of a "fixed" system is almost certain to yield a net loss in good consequences, however these are construed. Whatever gain there might be from establishing a system that markedly reduced the probability of executing the innocent, it would be outweighed by the other factors that must be part of the calculation. And this is surely the case when alternative sanctions—such as life imprisonment or life without parole—are considered, as they must be. It is unfortunate that justifications of the death penalty, whether utilitarian or retributivist, frequently neglect the need for arguments to establish the comparative superiority of the death penalty as punishment. As Stephen Nathanson notes, "[I]f the death penalty is to be justified . . . it must be the case that there are no feasible, morally preferable alternatives to the death penalty, no policies that are available to us and that would be equally effective in saving these innocent lives."[89]

Pure, or thoroughgoing, retributivists will know that there is no possible way of fixing the system to *insure* that only the guilty are executed. The same is true, of course, for commonly advanced alternatives, such as long-term imprisonment or even life without parole; there is no way to guarantee that the innocent will not receive these sanctions. It is here that the issues of finality and of irrevocability are pivotal. Alternative sanctions reserve an appropriately severe sanction for those guilty of the most heinous crimes, but also preserve the possibility of discovering and reversing miscarriages of justice, and of making restitution to those unjustly sentenced. Whether the pure retributivist principle of justice is construed along Kantian lines, social contractarian lines, or on simple concern for merit, it requires that mistakes be rectified and that justice be done to those who have been wrongly convicted. This is not possible when they have been wrongly executed. So—like those of the utilitarian—thoroughgoing retributivist calls for a moratorium to fix the system so that executions may resume are ill founded. In both cases, commitment to their respective principles can lead only to an endorsement of a moratorium that ends the system, one that provides for an alternative sanction reserved for the most heinous of crimes, such as long-term imprisonment or life without parole.[90]

What of partial retributivism? Does the innocence argument have the same implications for partial retributivism as it does for utilitarianism and thoroughgoing retributivism, with respect to a moratorium? We have seen that partial retributivism must be responsive to the empirical situation that gives rise to the innocence argument (i.e., the rise in exonerations, the statistical data regarding the frequency of erroneous convictions, the massive erosion in due process constitutional safeguards, etc.). This may well—and, indeed, ought to—lead to the call for a moratorium to fix the system. So an amelioration of the empirical situation is possible, perhaps, through the restoration and enhancement of the safeguards that the Supreme Court has undermined in its recent death penalty decisions.

The system might, indeed, be "fixed" such that an argument could at least be made that it results in the execution of substantially fewer innocent people. Unlike the thoroughgoing retributivist, partial retributivists will not be unsettled by the fact that, even under such an "improved" system, some innocent people would indeed be executed. For, as we have seen, they will contend that tolerating this is for the greater good, that the unintentional conviction and execution of a few innocent people is the price that must be paid.[91] The price that must be paid for making this argument, however, is that it threatens to "reduce" retributivism back into a utilitarian position on the execution of the innocent—the very issue which drove retributivists to adopt a principle of retributive justice mandating guilt as a necessary condition for punishment. Beyond charging partial retributivists with theoretical inconsistency or collapse, beyond criticizing the adequacy of whatever argument they offer for death as a proportionately more fit sanction than life without parole, is there anything more that can be said?

Indeed there is. For suppose that they have accepted the onus of proof and actually managed to improve the system in various ways during the moratorium so that the likelihood of executing the innocent would seem to be substantially reduced. The only way to determine if they are correct in their predictions about the virtues of the improved system is to actually test it. This would take some time, a period of years certainly, to establish an adequate "sample" of actual executions. And plainly it could not be done without running the risk of taking yet more innocent lives. Should the killing then resume, so that the system can be tested? Only if such social experimentation is justifiable. And it is hard to see how it could be. We have, after all, a clear case—the current case—where a system of capital punishment has, despite initial (but subsequently eroded) safeguards, resulted in a substantial number of erroneous convictions. This is an unpromising track record, which at least warrants healthy doubt as to whether an improved system with new safeguards in place would not suffer the same erosion. Moreover, since during the moratorium a suitably severe alternative sanction would have replaced death as the sanction reserved for the most heinous crimes, the need to demonstrate that this alternative sanction is an inadequate response to the demands of justice would be rhetorically, if not philosophically, much greater.

But more importantly, testing such a system would amount to unwarranted, and unjustifiable, social experimentation on the lives of the innocent.[92] They have not consented to such an experiment, and if they are well informed about the vicissitudes of the current system, they would be most unlikely to do so. Why, after all, subject oneself or one's fellow citizens to maximal risk—death—with no demonstrable accompanying benefits, given the fact that the death penalty does not have a greater deterrent effect than does life without parole? Some partial retributivists with strong convictions about the inadequacy of alternative sanctions (whether long-term imprisonment or life without parole) might still be willing to participate in a test of the improved system, but there is no way to conduct such a test without involving those of us who are unwilling.

ENDING THE SYSTEM

Calls for a moratorium to fix the system so that executions may resume fail to appreciate the full force of the innocence argument and cannot be sustained. As Unnever and Cullen observe, "[T]he prospect of innocents being arrested, placed on death row, and executed is not prevented by fine-tuning the punishment process but rather is systematic and inevitable."[93] The only way to "fix" the American system of capital punishment so as to avoid execution of the innocent is to end it. Efforts can then be directed to fixing the criminal justice system so as to ensure that some alternative sanction is a viable option for the most heinous crimes. There is no way to guarantee that the innocent will not receive this sanction. But this is where the issues of finality and of irrevocability become key. Long-term imprisonment, and certainly life without parole, reserves an appropriately severe sanction for those guilty of the most heinous crimes while also preserving the possibility of reversing miscarriages of justice, and of making restitution to those unjustly sentenced. Whatever the precise form the retributivist principle of justice takes (punishment as payback, as rebalancing the social ledger, as respecting criminals as an ends-in-themselves, and so on), it mandates justice, however belated, for those who have been wrongly convicted. Death rules out all of this; calls for a moratorium to fix the system so that executions may resume are therefore ill founded. Commitment to retributivist principles can lead only to an endorsement of a moratorium that ends the system, one that provides an alternative sanction reserved for the most vile crimes.

Nor do these calls for fixing, as opposed to ending, the death penalty take into account the international implications of imposing and then lifting a moratorium. The international community's objections to the American death penalty do not confine themselves to its current administration; they focus primarily on the fact that execution by the state violates human rights and is an intolerable abuse of state power. The rest of the world continues to pursue effective measures that make it increasingly difficult for the shrinking handful of death penalty states to persist in executing. For a growing number of countries, it is becoming routine to shelter American defendants from the American death penalty.

France, for example, refused to turn over the fugitive Charles Kopp to the United States until the Justice Department agreed that the death penalty would not be "requested, pronounced or applied."[94] In 2001, the United States was initially threatened with the loss of its observer status in the Council of Europe if it did not impose a national death penalty moratorium within two years.[95] Observer states, the council's rapporteur on the death penalty asserted, must "accept the principles of human rights and democracy to which all members commit themselves. The United States is no exception."[96] (The Council of Europe, however, has not as yet followed through on this threat.) The South African Constitutional Court's ruling disallowing extradition of al-Qaeda terrorists involved in the embassy bombings at Nairobi and Dar es Salaam insures that there will be no exceptions.[97] This decision was particularly powerful, and seems likely to be persuasive internationally and to have impact beyond South Africa. Indeed, a U.N. Human Rights Committee ruling two years later, in *Judge v. Canada*, confirmed this, taking Canada to task for violating the International Covenant on

Civil and Political Rights by deporting Roger Judge to the United States and failing to obtain assurances that the death penalty would not be imposed.

America will not be able to enforce even a tiny, narrowly circumscribed death penalty without raising vigorous protest and resistance from ever-larger portions of the world. Even beyond balking at extradition, some nations of Europe (prior to the extradition treaty of 2003) had originally refused to cooperate in providing evidence to American courts when that evidence could lead to a conviction that might result in an execution.[98] Thus, evidence that could be used to convict terrorists in American courts has not been available because of the death penalty. This trend away from cooperation with nations that execute is likely to expand.

Even in the Americas, the movement to abolish the death penalty by international treaty is strengthening as more and more nations ratify the protocol to the American Convention on Human Rights to Abolish the Death Penalty. Canada's startling reversal on extradition of death eligibles and Mexico's similar refusal to extradite further complicate U.S. foreign policy. As Bruce Shapiro observes, "In an exquisite irony, Fidel Castro—along with a few tiny Caribbean commonwealth states—joins the United States in keeping capital punishment alive in the Western Hemisphere."[99] Geography guarantees America continued friction on this issue with its nearest and most important neighbors.

While a moratorium might delay and even partially mitigate the problem, the pressures would be exponentially greater whenever the United States resumed executions. A moratorium could not admit of the smallest exception or relapse without strong and sustained international resistance. The cost to the United States would only increase at each such juncture. Moreover, simply having death penalty legislation, subject to resurrection by popular demand at every political whim, would insure constant international irritation. The United States has not just been slow on this issue; it has steadily pulled in the opposite direction from the rest of the world.

> The maintenance of the death penalty in the United States is becoming more and more anachronistic. International organizations like the United Nations, the Council of Europe and the European Union have issued calls for a moratorium on executions. There is a clear trend toward abolition, often preceded by the institution of a moratorium.[100]

The tension created can only get worse; the costs to the United States can only go higher. A moratorium will backfire unless followed by abolition. The world's tolerance of continued American violations of international human rights norms is rapidly faltering.

10 : Conclusion

Abolition of the death penalty is a hard-core human rights principle and therefore non-negotiable for the Council of Europe.
—Walter Schwimmer, Secretary General of the Council of Europe[1]

Clarence Darrow once predicted that "[t]he time will come when all people will view with horror the light way in which society and its courts of law now take human life."[2] The American people have not gotten this far yet, though most of the rest of the world has. They are waiting impatiently for the country that regards itself as the guardian of human rights to follow their lead in banning state execution as a grave human rights violation. They are doing all they can to raise the consciousness, and awake the conscience, of the last superpower to the fact that sanctioning the state's use of lethal violence against its own citizens, and against foreign nationals caught up in its criminal justice system, is an egregious, intolerable abuse of state power. They are enacting a form of sovereignty that places responsibility for ending egregious human rights abuses in the hands of the international community, a form of sovereignty that calls upon governments to set aside the idea that the rights of the nation-state within its own territorial borders are overriding and unassailable.

It is an effort being played out, as we have seen above, in many significant ways—from calls for an international moratorium on executions by the United Nations, the Council of Europe, and the European Union; to refusals to cooperate with the United States on extradition matters if the death penalty is at issue; to demands that the United States honor its commitments to the treaties and international legal instruments it has signed. Americans are largely unaware of all of this, as they are of many matters international; even in an era when borders are losing the power they once had to keep peoples apart, many Americans are ignorant of or indifferent to what is happening to others. Books such as this are written to remedy that lack of awareness. They are written largely as an act of faith that such knowledge will matter, as Justice Thurgood Marshall hypothesized, and that the American public is able and willing to reconsider deeply entrenched convictions about the morality and justice of death as a form of state punishment.

Deeply entrenched convictions, however, rarely drop away as soon as facts and arguments are waved at them. They are far more often slowly, uneasily, shed, sometimes with huge reluctance, as they grow increasingly untenable.

It takes effort and time to promote awareness in society that humane alternatives to the death penalty must be pursued . . . [E]xperience in many countries shows that public opinion is capable of discovering the fallacies of such simple retributive attitudes. People can come to realize that it is possible for society to be tough on crime and attentive to the concerns of victims' families without resorting to this inhumane punishment. But this presupposes that the public is made aware of the fundamental issues and facts surrounding the death penalty.[3]

Americans who support the death penalty do so for many reasons. Some of these reasons—it deters and incapacitates, is cost-effective, is fairly administered—are clearly mistaken and can readily be demonstrated to be so, provided minds remain open enough to take in the empirical evidence. Others have proven more resilient, harder to readily rebut—such as the idea that justice demands death in some cases, that it is deserved, a form of retributive payback for a serious violation of the social contract. We have tried here both to dispel the myths in the former case and to focus carefully on the retributive justifications for the death penalty and their moral Achilles heel, the innocence argument.

This last, we have wanted to stress, is not simply one more administrative objection to the current death penalty regime. Because retributive retentionists believe that only the guilty should be put to death, and because that is and will always be an evasive dream for a criminal justice system administered by the fallible, by the human, any punishment as thoroughly irrevocable as the death penalty is morally unacceptable. The retributivist believes it is wrong for the state to execute the innocent; but it is not possible for any system of capital punishment, no matter how well and persistently tinkered with, to avoid this. And because death is involved, it is not possible for the state to correct its error, to make reparation, as it is in the case of long-term imprisonment. That no series of incremental changes or refinements will succeed in changing this state of affairs is the realization to which one former retentionist, Justice Harry Blackmun, was finally led:

> From this day forward, I no longer shall tinker with the machinery of death. For more than 20 years I have endeavored—indeed, I have struggled—along with a majority of this Court, to develop procedural and substantive rules that would lend more than the mere appearance of fairness to the death penalty endeavor. Rather than continue to coddle the Court's delusion that the desired level of fairness has been achieved and the need for regulation eviscerated, I feel morally and intellectually obligated simply to concede that the death penalty experiment has failed.[4]

We have also suggested that the innocence argument serves to enhance other arguments against the death penalty that appeal to fairness—such as the presence of sustained racial and socioeconomic disparities, which means that those erroneously convicted and executed will almost certainly be poor and that issues of race and ethnicity will continue to haunt the system in a myriad of ways, only some of which we have managed to identify. The unjustness of a criminal justice system in which whom the state executes "is a lottery . . . shaped by the constraints of poverty, race, geography and local politics,"[5] is massively compounded by the fact that significant numbers of those thus selected are innocent.

Our argument is not that it is wrong for the state to execute the innocent but not the guilty, but that it is wrong for the state to execute, period. The innocence argument does not imply that there is no problem with the death penalty when it takes the lives of the guilty. It shows what happens when the state does so, contends that this is inconsistent with the retributive principle of justice, and suggests that retributivists should be so troubled by this as to support, instead, an alternative form of punishment that permits the state to remedy its errors and make some restitution to the innocent it punishes. No criminal justice system can avoid error, but it can avoid the irremediable error of destroying human life as a result of its errors.

If sovereignty means not that the state may do what it will with impunity within its own borders, but that it must be responsible for governing and promoting the well-being of a human community, such lethal violence, administered in the name of justice, has no place within those borders. The fact that it is also riddled with systemic error that cannot be eliminated, and marred by race, ethnic, and class biases, puts it in further conflict with the state's sovereign responsibilities. Virtually the entire international community has recognized this, seizing on the empirical evidence of error and unfairness to buttress its position that state execution is a human rights violation of a magnitude that cannot, must not, be tolerated. Yet America, and the American people, have not.

In fact, the American criminal justice system continues to "tinker with the machinery of death" in ways that render it only more morally problematic, elevating the interests of procedural efficiency over due process and of finality over human life, even innocent human life. It does so in Supreme Court decisions like *Herrera v. Collins*, where new evidence of actual innocence must be coupled to some constitutional error to be heard;[6] in *Sanchez-Llamas* and *Bustillo*, where state procedural default rules override the right to consular assistance; in new state court rules, such as Virginia's twenty-one-day rule, where even conclusive evidence of innocence cannot be considered and a death sentence revoked, if more than three weeks have lapsed since the date of sentencing.[7] These are strange fruits indeed, which the international community contemplates with astonishment:

> The United States is very much the great enigma in the death penalty debate, viewed from an international perspective. Its stubborn attachment to capital punishment puzzles Europeans, who see abolition as a logical outgrowth of democratic development and who are mystified about why a country so similar to themselves in so many ways can behave so differently.[8]

Americans are by and large blissfully unaware of the United States' "growing status as an international pariah" because of its commitment to state execution.[9] Such a status conflicts strongly with the preferred national self-conception. In 1997, Jesse Helms, then chair of the Senate Foreign Relations Committee, described U.N. Special Rapporteur Bacre Waly Ndiaye's visit to the United States to conduct a two-week death penalty fact-finding mission as "an absurd U.N. charade." He complained, in a letter to the U.S. permanent representative to the United Nations, William Richardson, "Bill, is this man confusing the United States with some other country or is this an intentional insult to the United States and to our nation's legal system?"[10]

Americans are also, for the most part, unaware of the empirical facts about the death penalty. A resolution adopted by the U.N. Commission on Human Rights in 2000,[11] addressed such ignorance, urging states retaining the death penalty "to make available to the public information with regard to the imposition of the death penalty"[12] as well as to establish a moratorium on executions "with a view to completely abolishing the death penalty."[13] It also reaffirmed its ongoing conviction that "abolition of the death penalty contributes to the enhancement of human dignity and to the progressive development of human rights."[14] The United States was not among the sixty-three signatories. It was, however, singled out quite recently by the U.N. Human Rights Committee for failing to fully acknowledge "studies according to which the death penalty may be imposed disproportionately on ethnic minorities as well as on low-income groups." The committee urged the United States to place a moratorium on executions, citing the International Covenant on Civil and Political Rights, which the United States has both signed and ratified.[15]

This lack of awareness of the basic facts about state execution domestically, and this insularity with respect to human rights standards internationally, must change. When they do change, will it make a difference? There is some reason to think it will. We have mentioned empirical studies, where such facts have lessened support for the death penalty all along the scale. There has been movement in the courts as well. The Supreme Court, in *Atkins v. Virginia*, appealed to "evolving standards of decency that mark the progress of a maturing society" in abolishing the death penalty for the mentally retarded.[16] They did so again in *Roper v. Simmons*, in abolishing the juvenile death penalty. In both cases, moreover, they took into account the views of the international community. There is movement detectible even within the current Bush administration (though this may have little to do with standards of decency): the president's memorandum for the attorney general directs state courts to suspend procedural default rules in certain cases in which the Vienna Convention on Consular Relations has been violated. And there is movement in the American public, with recent polls showing declines in support for the death penalty and increased support for a moratorium. There are, indeed, a good number who share one commentator's assessment that "the end game for American capital punishment has already begun but . . . the struggle will be intense."[17]

For the endgame to be successfully played out, not only must lack of awareness be remedied, but so must America's long struggle with racism. It is not merely coincidence that in the United States "the death penalty is imposed predominantly on people belonging to ethnic or other minorities or for crimes committed against persons belonging to majorities;"[18] that 69 percent of American executions take place in the "death belt" of southern, former slave-holding states;[19] or that the largest mass judicial execution in American history was of thirty-eight American Indians.[20] Increasingly, scholars attempting to explain America's inability to free itself from the hold of state execution are singling out its history of racial violence, vigilantism, and lynching.

> The explanations must necessarily be complex, but one element clearly stands out, and that is the racism that is endemic in the United States justice system . . . There are major deformations in United States law and society that can only be explained by the legacy of oppression, through slavery and subsequently through segregation.[21]

They point out that during the 1930s, as the frequency of lynchings abated in the southern states, judicial execution rose sharply.[22] "With the decline of lynching, many southern whites renounced the inhumanity of the mob, preferring instead to rely on the harsh justice of the state."[23] In virtually all of the "death belt" states, resistance to centralized government is strong, as is sentiment for limiting the powers of the state. And yet, as we noted in chapter 2, this does not translate into resistance to the most potent manifestation of state power—judicial execution. The reason may well have to do with the practice of lynching and the legacy of vigilantism. "The most substantive feature of the

American experience that has encouraged executions and protected them from being associated with excessive government power is a mythology of local control that appears to be linked to historical traditions of vigilante violence."[24]

In recent years, there has been substantial historical research enhancing our understanding of lynching, as well as its connection to state execution as demonstrated in chapter 5. One early argument in favor of capital punishment, for example, was that without it, people would resort to lynchings.[25] Efforts to read lynching and state execution as situated along a historical continuum take their cue from the series of procedural "refinements" that characterize the history of capital punishment in the twentieth century.

> If we think of opposition to the death penalty as having been effective mostly along the lines of incremental procedural fixes, it does not take much of a stretch to see that the current system of capital punishment is really in continuity with the American history of extra-legal violence and lynching—it is just more procedurally protected and has the minor additional virtue of being legal.[26]

That "minor additional virtue," however, is significant. There are some striking differences when a mob lynches and a state executes. When a mob lynches, those not involved in the killing can more readily convince themselves that they had nothing to do with it. They can say that what was done by the mob was not done with their approval or knowledge; that since what the mob did occurred in a sudden, passionate outrage, they were unaware it was going to happen and had no power to challenge or prevent it. They can say that the mob was not acting in their name, or in the name of justice. None of these things can be said when a democratic state executes.

When the United States overrides the right to life of those within its territorial boundaries and extinguishes those lives, its power to do so is sanctioned by Americans. Yet the system of justice they allow to kill on their behalf is riddled with error that cannot be eradicated and bias whose resilience persists. The crude machinery of death that is capital punishment cannot be justified as a form of protection, and, since it mauls the innocent as well as the guilty, it cannot be justified as a form of retribution. It is a machine that most of the rest of the world has thought fit to dismantle, in a committed effort to become a community of nations where human rights are not subjugated to the rights of sovereign states. America should be part of that community.

Notes

1. Introduction (pp. 1–8)

1. Abel Meeropol (music and lyrics), "Strange Fruit," first performed by Billie Holiday at Barney Josephson's Cafe Society, New York's first integrated nightclub, in 1939. Song lyrics based on Meeropol's poem "Bitter Fruit," (1937).

2. So claimed U.S. District Judge Learned Hand in 1923, who is quoted at length in chapter 6. *United States v. Garsson.* 291 F. 646, 649 (1923).

3. As of December 12, 2006, 69 nations were retentionist, while 128 nations were abolitionist in law or in practice. Of the latter, 88 were abolitionist for all crimes, 11 for ordinary crimes only, and 29 were abolitionist in practice. See Amnesty International, at http://webamnesty.org/pages/deathpenalty-countries-eng (accessed on 23 February 2007).

4. As of October 5, 2006, 120 foreign nationals, representing 32 different countries, were under sentence of death in the United States. Mark Warren, Death Penalty Information Center, http://www.deathpenaltyinfo.org/article.php?did=198&scid=31 #Reported-DROW (accessed December 3, 2006).

5. Daniel Klau, "Appellate Activism May Help Free the Innocent," *Connecticut Law Tribune*, vol. 27, no. 34 (2001): 18.

6. Sandra Day O'Connor, J., Concurring. *Herrera v. Collins*, 506 US 390 (1993).

7. Walter Schwimmer, "Death Penalty in U.S. Must Be Rethought," *International Herald Tribune*, January 25, 2001, http://www.iht.com/articles/2001/01/25/edwalt.t.php (accessed December 3, 2006).

2. Human Rights and the Erosion of Absolute Sovereignty (pp. 11–30)

1. William Connolly, *The Ethos of Pluralization* (Minneapolis: University of Minnesota Press, 1995): 157.

2. Michael R. Fowler and Julie M. Bunck, *Law, Power and the Sovereign State* (University Park: Penn State University Press, 1995): 151.

3. Michael Joseph Smith, "Sovereignty, Human Rights and Legitimacy in the Post–Cold War World" (1980), http://faculty.virginia.edu/irandhumanrights/mjsonsovty.htm. There is, however, reason to be wary of supposing that appeals to human rights are themselves absolute, and automatically trump other moral claims. See: Joy Gordon, "The Concept of Human Rights: The History and Meaning of its Politicization," *Brooklyn Journal of International Law*, vol. 23 (1998): 689, who argues this and suggests alternative models of human rights not committed to such absolutism. See also: Michael Ignatieff, *Human Rights and Politics and Idolatry* (Brooklyn, N.Y.: Princeton Uni-

versity Press, 2001), who opposes the tendency to regard human rights as a "secular religion."

The concept of human rights has been the centerpiece of Western political thought for several centuries. As a product of the Western intellectual heritage, its claim to universality has been challenged and it has been critiqued as an example of Western legal imperialism. It is important to recognize the existence of this debate and the need to develop a pluralistic approach to human rights that embraces diversity, although we will not engage these pressing issues here. See, however: Douglas Lee Donohoo, "Autonomy, Diversity and the Margin of Appreciation: Developing A Jurisprudence of Diversity within Universal Human Rights," *Emory International Law Review*, vol. 15 (1991): 319.

4. Bacre Waly Ndiaye, "Extrajudicial, Summary or Arbitrary Executions: Report of the Special Rapporteur," The Commission on Human Rights, U.N. Document, e/CN .4/1997/60 (1997): 20, 22.

5. However, as Anthony Anghie has argued, colonialism had a constitutive effect on the sovereignty doctrine:

The history of sovereignty doctrine in the nineteenth century, then, is a history of the processes by which European states, by developing a complex vocabulary of cultural and racial discriminations, set about establishing and presiding over a system of authority by which they could determine who was and was not sovereign.

Anthony Anghie, "Finding the Peripheries: Sovereignty and Colonialism in Nineteenth Century International Law," *Harvard International Law Journal*, vol. 40 (1999): 1, 66; Thomas Hobbes, *Leviathan*, 2nd ed. (orig. pub. London: Green Dragon, 1651; New York: Washington Square Press, 1969).

6. The only exception is for humanitarian intervention in the case of a severe violation of human rights. UN General Assembly, "Declaration on Principles of International Law" (October 24, 1970), http://www.un.org/documents/ga/res/25/ares25.htm (accessed December 3, 2006).

7. Hobbes, *Leviathan*, 250.

8. 1791 French Constitution, article 3 (Paris), adopted by the French National Constituent Assembly (Paris: September 1791).

9. See the opinion of Arbitrator Max Huber, *Island of Palmas Case* (*United States v. Netherlands*), 2 R.I.A.A. 829, 838 (Judge Anzilotti), (1928).

10. Daniel Philpott, "Sovereignty: An Introduction and Brief History," *Journal of International Affairs*, vol. 48, no. 2 (1995): 358.

11. "Ashcroft to announce a decision on Moussaoui in coming week," Agence France Presse, March 24, 2002. This parallels China's response to international criticism:

Such arguments as "human rights taking precedence over sovereignty" and "humanitarian intervention" seem to be in vogue these days. Some countries even put such arguments into practice. . . Sovereign equality, mutual respect for state sovereignty and noninterference in each other's internal affairs are the basic principles governing international relations today. . . Any deviation from or violation of these principles would destroy the universally-recognized norms governing international relations.

Tang Jiaxuan, "Statement by Foreign Minister Tang Jiaxuan at the 54th Session of the UN General Assembly," United Nations General Assembly, 54th Session (November 15, 2000), http://www.fmprc.gov.cn/eng/gjwt/gjzzyhy/2594/2602/t15218.htm (accessed November 27, 2006).

12. See: Michael Jacobsen and Stephanie Lawson, "Between Globalization and Localization: A Case Study of Human Rights Versus State Sovereignty," *Global Governance*, vol. 5 (1999): 216.

13. William Wirt, quoted in Glenn W. Morris, "International Law and Politics: Toward a Right to Self-Determination for Indigenous Peoples," in *The State of Native America*, edited by M. Annette Jaimes, (Boston: South End Press, 1992): 65.

14. Robert Porter, "The Meaning of Indigenous Nation Sovereignty," *Arizona State Law Journal*, vol. 34, no. 75 (2002): 82.

15. *Cherokee Nation v. Georgia*, 30 U.S. 1; 8 L. Ed. 25 (5 Pet.) (decided March 18, 1831): 17–18.

16. *United States v. Wheeler*, 435 U.S. 313 (argued January 11, 1978; as amended, March 22, 1978), 323.

17. Morris, "International Law and Politics," 66.

18. Paul W. Kahn, "American Hegemony and International Law," *Chicago Journal of International Law*, vol. 1 (2000): 1, 5.

19. See, for example: Fowler and Bunck, *Law, Power and the Sovereign State*, 1–3.

20. Louis Henkin, "That 'S' Word: Sovereignty, Globalization and Human Rights, et cetera," *Fordham Law Review*, vol. 68, no. 1 (1999): 1.

21. Fowler and Bunck, *Law, Power and the Sovereign State*, 3.

22. Charles Merriam, quoted in Fowler and Bunck, *Law, Power and the Sovereign State*, 3.

23. Kim Levin, quoted in Okwui Enwezor, "The CNN Documenta," *Village Voice*, July 9, 2002, p. 57. Available at: http://www.villagevoice.com/art/0227,levin,36174,13.html.

24. R. B. J. Walker and Saul H. Mendlovitz, *Contending Sovereignties: Redefining Political Community* (Boulder, Colo: Lynne Rienner Publishers, 1990): 181–82.

25. Dinah Shelton, "Globalization and the Erosion of Sovereignty," *Boston College International and Comparative Law Review*, vol. 25 (2002): 273, 279.

26. See: Michael Hardt and Antonio Negri, *Empire* (Cambridge, Ma.: Harvard University Press, 2001).

27. Helen Stacy, "Relational Sovereignty," *Stanford Law Review*, vol. 55 (2003): 2029, 2038.

28. "Helsinki Summit Declaration 1992," http://www1.umn.edu/humanrts/peace/docs/helsnk92.htm (accessed November 27, 2006).

29. The Copenhagen European Council, in 1993, recognized the right of central and eastern European countries to join the European Union provided they meet various criteria. These include having stable political institutions guaranteeing human rights and respect for minorities. See: http://europa.eu/scadplus/glossary/accession_criteria_copenhagen_en.htm (accessed August 20, 2006).

30. Stacy, "Relational Sovereignty," 2034.

31. Vaclav Havel, quoted in Smith, "Sovereignty, Human Rights, and Legitimacy."

32. See: Iris Marion Young, "Responsibility and Global Labor Justice," *Journal of Political Philosophy,*" vol. 12, no. 4 (December 2004): 365–88.

33. It is no longer so clear, however, that the United States government regards torture as unconscionable. In 2002, U.S. Attorney General Alberto Gonzales, while serving as counsel to President Bush, characterized the Geneva Convention's restrictions on treatment of the enemy as "quaint" and "obsolete." Draft Memorandum from Alberto R. Gonzales, White House Counsel, to George W. Bush, President, "Decision Re: Application of the Geneva Convention on Prisoners of War to the Conflict with al Qaeda and the Taliban" (January 25, 2002), available at http://www.chelsea green.com/2004/items/guantanamo/Excerpt3 (accessed December 3, 2006).

34. Bruce Shapiro, "Dead Reckoning," Nation (*August 6/13, 2001*):18.

35. Stacy, Relational Sovereignty," 2044.

36. Ibid., 2036.

37. Ibid., 2058.

38. Wallace Coffey and Rebecca Tsosie, "Rethinking the Tribal Sovereignty Doctrine: Cultural Sovereignty and the Collective Future of Indian Nations," *Stanford Law and Policy Review*, vol. 12 (2001): 191, 195.

39. Ibid., 197.

40. Ibid., 199.

41. Ibid., 198.

42. Ibid.

43. Craig Scott, "Indigenous Self-Determination and Decolonization of the International Imagination: A Plea," *Human Rights Quarterly*, vol. 18 (1996): 814, 819.

44. Iris Marion Young, "Two Concepts of Self-Determination," in *Human Rights: Concepts, Contests, Contingencies*, edited by Austin Sarat and Thomas R. Kearns (Ann Arbor: University of Michigan Press, 2001): 40.

45. Iris Marion Young, "Hybrid Democracy: Iroquois Federalism and the Postcolonial Project," in *Political Theory and the Rights of Peoples*, edited by Duncan Ivison, Paul Patton, and Will Sanders, (Cambridge, Eng.: Cambridge University Press, 2000): 255.

46. Adeno Addis, "The Thin State in Thick Globalism: Sovereignty in the Information Age," *Vanderbilt Journal of Transnational Law*, vol. 37 (2004): 1, 66.

47. Ibid., 71.

48. Ibid., 106.

49. Henkin, "That 'S' Word," 7.

50. Understanding sovereignty in terms of such compliance has been supported by Abram Chayes and Antonia Handler Chayes, *The New Sovereignty: Compliance with International Regulatory Treaties* (Cambridge, Mass.: Harvard University Press, 1995).

51. Young, "Self-Determination," (2001), 35. Our discussion here is indebted to Young's work in this article, as well as in Young, "Responsibility and Global Labor Justice."

52. See: Young, "Self-Determination," especially p. 39. Young makes these points concerning the concept of relational self-determination, while we have adapted them here to a discussion of sovereignty. We note, though, that in her article on hybrid democracy (2000), Young questions the system of state sovereignty, and argues instead for a decentered, diverse, democratic federalism.

53. Young, "Self-Determination," 40.

54. Ibid., 44.

55. Ibid., 40.

56. Ibid., 44.

57. Joan Fitzpatrick, "The Unreality of International Law in the United States and the LaGrand Case," *Yale Journal of International Law*, vol. 27 (2002): 427, 428.

58. In addition to the Convention on the Rights of the Child, the United States has not ratified the Convention of the Elimination of All Forms of Discrimination against Women and the International Covenant on Economic, Social and Cultural Rights. For the status of these and other international human rights treaties, see Office of the High Commissioner for Human Rights, "Status of Ratifications of the Principal International Human Rights Treaties" http://www.unhchr.ch/pdf/report.pdf. See also: Malvina Halberstam, "United States Ratification of the Convention on the Elimination of All Forms of Discrimination against Women," *George Washington Journal of International Law and Economics*, vol. 31 (1997): 51; Kathleen M. Sullivan, "Constitutionalizing Women's Equality," *California Law Review*, vol. 90 (2002): 735, 762. For a discussion of efforts by former UN high commissioner Mary Robinson to hold the United States accountable to international human rights standards, see: Amy Edelstein, "Think Globally, Act Globally," *Women's Review of Books*, vol. 20, no. 5 (2003): 8–11.

59. William A. Schabas, *The Abolition of the Death Penalty in International Law*, 2nd ed. (Cambridge, Eng.: Cambridge University Press, 1997): 184.

60. Ibid., 184. The signing of an international treaty by a state is not sufficient to create a legally binding obligation; it creates "an obligation of good faith to refrain from acts calculated to frustrate the objects of the treaty", (Ian Brownlie, *Principles of Public International Law*, 5th ed. [Oxford: Oxford University Press, 1998]: 610–11) An international treaty does not have binding, legal force internationally unless the state

has not only signed but ratified it through, for example, a legislative vote. A ratified treaty may or may not also be incorporated into domestic law, and so be able to be upheld in domestic courts.

61. Amnesty International, http://web.amnesty.org/library/Index/ENGACT50002 2003.

62. Somalia is the other nation to do so. See: Amnesty International, http://web.amnesty.org/library/index/engact500042003.

63. *Roper v. Simmons*, 543 U.S. 551 (2005). *Roper* overruled *Stanford v. Kentucky*, where Justice Scalia writing for the majority expressly disavowed the relevance of international practices and standards "[f]or purposes of determining whether a particular form of punishment is contrary to evolving standards of decency, so as to violate the cruel and unusual punishment clause of the Federal Constitution's Eighth Amendment." 492 U.S. 361; 369, 370 n. 1 (1989).

64. John Ashcroft, testimony, Senate Subcommittee on International Operations of the Committee on Foreign Relations, S.Hrg. 105–724: *Is a U.N. International Criminal Court in the U.S. National Interest?* 105th Congress, 2d sess., July 23, 1998, 8. See: http://www.access.gpo.gov/congress/senate.

65. See, for example: William A. Schabas, "The ICJ Ruling Against the United States: Is it Really about the Death Penalty?" *Yale International Law*, vol. 27 (2002): 445, 447. (The United States, of course has been hostile to the International Court of Justice since the mid-1980s, when it was condemned for supporting the Contras in Nicaragua.)

66. The United States is a staunch supporter of the World Trade Organization and regularly submits to its jurisdiction in trade disputes. Various scholars have also commented upon the United States' "unilateral interpretation of sovereign immunity to exclude acts which are commercial by nature." Beth A. Simmons, "Is Sovereignty Still Relevant?" review of *Sovereignty through Interdependence* by Harry G. Gelber, *American Journal of International Law*, vol. 94 (2000): 226, 228. It is in the human rights realm that the United States consistently objects to international judicial proceedings. See, for example: World Trade Organization, "Settling Disputes: Case Study: The Time Table in Practice," http://www.wto.org/english/thewto_e/whatis_e/tif_e/disp3_e.htm.

67. For example, the United States has not ratified the American Convention on Human Rights, thus depriving the Inter-American Court of Human Rights of jurisdiction. For the ratification and accession information on this treaty, see: "American Convention on Human Rights," "Pact of San Jose, Costa Rica," *Multilateral Treaties B-32*, http://www.oas.org/juridico/english/Sigs/b-32.html (accessed December 3, 2006). Similarly, the United States has not ratified the Optional Protocol to the International Covenant on Civil and Political Rights and thus has not acceded to the jurisdiction of the U.N. Human Rights Committee. The Optional Protocol is available from the office of the United Nation's high commissioner for human rights, http://www.unhchr.ch/

html/menu3/b/a_opt2.htm (accessed December 3, 2006). The status of ratifications is available in a PDF format linked thereto. The U.S. reservation to ratification of the Genocide Convention also specifically excludes jurisdiction of the International Criminal Court. See also: Shabas, "ICJ Ruling," 447.

68. See, for example: David J. Scheffer, "The United States and the International Criminal Court," *American Journal of International Law*, vol. 93 (1999): 12; Seth Harris, "The United States and the International Criminal Court: Legal Potential for Non-Party State Jurisdiction," *Hawaii Law Review*, vol. 23 (2000): 277, 296–98.

69. James Bacchus, "The Garden," *Fordham International Law Journal*, vol. 28 (2005): 308, n. 139.

70. Ibid.

71. John Ashcroft, testimony, Senate Subcommittee, S. Hrg. 105–724, 10.

72. The Web site for the International Criminal Court is available at http://www .un.org/law/icc (accessed October 22, 2006). There are now one hundred state parties to this agreement.

73. Article 77 of the *Rome Statute of the International Criminal Court* provides that the Court may impose:

(a) Imprisonment for a specified number of years, which may not exceed a maximum of 30 years; or

(b) A term of life imprisonment when justified by the extreme gravity of the crime and the individual circumstance of the convicted person.

Rome Statute of the International Criminal Court, art. 77, http://www.un.org/law/icc/ statute/romefra.htm, (accessed: December 3, 2006).

74. Michael B. Sharf, testimony, Senate Subcommittee, S. Hrg. 105–724, 73.

75. These are only the most immediate of an appalling string of twentieth-century atrocities. See: Rudolph J. Rummel and Irving L. Horowitz, *Death by Government*, 5th ed. (New Brunswick, Can.: Transaction Publishers, 2004), who documents 170 million civilian deaths as the result of genocide, war crimes, and crimes against humanity. As Michael Scharf notes in his testimony to the Senate Subcommittee on International Operations, "We have lived in a golden age of impunity, where a person stands a much better chance of being tried for taking a single life than for killing ten thousand or a million." (Senate Subcommittee, S. Hrg. 105–724, 72.)

76. "Establishing a Just, Fair and Effective International Criminal Court," 1 October 1994: p. 1. Available on the Amnesty International Library, http://web.amnesty .org/library/index/engior400051994?open&of=eng-385.

77. According to M. Cherif Bassiouni, international criminal law is in many respects a continuum of internationally protected human rights. International penal prescriptions, whether or not established for the preservation and protection of human rights, "require that each crime have an international or transnational element." A crime has an international element when its impact affects the collective se-

curity interests of the world community, or when the seriousness of magnitude of the conduct is such that it poses a threat to the peace and security of humankind. M. Cherif Bassiouni, ed., *Introduction to International Criminal Law* (Ardsley, N.Y.: Transnational Publishers, 2003): 24.

78. John B. Quigley, "International Criminal Court; U.S. concerns ill-founded," *Milwaukee Journal Sentinel*, July 21, 2002: 5J.

79. Richard Dicker, testimony, Senate Subcommittee, S. Hrg. 105–724, 77.

80. Ibid.

81. Ibid.

82. Lee Casey, testimony, Senate Subcommittee, S. Hrg. 105–724, 64.

83. Ibid., 69.

84. Ibid.

85. Ibid.

86. Benjamin B. Ferencz, Rome Conference address, International Criminal Court (June 16, 1998), http://www.un.org/icc/speeches/616ppc.htm (accessed October 22, 2006).

87. Smith, "Sovereignty, Human Rights, and Legitimacy."

88. Fowler and Bunck, *Law, Power, and the Sovereign State*, 152.

89. A number of theorists of international justice have discussed transnational responsibilities, political responsibility, and shared responsibility. See: Iris Marion Young's valuable overview of these in "Responsibility and Global Labor Justice," to which our discussion here is indebted.

90. Amnesty International, "No return to execution: The US death penalty as a barrier to extradition," *Amnesty International Report*, http://www.web.amnesty.org/ai.nsf/recent/AMR511712001?OpenDocument (accessed December 3, 2006).

91. Amnesty International, "Facts and Figures on the Death Penalty," available at http://web.amnesty.org/pages/deathpenalty-facts-eng (last checked December 3, 2006).

92. Peter Schieder, "Council of Europe calls for international rejection of the death penalty," February 28, 2003, http://www.coe.int/NewsSearch/Default.asp?p5nwz&id52262&lmLangue=1 (accessed October 22, 2006).

93. Amnesty International, http://web.amnesty.org/pages/deathpenalty-facts-eng (accessed October 23, 2006). See also: the Council of Europe Web site, http://www.coe.int (accessed October 22, 2006).

94. Death Penalty Information Center, http://www.deathpenaltyinfo.org/ (accessed October 22, 2006).

95. Ibid. See also: Amnesty International, http://web.amnesty.org/pages/deathpenalty-facts-eng (accessed October 23, 2006).

96. See: Amnesty International, http://web.amnesty.org/pages/deathpenalty-facts-eng (accessed November 13, 2006).

97. "Brief for U.S. Diplomats et al. as Amici Curiae Supporting Respondent, State

ex rel. Simmons," 125 S. Ct. 1183 (2004) (No. 03–633), quoted in David Sloss, "Do International Norms Influence State Behavior?: The Limits of the International Law," review of The Limits of International Law by Jack L. Goldsmith and Eric A. Posner, *George Washington International Law Review*, vol. 38 (2006): 159, n. 106.

98. Felix G. Rohatyn, "Dead to the World," *New York Times* (January 26, 2006), A23.

99. Harold Hongju Koh, "A United States Foreign Policy for the 21st Century," St. *Louis University Law Journal*, vol. 46 (2002): 293, 309–10.

100. Death Penalty Information Center, 12 December 2005. Available on http://www.deathpenaltyinfo.org/newsanddev.php?seid=30&seyr=2005.

101. Shapiro, "Dead Reckoning," 16.

3. Extradition (pp. 31–49)

1. George W. Bush, quoted in Ed Vulliamy, Peter Beaumont, Kamal Ahmed, and Luke Harding, "Terror in America: Get ready for war, Bush tells America: The battle will be long, warns President: Pakistan 'to aid US' as Afghans flee target zone: Blair urges restraint as allies grow nervous," *Observer*, September 16, 2001, 1.

2. Oliver Wendell Holmes, "The Path of the Law," speech given at Boston University School of Law, January 8, 1897, *Harvard Law Review*, vol. 10 (1897): 457, 469.

3. There are two exceptions. One was the extradition treaty with Portugal in 1908 and the other with Venezuela in 1923, both of which included obligatory death penalty exceptions to extradition.

4. Starting with extradition treaties in 1972 with the United Kingdom, and 1976 with Canada, nations began to seek assurances in capital cases. But their executive branches were not generally required by the courts to seek such assurances. As explained below, the case law affecting such decision making changed radically in 1991 in that the rule of non-inquiry started to erode as a result of court decisions.

5. J. L. Brierly, *The Law of Nations*, 6th ed., edited by Humphrey Waldock (Oxford, Eng.: Oxford University Press, 1963): 277.

6. See: *United States v. Rauscher*, 119 U.S. 407; 7 S. Ct. 234; 30 L. Ed. 425 (1886), holding that an individual may invoke specialty as a defense to prosecution brought through extradition, without a requirement that the sending state protest the treaty breach.

See also: *State v. Vanderpool*, 39 Ohio St. 273 (1883), recognizing individual rights under extradition treaty. The United States was probably the first nation to recognize that individuals have private rights under extradition treaties, which they may invoke independently of the sending state.

7. But see: *The Alien Tort Claims Statute of 1789*, 28 U.S.C. § 1350, where the United States pioneered the perception of individuals as parties with standing to invoke international law.

8. *Cornejo-Barreto v. Seifert*, 218 F.3d 1004 (9th Cir. 2000) 1011, n. 5.

9. Mark Warren, "Returning Prisoners to Face the U.S. Death Penalty: Limitations under International Law," *Death Penalty Information Center (DPIC)*, (last updated: February 2006), http://www3.sympatico.ca/aiwarren/return.htm (accessed October 26, 2006).

10. *Glucksman v. Henkel*, 221 U.S. 508 (1911) at 512.

11. See: Andrew J. Parmenter, "Death by Non-Inquiry: The Ninth Circuit Permits the Extradition of a U.S. Citizen Facing the Death Penalty for a Non-Violent Drug Offense" [*Prasoprat v. Benov*, 421 F.3d 1009 (9th Cir. 2005)]," *Washburn Law Journal*, vol. 45 (2006): 657.

12. *Soering v. United Kingdom*, (1989) 161 Eur. Ct. H.R. (Sev. A) 217, 11 E.H.R.R. 439 [Soering].

13. Ibid.

14. Matthew W. Henning, "Extradition Controversies: How Enthusiastic Prosecutions Can Lead to International Incidents," *Boston College International and Comparative Law Review*, vol. 22 (1999): 356–57.

15. *Soering v. United Kingdom*, at 445–49.

16. Ibid., at 445–63.

17. The European Convention on Human Rights and Additional Protocols is available at the European Court of Human Rights Web site, Basic Texts, European Court of Human Rights, "Convention for the Protection of Human Rights and Fundamental Freedoms as Amended by Protocol No. 11," http://www.echr.coe.int/ECHR/EN/Header/Basic+Texts/Basic+Texts/The+European+Convention+on+Human+Rights+and+its+Protocols/ (last visited October 22, 2006).

18. Ibid.

19. Ibid.

20. *Pratt v. Attorney General of Jamaica*, 2 A.C.1, 4 All E.R. 769 (P.C. 1993).

21. The *Soering* decision noted that the "automatic appeal of the Supreme Court of Virginia normally takes no more than six months," and held that the consequence of available collateral habeas procedures is that "the condemned prisoner has to endure for many years the conditions on death row and the anguish and mounting tension of living in the ever-present shadow of death." *Soering v. United Kingdom*, (1989) 161 Eur. Ct. H.R. (sev. A) 217, 11 E.H.R.R. 439 [Soering].

22. *Cornejo-Barreto*, at 1009, n. 5.

23. Iain Murray, "The International Politics of Death," *The American Enterprise Online*, January 14, 2002. http://www.clarkprosecutor.org/html/links/dplinks.htm.

24. Patrick Anidjar, "Washington, EU to sign multilateral extradition treaty," Agence France Presse, June 26, 2003. Available on Lexis.

25. *Venezia v. Ministero di Grazia e Giustizia*, Judgment No. 223, 79, *Rivista di Diritto Internazionale* (1996) at 815.

26. *United States v. Alvarez-Machain*, 504 U.S. 655 (1992).

27. See: Matthew W. Henning, "Extradition Controversies: How Enthusiastic Pro-

secutions Can Lead to International Incidents," *Boston College International and Comparative Law Review*, vol. 22 (1999): 356–57.

28. "Mexico: Talks With U.S. to Ban Extraterritorial Kidnapping," IPS (Inter Press Service), June 23, 1993; see also: John Guendelsberger, "Two Kinds of Federal Kidnapping," *Plain Dealer*, July 2, 1993, 5B.

29. Roderigo Labardini, "Deportation in Lieu of Extradition from Mexico," *International Enforcement Law Reporter*, vol. 20 (2004): 239, n. 5.

30. Sue Doyle, "Bounty Hunter to Stand Trial in Luster's Capture," *Daily News of Los Angeles*, June 27, 2003, N6.

31. See: "3rd Roundup: European governments "ignored evidence of CIA flights," Deutsche Press-Agentur, February 23, 2006; "Euro MPs criticize Italy's inquiry into alleged CIA actions," Deutsche Press-Agentur, March 6, 2006; Dana Priest, "CIA Holds Terror Suspects in Secret Prisons; Debate Is Growing Within Agency About Legality and Morality of Overseas System Set Up After 9/11," *Washington Post*, November 2, 2005, A1; Tony Peterson, "Germans investigate CIA kidnap of innocent citizen," *Belfast Telegraph*, February 22, 2006; "Macedonia awaits Council of Europe report on CIA prisons," BBC *Monitoring Europe—Political*, supplied by BBC Worldwide Monitoring March 1, 2006.

32. "*Mohamed v. President of the Republic of South Africa*," BCLR 685 (South Africa), S.C. (2001).

33. Bruce Zagaris, "African Constitutional Court Rules Deporting Alleged Terrorist to U.S. Violated Rights," *International Enforcement Law Reporter*, vol. 17 (2001): 12.

34. *Roger Judge v. Canada*, Communication No. 829/1998, UNHRC, U.N. Document CCPR/C/78/D/829/1998 (2003). http://www.unhchr.ch/tbs/doc.nsf.

35. *Giry v. Dominican Republic*, Communication No. 193/1985, U.N. Document CCPR/C/39/D/193/1985 (1985). http://www.unhchr.ch/tbs/doc.nsf.

36. According to the Council of Europe's Web site, as of December 3, 2006, the member nations are Albania, Andorra, Armenia, Austria, Azerbaijan, Belgium, Bosnia and Herzegovina, Bulgaria, Croatia, Cyprus, Czech Republic, Denmark, Estonia, Finland, France, Georgia, Germany, Greece, Hungary, Iceland, Ireland, Italy, Latvia, Liechtenstein, Lithuania, Luxembourg, Malta, Moldova, Monaco, Netherlands, Norway, Poland, Portugal, Romania, Russian Federation, San Marino, Serbia, Slovakia, Slovenia, Spain, Sweden, Switzerland, "the former Yugoslav Republic of Macedonia," Turkey, Ukraine, United Kingdom. It has application from two more countries (Belarus and Montenegro) and has granted observer status to the Holy See, the United States, Canada, Mexico, and Japan.

37. Agreement on extradition between the European Union and the United States of America, (LexisNexis Academic, CELEX Database: Legislation, Publication date, July 19, 2003), (Document date, June 25, 2003).

38. Council of Europe Parliamentary Assembly, "Combating terrorism and re-

spect for human rights," Resolution 1271 (2002), http://assembly.coe.int/Documents/AdoptedText/ta02/ERES1271.htm (accessed October 31, 2006).

39. *Kindler v. Minister of Justice*, [1991] 2 S.C.R. 779; *Reference Re Ng Extradition* [1991] 2 S.C.R. 858 84 D.L.R. (4th): 498.

40. *Kindler v. Canada*, Communication No. 470/1991, U.N. Document. CCPR/48/D/470/1991 (views adopted July 30, 1993), in *Report of the Human Rights Committee*, United Nations General Assembly Official Records (UNGAOR) 48th Session, Supp. No. 40, U.N. Document A/48/40, vol. 2 (1993), annex XII. U, reprinted in 98 I.L.R. 426 (1993), *Human Rights Law Journal*, vol. 14 (1994): 307, *Ng. v. Canada*, Communication No. 469/1991, U.N. Document CCPR/49/D/469/1991 (November 5, 1993), in *Report of the Human Rights Committee*, UNGAOR, 49th Session, Supp. No. 40, U.N. Document A/49/40, vol. 2 (1994), annex IX. CC, reprinted in *Human Rights Law Journal*, vol. 15 (1994): 1994, 1 I.H.R.R. 161.

41. The issue was whether Canada had violated its obligations under articles 6 or 7 of the International Covenant on Civil and Political Rights.

42. Matthew W. Henning, "Extradition Controversies: How Enthusiastic Prosecutions Can Lead to International Incidents," *Boston College International and Comparative Law Review*, vol. 22 (1999): 356–57.

43. The Human Rights Committee's *Kindler* decision says, "In determining whether, in a particular case, the imposition of capital punishment could constitute a violation of article 7, the Committee will have regard to the relevant personal factors regarding the author, the specific conditions of detention on death row, and whether the proposed method of execution is particularly abhorrent." (*Kindler v. Canada*, at ¶15.3)

44. *United States of America v. Burns*, [2001] 1 S.C.R. 283, 2001 SCC 7. The court's 1991 *Kindler* decision distinguishes *Soering* based on the personal attributes of the respective defendants and gives no weight to the death-row phenomenon. In contrast, the *Burns* court accepts the phenomenon as a relevant factor, citing *Soering* as authority.

45. Ibid. at ¶ 65.

46. Ibid. at ¶ 75.

47. Ibid. at ¶ 78.

48. Ibid. at ¶ 91.

49. James S. Liebman, Jeffrey Fagan, Valerie West, and Jonathan Lloyd, "Habeas: Capital Attrition: Error Rates in Capital Cases," *Texas Law Review*, vol. 78 (2000): 1839.

50. *Roger Judge v. Canada*.

51. *Roger Judge v. Canada*, Communication No. 829, (1998).

52. See: UN http://www.unhchr.ch/tbs/doc.nsf (accessed November 9, 2006).

53. See: Ibid.

54. Mark Warren, "Returning Prisoners to Face the U.S. Death Penalty: Limitation Under International Law," http://www3.sympatico.ca/aiwarren/return.htm (accessed October 24, 2006).

55. Death Penalty Information Center, cited in Amnesty International, http://www .deathpenaltyinfo.org (accessed November 28, 2006).

56. S v. Makwanyane and Another, 1995 (6) BCLR 665 (CC).

57. Mohamed v. President of the Republic of South Africa.

58. Ibid. at ¶ 67.

59. Ibid. at ¶ 73.

60. United States v. Bin Laden, 156 F. Supp. 2d 359 (2001).

61. See: Bruce Zagaris, "South African Constitutional Court Rules Deporting Alleged Terrorist to U.S. Violated Rights," International Enforcement Law Reporter, vol. 17, no. 2 (December 2001).

62. Rodrigo Labardini, "Extradition and Imprisonment," International Enforcement Law Reporter, vol. 21, no. 11 (2005).

63. Amnesty International, "Death Penalty News," June 2005, http://web.amnesty .org (accessed February 7, 2006).

64. Rodrigo Labardini, "Life Imprisonment and Extradition: Historical Development, International Context, and the Current Situation in Mexico and the United States," Southwestern Journal of Law and Trade in the Americas, vol. 11 (2005): 1, 19.

65. Labardini, "Life Imprisonment and Extradition," 23–26.

66. Bruce Zagaris, "Columbian Supreme Court Inquires about Potential U.S. Violations of Extradition Terms," International Enforcement Law Reporter, vol. 21, no. 6 (June 2005).

67. United States v. Campbell, 300 F.3d 202 (2002). The defendant was extradited from Costa Rica with the proviso that he not serve more than fifty years.

68. In United States v. Badalamenti, the defendant Gaetano Badalamenti had been extradited from Spain on the condition that "the maximum period of imprisonment may not in any event exceed 30 years." 2003 U.S. Dist. LEXIS 22817, 84 Cr. 236 (D.C. 2003).

69. OAS General Assembly Resolution, "The Protocol to the American Convention on Human Rights to Abolish the Death Penalty," Organization of American States, Washington, D.C., http://www.oas.org/main/main.asp?sLang=E&sLink=http://www.oas.org/ DIL/treaties_and_agreements.htm (accessed October 31, 2006).

70. The Inter-American Convention on Extradition provides:

The States Parties shall not grant extradition when the offense in question is punishable in the requesting State by the death penalty, by life imprisonment, or by degrading punishment, unless the requested State has previously obtained from the requesting State, through the diplomatic channel, sufficient assurances that none of the above-mentioned penalties will be imposed on the person sought or that, if such penalties are imposed, they will not be enforced.

Inter-American Convention on Extradition, article 9, http://www.oas.org/juridico/ English/treaties/b-47.html (accessed October 31, 2006).

71. Warren, "Returning Prisoners."

72. Bruce Schreiner, "Captured Kentuckian wouldn't be executed," Associated Press State and Local Wire, May 5, 2005.

73. *United States v. Sanchez*, 323 F. Supp. 2d 403 (2004).

74. Amnesty International, "Privy Council Abolishes Mandatory Death Sentence," Amnesty News Release, March 9, 2006, AI Index: 14/001/2006. http://www.amnesty usa.org/abolish/document.do?id=ENGAMR140012006.

75. Margaret A. Burnham, "Indigenous Constitutionalism and the Death Penalty: The Case of the Commonwealth Caribbean," *International Journal of Constitutional Law* (October 2005).

76. Amnesty International, "Privy Council Abolishes Mandatory Death Sentence."

77. Amnesty International, http://web.amnesty.org (visited May 23, 2006).

78. Roger Hood, *The Death Penalty: A Worldwide Perspective* (Oxford, Eng.: Oxford University Press, 2002): 43–55.

79. Amnesty International, "Death Penalty News," January 2006, http://web.amnesty .org (visited February 7, 2006).

80. Ibid.

81. Abdullahi Ahmed An-Na`im, "Human Rights in the Muslim World," in *The Philosophy of Human Rights*, edited by Patrick Hayden (St. Paul: Paragon House, 2001): 315–35.

82. M. Cherif Bassiouni, "Death as a penalty in the Shari`a," in *Capital Punishment*, edited by Peter Hodgkinson and William A. Shabas, (Cambridge, Eng.: Cambridge University Press, 2003): 169–85.

83. E-mail from human rights researcher Mark Warren, to the authors on January 31, 2006, stating in pertinent part: "King 'Abdallah II bin al-Hussein of Jordan stated in an interview with the Italian newspaper *Corriere della Sera* published on 16 November [2005] that 'In coordination with the European Union we would like to modify our penal code.' Jordan could soon become the first country in the Middle East without capital punishment." A copy of this e-mail is on file with the authors.

84. "Amnesty, EU Praise Death Penalty Freeze," *Manila Standard*, April 21, 2006.

85. "Anticrime Groups Slam Death Penalty Reduction," *Manila Standard*, April 17, 2006.

86. "Philippines President Signs law Abolishing Death Penalty," BBC Monitoring International Reports, July 4, 2006.

87. David Lague, "China Moves to Lessen the Broad Use of Death Sentences," *New York Times*, November 1, 2006, A3.

88. Daniel J. Sharfstein, "Human Rights Beyond the War on Terrorism: Extradition Defenses Based on Prison Conditions in the United States," *Santa Clara Legal Review*, vol. 42 (2002): 1137.

89. Melissa Eddy, "German supreme court backs extradition of Yemeni terror sus-

pect to U.S.," (*Salt Lake City*) *Deseret News* http://www.desnews.com/cgi-bin/cqcgi_
state/@state.env?CQ_SESSION_KEY=TTOVTRYLSCLX&CQ_CUR_DOCUMENT=14
&CQ_TEXT_MAIN=YES (accessed November 13, 2003).

4. Honoring Treaty Commitments (pp. 50–72)

1. Louis Henkin, Sibley Lecture, "Human Rights and State 'Sovereignty,'" *Georgia Journal of International and Comparative Law*, vol. 25 (fall 1995/winter 1996): 31, 45.

2. Memorandum for the Attorney General, "Subject: Compliance with the Decision of the International Court of Justice in Avena," February 28, 2005, http://www.white house.gov/news/releases/2005/02/20050228–18.html (accessed November 9, 2006).

3. *Ex Parte Jose Ernesto Medellin*, No. AP-75,207, 2006 Texas Criminal Appeals LEXIS 2236 (November 15, 2006).

4. Mark Warren, personal communication to the authors, November 18, 2006. Given that the case involves the power of the president to issue an order affecting foreign relations, the case appears to involve significant legal issues of national importance.

5. Editorial, *Detroit Free Press*, November 21, 2000, http://www3.sympatico.ca/ aiwarren/editorials.htm.

6. "Vienna Convention on Consular Relations," [1970] 21 U.S.T. 77, T.I.A.S. No. 6820 (April 24, 1963).

7. "Optional Protocol to the Vienna Convention on Consular Relations Concerning the Compulsory Settlement of Disputes," 596 U.N.T.S. 487 at 488, 21 U.S.T. (April 24, 1963): 325–26 (entered into force, March 19, 1967; accession by United States, December 24, 1969).

8. Letter from Condoleezza Rice, Secretary of State, to Kofi A. Annan, Secretary General of the United Nations, March 7, 2005; see Juliana Ochoa, *Berkeley Political Review*, http://www.ocf.berkeley.edu/~bpreview/old/international/capitalcrime.html (accessed December 6, 2006).

9. Brief for the United States as Amicus Curiae Supporting Respondent, in *Medellin v. Dredtke*, 12. See Web site of Debevoise and Plimpton, LLP, for all briefs in this case: http://www.debevoise.com/newseventspubs/news/RepresentationDetail.aspx?exp_id=70b4b744–00d6–4efo–94ae–0400cd3f255b (accessed December 6, 2006).

10. Ibid., 54.

11. Joan Fitzpatrick, "The Unreality of International Law in the United States and the LaGrand Case," *Yale Journal of International Law*, vol. 27 (2002): 427, 428.

12. Beth A. Simmons, "Is Sovereignty Still Relevant?" *American Journal of International Law*, vol. 94 (2000): 226, 228; see also: WTO (World Trade Organization), "Settling Disputes: Case Study: The Time Table in Practice," http://www.wto.org/english/ thewto_e/whatis_e/tif_e/disp3_e.htm (accessed November 13, 2006).

13. United States Constitution, art. 6, cl. 2.

14. *Foster v. Neilson*, 27 U.S. 253 (1829) at 314.

15. *Edye v. Robertson (Head Money Cases)*, 112 U.S. 580 (1884) at 598–99.

16. Ibid.

17. Karen DeYoung, "President Against Relaxing Cuban Economic Sanctions, Increase in U.S. Aid to Dissidents Supported," *Washington Post*, May 19, 2001: A5. In the same vein, the U.S. State Department Web site page devoted to human rights states:

> The protection of fundamental human rights was a foundation stone in the establishment of the United States over 200 years ago. Since then, a central goal of U.S. foreign policy has been the promotion of respect for human rights, as embodied in the Universal Declaration of Human Rights. The United States understands that the existence of human rights helps secure the peace, deter aggression, promote the rule of law, combat crime and corruption, strengthen democracies, and prevent humanitarian crises.

"Human Rights," U.S. Department of State, http://www.state.gov/g/drl/hr. The State Department provides detailed country reports of the world's worst human rights violators. While U.S. abuses certainly do not rival those of many more egregious human rights violators around the world, its record of flouting international human rights treaties does seem to weaken its message. For a comprehensive report on the U.S. human rights record, see: Human Rights Watch, *World Report 2006: Events of 2005* (2006): 502, 514. http://hrw.org/wrak6.

18. Death Penalty Information Center, http://www.deathpenaltyinfo.org/article.php?did=198&scid=31#Reported-DROW (accessed November 9, 2006).

19. Stuart Taylor Jr., "We Promised the World; Now President Bush should honor our treaty obligations to foreigners in U.S. courts," *Legal Times*, April 12, 2004: 62.

20. As Anthony N. Bishop has written on a related point, "[W]hile the United States should be applauded for maintaining pressure on countries with poor human rights records, America's disapproval of other countries seems hypocritical in light of its unwillingness to abide by international norms respecting the use of the death penalty." "The Death Penalty in the United States: An International Human Rights Perspective," *Southern Texas Law Review*, vol. 43 (2002): 115, 119.

21. *Breard v. Greene*, 523 U.S. 371 (1998) at 373.

22. *Breard v. Virginia*, 248 Va. 68 (Va. Sup. Ct. 1994).

23. Habeas corpus is the legal procedure by which a person is released from unlawful detention.

24. *Breard v. Netherland*, 949 F. Supp. 1255 at 1266 (E.D. Va. 1996).

25. The rule was changed in 2001 to allow after-acquired DNA or "biological" evidence. Other evidence of innocence remains subject to procedural default. The violations of the VCCR are wholly unaffected by this change. See: *Virginia Code Ann.* § 19.2–270.4:1 (2006); see also: Kathryn Roe Eldridge and Mathew L. Engle, "Case Notes: Code of Virginia: *Va. Code Ann.* Sec. 19.2–270.4:1," 14 *Capital Defense Journal* (2001): 217.

26. The rule is subject to narrow exceptions that do not apply in most cases. For a general overview of procedural default, see: Alan W. Clarke, "Procedural Labyrinths and the Injustice of Death: A Critique of Death Penalty Habeas Corpus," part 2, *University of Richmond Law Review*, vol. 30 (1996): 303, 328–74. These rules were originally judicial creations of the Rehnquist court, but were ultimately codified by the *Antiterrorism and Effective Death Penalty Act of 1996* (AEDPA). The AEDPA modifies 28 U.S.C. § § 2254–2255 and adds § § 2261–2266. The AEDPA did effect changes in existing judge-made law, but it did not change the procedural default doctrine—and, on the whole, the AEDPA is best viewed, as Professor David Gottlieb put it in a talk given at the New Mexico School of Law, as "a codification of much of the Court's work" on federal habeas corpus. David Gottlieb and Randal Coyne, "Habeas Corpus Practice in State and Federal Courts," *New Mexico Law Review*, vol. 31 (2001): 201–202. The Mexican government provided the ICJ with the following simplified version of procedural default: "[A] defendant who could have raised, but fails to raise, a legal issue at trial will generally not be permitted to raise it in future proceedings, on appeal or in a petition for a writ of *habeas corpus*." *Case Concerning Avena and Other Mexican Nationals (Mexico v. United States)*, March 31, 2004, General List No. 128, ¶ 111 [Avena], http://www.icj-cij .org/icjwww/idocket/imu/imnsfram.htm. While this definition is correct in so far as it goes, it fails to mention that facts or evidence can also be procedurally defaulted, and issues can be lost on appeal as well.

27. Alan W. Clarke, Laurie Anne Whitt, Eric Lambert, and Oko Elechi, "Does the Rest of the World Matter? Sovereignty, International Human Rights Law and the American Death Penalty," *Queen's Law Journal*, vol. 30, no. 1 (2004): 107.

28. *Breard v. Greene*, 523 U.S. 371 (1998): at 380 (Breyer, J., dissenting).

29. Paraguay, as noted in the text, filed suit at the ICJ and the ICJ had issued provisional measures *before* the Supreme Court ruled. The Supreme Court described that chain of events as "unfortunate," but found no reason under domestic law why Virginia could not proceed with the execution.

30. Press statement by James P. Rubin, spokesman, U.S. Department of State, November 4, 1998; text of statement released in Asuncion, Paraguay, http://www3 .sympatico.ca/aiwarren/editorials.htm.

31. Mark Warren, "Death, Dissent and Diplomacy: The U.S. Death Penalty as an Obstacle to Foreign Relations," *William and Mary Bill of Rights Journal*, vol. 13, no. 8 (2004): 309, 328.

32. Ibid., 329.

33. The AEDPA modifies 28 U.S.C. § § 2254–2255 and adds § § 2261–2266. In addition to adding strict time limits on the filing of a writ of habeas corpus and limitations on the filing of successive petitions, it also preserved judge-made procedural default, retroactivity, and exhaustion requirements.

34. *Germany v. United States of America*, 2001 I.C.J. 466 (LaGrand).

35. *Case Concerning Avena and Other Mexican Nationals (Mexico v. United States)*, March 31, 2004, General List No. 128, ¶ 111 [*Avena*].

36. Anthony N. Bishop, "The Unenforceable Rights to Consular Notification and Access in the United States: What's Changed Since the LaGrand Case?" *Houston Journal of International Law*, vol. 25 (2002): 1, 29.

37. Mexico became a party to the Optional Protocol to the Vienna Convention on Consular Relations on March 15, 2002. See also: multilateral treaties deposited with the secretary general, in the United Nations *Treaty Collection* on-line.

38. Advisory Opinion OC-16/99, Inter-American Court of Human Rights, "The Right to Information on Consular Assistance in the Framework of the Guarantees of the Due Process of Law," 64–65.

39. Bishop, "Unenforceable Rights," 28.

40. *LaGrand*, at ¶ 30.

41. *Federal Republic of Germany v. United States*, 526 U.S. 111 (1999).

42. *LaGrand*, at ¶ 110.

43. Ibid. at ¶ 77.

44. *Sanchez-Llamas v. Oregon and Bustillo v. Virginia*, 126 S.Ct. 2669 (2006).

45. Memorandum for the Attorney General, February 28, 2005.

46. *Avena*, February 5, 2003, at ¶ 59.

47. *Id.* at ¶ 2; see also: Death Penalty Information Center, available at http://www .deathpenaltyinfo.org/article.php?did=198&scid=31, which reports fifty-two as of May 24, 2006 (accessed November 1, 2006).

48. For an explanation of the penalty phase of a capital trial, see: Alan W. Clarke, "Virginia's Capital Murder Sentencing Proceeding: A Defense Perspective," *University of Richmond Law Review*, vol. 18 (1984): 341.

49. Subsequent Application for Post-Conviction Relief, in *Osbaldo Torres v. Oklahoma* (2003), at 2, filed in the Court of Criminal Appeals of the State of Oklahoma by Mark Henrickson, counsel for Osbaldo Torres, and available at: http://www.debevoise .com/publications/pdf/TorresFinal.pdf.

50. For an article detailing just how bad the lawyers for capital defendants can be, see: Alan W. Clarke, "Procedural Labyrinths and the Injustice of Death: A Critique of Death Penalty Habeas Corpus," pt. 1, *University of Richmond Law Review*, vol. 29 (1995): 1327.

51. Toby Sterling, "World Court to Rule on Stay of Execution for Mexicans on Death Row," *Worldstream*, Associated Press, February 4, 2003.

52. *Avena* (2004), at ¶ 32.

53. *Id.* at ¶ 153.

54. *Id.* at ¶ 143.

55. *Id.* at 121.

56. *Id.* at 153.

57. Id. at 138.

58. James C. Harrington, "This country must practice the same standards it asks of others," *Fulton County Daily Report*, vol. 9 (September 10, 2002), See also: Nicholas Wapshott, "Court tells US to spare Mexicans," *Australian*, February 7, 2003, 10.

59. Rodrigo Labardini, "International Court of Justice Finds U.S. Breached Its Obligations under the Vienna Convention on Consular Relations," *International Enforcement Law Reporter*, vol. 20, no.6 (2004): 250.

60. Bishop, "Unenforceable Rights," 84–91.

61. Patrick Timmons, "La Abogada de Mexico: Sandra Babcock's Battle against the Death Penalty," *Texas Observer*, October 25, 2002, http://www.texasobserver.org/show Article.asp?ArticleID=1123. Her work and that of the Mexican Capital Assistance Program are meticulously detailed by Michael Fleishman, in "The Role of the Mexican Government in Defense of Its Foreign Nationals in United States Death Penalty Cases," *Arizona Journal of International and Comparative Law*, vol. 20 (2003): 359.

62. "U.S. Holding 38 Mexican Citizens on Death Row," *News*, (Mexico) April 27, 1998.

63. Sam Dillon, "Mexico reacts bitterly to execution of one of its citizens in Texas," *New York Times*, June 20, 1997, 6.

64. Ibid.

65. Brian Knowlton, "Execution pits Mexico against U.S.; Fox echoes world on the death penalty," *International Herald Tribune* August 16, 2002, 1.

66. Paul English, "Torres' court fight could continue, his attorney says," *The Tulsa World*, May 15, 2004, A12.

67. Sean Murphy, "Governor Commutes Mexican national's death sentence," Associated Press, State and Local Wire, May 14, 2004.

68. *Torres v. Oklahoma*, 2005 OK CR 17, 120 P.3d 1184 (2005), at 1188.

69. See: chapter 7 for an explanation of the concept "innocent of the death penalty."

70. English, "Torres' Court Fight," Sect A, p. 12.

71. Mark Warren, Personal communication to authors. Torres was convicted as an accomplice who aided and abetted. Torres concedes that he went to the victim's apartment to help recover a friend's debt, but asserts he had no idea that the codefendant was going to kick the apartment door down and start shooting. The sole evidence of malice aforethought was the testimony (since recanted) of a neighbor who claimed that she saw Torres put something in the waist of his pants that looked like a pistol before entering the building. No second gun was used or recovered, however.

72. James H. Carter, "Avena in an Oklahoma Court," http://www.asil.org/pdfs/ Carter_Avena_Notes.pdf (accessed November 13, 2006). Carter is president of the American Society of International Law.

73. Bradley B. Clarke, "Honduras asks Perry to spare two killers' lives," Associated

Press, State and Local Wire, May 15, 2004, Texas Law blog, http://texaslaw.blogspot
.com/archives/2004_05_01_texaslaw_archive.html.

74. A San Bernardino County judge ruled, in a capital case involving a Honduran
national, that there is no remedy for a VCCR violation; see: Rod Leveque, "Ultimate
penalty in play for foreigner; Judge: Treaty no aid to murder suspect," *San Bernardino
Sun*, June 18, 2004.

75. Henkin, Sibley Lecture, 31, 45.

76. Memorandum for the Attorney General. Comity in this context means as
a matter of respect, rather than as a legally binding obligation. Thus, the president's
directive tells the state courts that they should give the opinion effect not because of
a binding legal obligation, but as a matter of respect for the opinion in international law.

77. Cases were consolidated on appeal. *Sanchez-Llamas v. Oregon* and *Bustillo v. Virginia*, 126 S.Ct. 2669 (2006).

78. *Sanchez-Llamas v. Oregon* and *Bustillo v. Virginia*, at 2681.

79. Brief for Petitioner Mario Bustillo, In the Supreme Court of the United States,
2; available at: http://www.debevoise.com/VCCR/ (accessed November 9, 2006).

80. Ibid., 2.

81. Ibid., 3.

82. *Sanchez-Llamas*, at 2684.

83. Ibid. at 2688.

84. Ibid. at 2688; (concurring opinion by Justice Ginsberg).

85. See: Clarke, "Procedural Labyrinths and the Injustice of Death: A Critique of
Death Penalty Habeas Corpus," pt. 1, *University of Richmond Law Review*, vol. 29 (1995):
1327; Clarke, "Procedural Labyrinths and the Injustice of Death: A Critique of Death
Penalty Habeas Corpus," pt. 2, *University of Richmond Law Review*, vol. 30 (1996): 303.

86. *Sanchez-Llamas*, at 2709.

87. Ibid.

88. Ibid.

89. Memorandum for the Attorney General.

90. For a complete discussion of the memorandum and its extraordinary nature,
see: Mark Warren, "Additional Updates," DPIC, Human Rights Research, http://www
.deathpenaltyinfo.org/article.php?scid=31&did=579 (accessed November 11, 2006).

91. *Ex Parte Jose Ernesto Medellin*.

92. A San Bernardino County judge ruled, in a capital case involving a Honduran
national, that there is no remedy for a VCCR violation; see also: Leveque, "Ultimate
penalty."

93. See: Clarke, "Procedural Labyrinths" (1995); and Clarke, "Procedural Labyrinths"
(1996), for an extended discussion of state procedural default rules and their enforcement by the federal courts. In this study of procedural default rules' application to Vir-

ginia death penalty jurisprudence, procedural default was found to have played a role in the dismissal of capital appeals in eighty-four of ninety-one capital cases during the period studied. If these numbers hold for other states (or are even close), procedural default trips up more death penalty appeals than any other doctrine. This is at the very least one of the more common ways in which a capital appeal is lost.

94. Anthony N. Bishop, "The Death Penalty in the United States: An International Human Rights Perspective," *Southern Texas Law Review*, vol. 43 (2002): 1115, 1216; cited in Brook A. Masters, "U.S. Deprived Mexican of Fair Trial, Appeal Says," *Washington Post*, August 23, 2001, A8.

95. English, "Torres' court fight," sect. A, p. 12; "Governor commutes Mexican national's death sentence," *Boston Herald*, May 14, 2004, http://news.bostonherald.com/national/view.bg?articleid=27877&format= (accessed November 28, 2006).

96. Toby Sterling, "World Court rules US must stay execution of 3 Mexicans," *Chicago Tribune*, February 5, 2003, 3.

97. Amy Edelstein, "Think globally, act globally," *Women's Review of Books*, vol. 20 (2003): 5. Following the World Trade Center attacks on September 11, 2001, Robinson continued, the United States was not complying with international human rights norms and standards with regard to Guantanamo Bay prisoners and the detention of immigrants. "[This] was being viewed by the rest of the world as a signal that those standards had changed. I had to say, as UN High Commissioner, that *those standards had not changed*. They are a legal technical apparatus. They don't change because one country is not upholding them fully." (11, Emphasis in original).

5. Death Penalty Myths (pp. 75–96)

1. Mark Twain, http://www.quotationreference.com; full hyperlink, http://www.quotationreference.com/quotefinder.php?strt=11&subj=Mark+Twain&bya=&byq=&bys=&byex=&byax=1&subind=&lr= (accessed November 3, 2006).

2. Roger Hood, *The Death Penalty: A Worldwide Perspective*, 3d ed. (Oxford, Eng.: Oxford University Press, 2002): 225.

3. Travis C. Pratt and Francis C. Cullen, "Assessing Macro-Level Predictors and Theories of Crime: A Meta-Analysis," *Crime and Justice*, vol. 32 (2005): 373.

4. Roper Center/*Newsweek* Poll, sponsor: Princeton Survey Research Associates, ACC-NO: 0382405, May 12, 2001.

5. Roper Center Poll, sponsors: *Time* and CNN ACC-NO: 0290610, June 6, 1997.

6. Michael L. Radelet and Ronald L. Akers, "Deterrence and the Death Penalty: The Views of the Experts," *Journal of Criminal Law and Criminology*, vol. 87 (1996): 7–8.

7. Ibid., 8.

8. Douglas Hay, "Property, Authority and the Criminal Law," in *Albion's Fatal Tree: Crime and Society in Eighteenth-Century England*, edited by Allen Lane (New York: Pantheon Books, 1975): 23.

9. Ibid.

10. Ibid.

11. Louis P. Mazur, *Rites of Execution: Capital Punishment and the Transformation of American Culture, 1776–1865* (Oxford, Eng.: Oxford University Press, 1989): 63.

12. Jim Hornby, *In the Shadow of the Gallows* (Charlottetown, Prince Edward Island: Institute of Island Studies, 1998): 74 (quoting from the *North Star* (Charlottetown, 1869).

13. Anthony Amsterdam, et al., "Brief of Amici Curiae," *New York University Review of Law and Social Change*, vol. 27 (2001/2002): 399.

14. Mazur, *Rites of Execution*, 143.

15. Eugene G. Wanger, "Historical Reflections on Michigan's Abolition of the Death Penalty," *Thomas M. Cooley Law Review*, vol. 13, no. 3 (1996): 755–763.

16. John D. Bessler, *The "Midnight Assassination Law" and Minnesota's Anti-Death Penalty Movement, 1849–1911* (Minneapolis: University of Minnesota Press, 1996): 605.

17. E. H. Sutherland, "Murder and the Death Penalty," *Journal of the American Institute of Criminal Law and Criminology*, vol. 15 (1925): 522–29.

18. Ibid., 529.

19. Karl F. Schussler, "The Deterrent Influence of the Death Penalty," *Annals of the American Academy of Political and Social Science*, vol. 284 (1952): 54–62.

20. Johan Thorsten Sellin, *Capital Punishment* (New York: Harper and Row, 1967): 135–38.

21. Keith Harries and Derral Cheatwood, "Capital Punishment and the Deterrence of Violent Crime in Comparable Counties," in *Capital Punishment: A Balanced Examination*, edited by Evan J. Mandery (Boston: Jones and Bartlett, 2005): 49–56.

22. Ibid., 55.

23. This is drawn from table 1, Ruth D. Peterson and William C. Bailey, "Is Capital Punishment an Effective Deterrent for Murder?: An Examination of Social Science Research," in *America's Experiment with Capital Punishment*, 2nd ed., edited by James R. Acker, Robert M. Bohm, and Charles S. Lanier (Durham, N.C.: Carolina Academic Press, 2003): 254.

24. Death Penalty Information Center (DPIC), calculations provided by David Cooper, "Deterrence: States without the Death Penalty Fared Better over Past Decade," Death Penalty Information Center, http://www.deathpenaltyinfo.org/article.php?scid=12&did==168 (accessed November 3, 2006).

25. John K. Cochran and Mitchell B. Chamblin, "Deterrence and Brutalization: The Dual Effects of Executions," in Mandery, ed., *Capital Punishment*, 68.

26. See: Peterson and Bailey, "Is Capital Punishment an Effective Deterrent?" ch. 8, for discussion of the social science evidence on both deterrence and brutalization.

27. Erica Templeton, "Killing Kids: The Impact of *Domingues v. Nevada* on the Juvenile Death Penalty as a Violation of International Law," *41 Boston College Law Review*

1175 (2000) at 1182; citing Death Penalty Information Center, http://www.deathpenalty info.org/whatsnew/html.

28. Ted Goertzel, "Capital Punishment and Homicide: Sociological Realities and Econometric Illusions," *Skeptical Inquirer*, Vol. 28, no. 4 (July/August 2004), Death Penalty Information Center, http://www.deathpenaltyinfo.org/article.php?scid=12& did=1176 (accessed December 11, 2006).

29. National Academy of Sciences, "Deterrence and Incapacitation: Estimating the Effects of Criminal Sanctions on Crime Rates, Report of the Panel of Deterrence and Incapacitation," Alfred Blumstein, Jaquelin Cohen, and Daniel Nagin, eds. (Washington, D.C.: National Academy of Sciences, 1978).

30. Cass R. Sunstein and Adrian Vermeule, "Is Capital Punishment Morally Required? Act, Omission, and Life-Life Trade-offs," *Stanford Law Review*, vol. 58 (2005): 703, 711, summarizing the newer econometric studies and concluding "that on average, each execution results in eighteen fewer murders."

31. Jeffrey Fagan, Franklin E. Zimring, and Amanda Geller, *Texas Law Review*, vol. 84 (2006): 1803, 1859.

32. Ibid., 1822.

33. Ibid., 1860.

34. Ibid.

35. Ibid., 1827–32.

36. Richard Berk, "New Claims about Executions and General Deterrence: Déjà vu All Over Again?" *Journal of Empirical Legal Studies*, vol. 2 (2005): 303, 305.

37. Jeffrey Fagan, "Deterrence and the Death Penalty: A Critical Review of New Evidence," testimony before the New York State Assembly Standing Committee on Codes, Standing Committee on Judiciary, and Standing Committee on Correction; Hearings on the Future of Capital Punishment in the State of New York, January 21, 2005, http://www.deathpenaltyinfo.org.

38. Goertzel, "Capital Punishment and Homicide."

39. Jon Sorensen and Rocky LeAnn Pilgrim, *Lethal Injection: Capital Punishment in Texas during the Modern Era* (Austin: University of Texas Press, 2006): 36.

40. Ibid., 48, n. 30.

41. Lisa Stolzenberg and Stewart J. D'Allesio, "Capital Punishment, Execution Publicity and Murder in Houston, Texas," *Journal of Criminal Law and Criminology*, vol. 94 (2004): 362.

42. Ibid., 374.

43. Geofrey Rapp, "The Economics of Shootouts: Does the Passage of Capital Punishment Laws Protect or Endanger Police Officers?" *Albany Law Review*, vol. 65 (2002): 1067.

44. John J. Donohoe and Justin Wolfers, "Uses and Abuses of Empirical Evidence in the Death Penalty Debate," *Stanford Law Review*, vol. 58 (2005): 791, 794.

45. Ibid., 798.

46. These arguments draw upon and to some extent summarize Donohoe and Wolfers, "Uses and Abuses of Empirical Evidence," 791–845.

47. Ted Goertzel, "Econometric Modeling as Junk Science," *Skeptical Inquirer*, vol. 26, no. 1 (January/February 2002): 19–23, http://crab.rutgers.edu/%7Egoertzel/mythsof murder.htm (accessed November 13, 2006).

48. Peterson and Bailey, "Is Capital Punishment an Effective Deterrent?" 274.

49. William J. Bowers and Glenn J. Pierce, "Deterrence or Brutalization: What is the Effect of Executions?" *Crime and Delinquency*, vol. 26 (1980): 453–84.

50. William C. Bailey, "Deterrence, Brutalization, and the Death Penalty: Another Examination of Oklahoma's Return to Capital Punishment," *Criminology*, vol. 36 (1988): 711.

51. John K. Cochran and Mitchell B. Chamblin, "Deterrence and Brutalization: The Dual Effects of Executions," in Mandery, ed., *Capital Punishment*, 71–72.

52. Jon Sorensen, Robert Winkle, Victoria Brewer, and James Marquart, "Capital Punishment and Deterrence: Examining the Effect of Executions on Murder in Texas," in Mandery, ed., *Capital Punishment*, 75.

53. Radelet and Akers, "Deterrence and the Death Penalty," 1.

54. *Furman v. Georgia*, 408 U.S. 238; 92 S. Ct. 2726; 33 L. Ed. 2d 346; 1972 U.S. LEXIS 169 (1972).

55. Ibid., at 309–10.

56. In *Furman*, a divided Supreme Court struck down all death penalty statutes. Four years later, the Court sustained "guided discretion" death penalty regimes in *Gregg v. Georgia*, 428 U.S. 153 (1976), *Proffit v. Florida*, 428 U.S. 242 (1976), and *Jurek v. Texas*, 428 U.S. 262 (1976). At the same time, the Court struck down mandatory death penalty laws in *Woodson v. North Carolina*, 428 U.S. 280 (1976), and *Roberts v. Louisiana*, 428 U.S. 325 (1976).

57. James W. Marquart and Jon Sorensen, "A National Study of the Furman-Commuted Inmates: Assessing the Threat to Society from Capital Offenders," *Loyola of Los Angeles Law Review*, vol. 23 (1989): 5–28.

58. Given various inconsistencies in the data, Marquart and Sorensen were not able to definitively state the precise number of persons whose sentences were commuted by *Furman*. The 558 tracked, however, constitute the large majority, and a good sampling, of these prisoners. Their conclusions, therefore, appear sound.

59. Marquart and Sorensen, "A National Study," 10 n. 45.

60. Michael L. Radelet and James W. Marquart, "Assessing Nondangerousness during Death Penalty Phases of Capital Trials," *Albany Law Review*, vol. 54 (1990): 845–61, summarizing research on the issue of recidivism among convicted murderers.

61. Ibid.; see also: Michael L. Radelet and Marian J. Borg, "The Changing Nature of the Death Penalty Debates," *Annual Review Sociology*, vol. 26 (2000): 43–61, 46.

62. Radelet and Marquart, "Assessing Nondangerousness."

63. Ibid.

64. John Monahan, "The Scientific Status of Research on Clinical and Actuarial Predictions of Violence," in *Social Science and the Law*, David L. Faigman et al., ed., vol. 1 (St. Paul, Minn.: West Group, 2002): 90–112.

65. Radelet and Marquart, "Assessing Nondangerousness."

66. Death Penalty Information Center, http://www.deathpenaltyinfo.org/article .php?did=555&scid5=59 (accessed November 10, 2006).

67. From testimony in the case of Clarence Brandley (later exonerated) and quoted in Penny J. White, "A Response and Retort," *Connecticut Law Review*, vol. 33 (2001): 899, n. 100. See also: Death Penalty Information Center, http://www.deathpenaltyinfo.org/ article.php?scid=6&did=109 (last visited July 24, 2006). According to the center, Brandley was awarded a new trial when evidence showed prosecutorial suppression of exculpatory evidence and perjury by prosecution witnesses. An investigation by the Department of Justice and the FBI uncovered more misconduct, and in 1989 a new trial was granted. Prior to the new trial, all of the charges against Brandley were dropped. Brandley is the subject of the book *White Lies* by Nick Davies. (*Ex Parte Brandley*, 781 S.W.2d 886, (Tex. Crim. App. 1989), *The Dallas Times Herald*, (10/2/90), and *Washington Post*, (2/1/95).

68. Death Penalty Information Center, http://www.deathpenaltyinfo.org/article .php?scid=5&did==184 (accessed June 4, 2006).

69. Determined by counting all Native Americans as listed March 2006 in the Death Penalty Information Center's Execution Database. This database lists, where known, the race of both defendant and victim, as well as the state conducting the execution.

70. "U.S. Census Bureau, State and County QuickFacts," http://www.deathpenalty info.org/article.php?scid=5&did=184 (last accessed June 4, 2006).

71. David C. Baldus, George Woodworth, David Zuckerman, Neil Alan Weiner, and Barbara Profitt, "Racial Discrimination and the Death Penalty in the Post-*Furman* Era: An Empirical and Legal Overview, with Recent Findings from Philadelphia," *Cornell Law Review*, vol. 83 (1998): 1638, n. 61.

72. Richard C. Dieter, *The Death Penalty in Black and White: Who Lives, Who Dies, Who Decides*, Washington, D.C.: Death Penalty Information Center, 1998. Available at http://www.deathpenaltyinfo.org/article.php?scid=45&did=539.

73. David Baldus, "Race Discrimination and the Legitimacy of Capital Punishment: Reflections on the Interaction of Fact and Perception," *DePaul Law Review*, vol. 53 (2004): 1411–95.

74. David C. Baldus and George Woodworth, "Race Discrimination in the Administration of the Death Penalty: An Overview of the Empirical Evidence with Special Emphasis on the Post-1990 Research," *Criminal Law Bulletin*, vol. 39 (2003): 214.

75. Glenn L. Pierce and Michael L. Radelet, "The Impact of Legally Inappropriate Factors on Death Sentencing for California Homicides, 1990–99," *Santa Clara Law Review*, vol. 46 (2005): 1–47.

76. Jennifer L. Eberhardt, Paul G. Davies, Valerie J. Purdie-Vagns, and Sheri Lynn Johnson, "Looking Deathworthy: Perceived Stereotypicality of Black Defendants Predicts Capital-Sentencing Outcomes," *Psychological Science*, vol. 17 (2006): 383, 384.

77. Ibid., 384.

78. Ibid., 385.

79. Baldus and Woodworth, "Race Discrimination," 221.

80. *Ring v. Arizona*, 536 U.S. 584 (2002).

81. See: Stephen B. Brauerman, "Balancing the Burden: The Constitutional Justification for Requiring the Government to Prove the Absence of Mental Retardation before Imposing the Death Penalty," *American University Law Review*, vol. 54 (2004): 401, 408.

82. It is difficult to overstate David Baldus and George Woodworth's influence and importance in this area, and many of the ideas for this section have been strongly influenced by their work. Michael L. Radelet and Glenn L. Pierce have also done pioneering work in this area with definitive studies of Illinois, Florida, and California.

83. See, generally, the work of Baldus and Woodworth, cited above.

84. *McCleskey v. Kemp*, 481 U.S. 279 (1987); for more on this, see: Anthony G. Amsterdam and Jerome Bruner, *Minding the Law* (Cambridge, Mass.: Harvard University Press, 2000): chap. 7.

85. *McCleskey v. Kemp*.

86. *Miller-El v. Dretke*, 545 U.S. 231 (2005).

87. William J. Bowers, Marla Sandys, and Thomas W. Brewer, "Crossing Racial Boundaries: A Closer Look at the Roots of Racial Bias in Capital Sentencing When the Defendant is Black and the Victim is White," *DePaul Law Review*, vol. 53 (2004): 1497–1537.

88. Ibid.

89. David C. Baldus et al., "Racial Discrimination."

90. Jack Greenberg, "Against the American System of Capital Punishment," *Harvard Law Review*, vol. 99 (1986): 1670–80.

91. Death Penalty Information Center, http://www.deathpenaltyinfo.org/Fact Sheet.pdf (accessed November 12, 2006).

92. Margaret Vandiver, David J. Giacopassi, and Mazie S. Curley, "The Tennessee Slave Code: A Legal Antecedent to Inequities in Modern Capital Cases," *Journal of Ethnicity in Criminal Justice*, vol. 1 (2003): 67–89.

93. David Jacobs, Stephanie L. Kent, and Jason T. Carmichael, "Vigilantism, Current Racial Threat, and Death Sentences," *American Sociological Review*, vol. 70 (2005): 656–77.

94. Franklin E. Zimring, *The Contradictions of American Capital Punishment* (Oxford, Eng.: Oxford University Press, 2003): 89.

95. Jacobs, Kent, and Carmichael, "Vigilantism."

96. Death Penalty Information Center, http://www.deathpenaltyinfo.org (accessed November 12, 2006).

97. Phillip J. Cook and Donna B. Slawson, "The Costs of Processing Murder Cases in North Carolina," Terry Stanford Institute of Public Policy, (Durham, N.C.: Duke University Press, 1993).

98. Death Penalty Information Center, http://www.deathpenaltyinfo.org/article .php?did=108&scid=7 (accessed July 24, 2006).

99. Robert M. Bohm, "The Economic Costs of Capital Punishment: Past, Present, and Future," in Acker, Bohm, and Lanier, eds., *America's Experiment with Capital Punishment*, 578; cited in M. Garey, "The Cost of Taking a Life: Dollars and Sense of the Death Penalty," *University of California Davis Law Review*, vol. 18 (1989):1221–73; and Robert L. Spangenberg and Elizabeth R. Walsh, "Capital Punishment or Life Imprisonment? Some Cost Considerations," *Loyola of Los Angeles Law Review*, vol. 23 (1989): 45–58.

100. James S. Liebman, Jeffrey Fagan, Valerie West, and Jonathan Lloyd, "Habeas: Capital Attrition: Error Rates in Capital Cases, 1973–1995," *Texas Law Review*, vol. 78 (2000): 1839–65.

101. Death Penalty Information Center, http://www.deathpenaltyinfo.org (accessed November 28, 2006).

6. Attitudes toward Capital Punishment (pp. 97–112)

1. *Furman v. Georgia*, 408 U.S. 238 at 362 (1972) (Justice Marshall concurring).

2. Polls concerning capital punishment have been collected and are available on the Internet in two places. The *Sourcebook for Criminal Justice Statistics* is available at http:// www.albany.edu/sourcebook (accessed November 28, 2006). The Death Penalty Information Center also collects a variety of polls and other statistics on capital punishment and is available at http://www.deathpenaltyinfo.org (accessed November 28, 2006).

3. *Gregg v. Georgia*, 428 U.S. 153 (1976).

4. *Proffit v. Florida*, 428 U.S. 242 (1976).

5. *Jurek v. Texas*, 428 U.S. 262 (1976).

6. Bryan Stevenson, "Politics and the Death Penalty: Can Rational Discourse and Due Process Survive the Perceived Political Pressure?" *Fordham Urban Law Journal*, vol. 21 (1994): 239, 254.

7. Richard Cohen, "Playing Politics with the Death Penalty," *Washington Post*, March 20, 1990, A19.

8. Hugo Adam Bedau, "The Decline of Executive Clemency in Capital Cases," *New York University Review of Law and Social Change*, vol. 18, (1990–91): 255.

9. See: Alan W. Clarke, "Procedural Labyrinths and the Injustice of Death: A Cri-

tique of Death Penalty Habeas Corpus," pt. 1, *University of Richmond Law Review*, vol. 29 (1995): 1327; Alan W. Clarke, "Procedural Labyrinths and the Injustice of Death: A Critique of Death Penalty Habeas Corpus," pt. 2, *University of Richmond Law Review*, vol. 30 (1996): 303.

10. Ann L. Pastone and Kathleen Maquine, eds., *Sourcebook of Criminal Justice Statistics*, 31st ed. (Bureau of Justice Statistics, 2002): 143. Available at http://www.albany .edu/sourcebook (accessed November 21, 2006).

11. Death Penalty Information Center, http://www.deathpenaltyinfo.org/newsand-dev.php?scid=23 (accessed November 17, 2006.

12. Death Penalty Information Center http://www.deathpenaltyinfo.org/article .php?did=555&scid=59 (accessed November 17, 2006).

13. "Equal Justice USA," Quixote Center, http://www.quixote.org/ej (accessed (December 7, 2006).

14. Fredric U. Dicker and Kenneth Lovett, "New Yorkers Oppose New Death Penalty," *New York Post*, March 9, 2005, 28.

15. Errol A. Cockfield, "Poll: Education voters' top issue; Economy and health care next in NY survey that also shows sharp split by regions; LI big on property taxes," *Newsday* (New York), March 10, 2006, A22.

16. Allan Turner, "Bloodthirsty image at odds with local poll," *Houston Chronicle*, February 3, 2001, http://www.HoustonChroncle.com/cs/CDA/ssistroy.mpl/special/ penalty/813659 (accessed November 28, 2006).

17. Death Penalty Information Center, http://www.deathpenaltyinfo.org, citing a statewide poll conducted by Capital Survey Research Center, the polling arm of the Alabama Education Center.

18. Samuel R. Gross and Phoebe C. Ellsworth, "Second Thoughts: Americans' Views on the Death Penalty at the Turn of the Century," *Capital Punishment and the American Future* (Durham, N.C.: Duke University Press, 2001): 8.

19. Texas' first post-*Furman* execution was of Charlie Brooks in 1982; it has since executed 379 persons for an annual rate, as of November 2006, of 15.79 (379 divided by 24). If one calculates the numbers from the *Gregg, Jurek*, and *Proffit* decisions of 1976, the rate is 12.63 (379 divided by 30). Data from the Death Penalty Information Center, http://www.deathpenaltyinfo.org/executions.php.

20. The Espy Database (which contains the best source of execution data before 1976), http://www.deathpenaltyinfo.org/article.php?scid=8&did=269 (accessed November 22, 2006).

21. These percentages were calculated by the authors, using the data from the Death Penalty Information Center, "Facts About the Death Penalty," http://www.death penaltyinfo.org/FactSheet.pdf (accessed November 17, 2006).

22. Frank Zimring and Gordon Hawkins, *Capital Punishment and the American Agenda* (Cambridge, Eng.: Cambridge University Press, 1986): 12.

23. University of Wisconsin Badger Poll (July 17, 2006), Death Penalty Information Center, http://www.deathpenaltyinfo.org/article.php?did=1850&scid=64 (accessed November 10, 2006).

24. These polls are summarized by: the Death Penalty Information Center, http://www.deathpenaltyinfo.org/newsanddev.php?scid=23 (visited August 10, 2006).

25. Phoebe Ellsworth and Sam Gross, "Hardening of the attitudes: Americans' Views on the Death Penalty," *Journal of Social Issues*, vol. 50 (1994): 19–52, 21–22.

26. Ibid., 23.

27. Ibid., 36, 36.

28. Eric Lambert, Alan W. Clarke, and Janet Lambert, "Crime, Capital Punishment, and Knowledge: Are Criminal Justice Majors Better Informed Than Other Majors About Crime and Punishment?" *Social Science Journal*, vol. 41 (2004): 53. See also, Eric Lambert and Alan Clarke, "The Impact of Information on an Individual's Support of the Death Penalty: A Partial Test of the Marshall Hypothesis among College Students," *Criminal Justice Policy Review*, vol. 12 (2001): 215–34, for a summary of the studies on this topic.

29. Austin Sarat and Neil Vidmar, "Public Opinion, the Death Penalty, and the Eighth Amendment: Testing the Marshall Hypothesis," *Wisconsin Law Review* (1976): 171.

30. For an excellent summary of the research on Robert Bohm's work, as well as other aspects of death penalty opinion, see: Robert Bohm, "American Death Penalty Opinion: Past, Present, and Future," in *America's Experiment with Capital Punishment*, 2nd ed., edited by James R. Acker, Robert M. Bohm, and Charles S. Lanier (Durham, N.C.: Carolina Academic Press, 2003): 27–54.

31. For a short summary of this literature, see: Alan W. Clarke, Eric Lambert, and Laurie Anne Whitt, "Executing the Innocent: The Next Step in the Marshall Hypotheses," *New York University Review of Law and Social Change*, vol. 26 (2000/2001): 309–45; Lambert and Clarke, "Impact of Information."

32. Bohm, "American Death Penalty Opinion," 43.

33. Learned Hand, *United States v. Garsson*, 291 F. at 649 646 (1923).

34. These cases are among those summarized in "Catalogue of Defendants," found in Hugo Adam Bedau and Michael Radelet, "Miscarriages of Justice in Potentially Capital Cases," *Stanford Law Review*, vol. 40 (1987): 21. Both the Joe Hill and Sacco-Vanzetti cases are still contested, however, and a great deal of scholarship has weighed in on the guilt or innocence of both. While both prosecutions were, in the hindsight of history, shaky, nonetheless, their guilt or innocence remains uncertain.

35. Tom R. Tyler and Renee Weber, "Support for the Death Penalty: Instrumental Response to Crime of Symbolic Attitude," *Law and Society Review*, vol. 20 (1982): 21.

36. Alan Clarke, Eric Lambert, and Laurie Anne Whitt, "Debating the Death Penalty: The Impact of Innocence," *Guild Practitioner*, vol. 59, no. 2 (2002): 116–28.

37. Bureau of Justice Statistics, *Criminal Justice Statistics*, 148 (accessed November 21, 2006).

38. Bedau and Radelet, "Miscarriages of Justice," 21. Later, their updated and revised research was included in a book coauthored with Constance E. Putnam: Bedau, Radelet, and Putnam, *In Spite of Innocence* (Evanston, Ill.: Northwestern University Press, 1992).

39. Stephen J. Markman and Paul G. Cassell, "Protecting the Innocent: A Response to the Bedau-Radelet Study," *Stanford Law Review*, vol. 41 (1988): 121–60.

40. Death Penalty Information Center, http://www.deathpenaltyinfo.org/article .php?did=412&scid=6 (accessed November 18, 2006).

41. James D. Unnever and Francis T. Cullen, "Executing the Innocent and Support for Capital Punishment: Implications for Public Policy," *Criminology and Public Policy*, vol. 4, no.1 (2005): 3–38, 24.

42. *Illinois v. Anthony Porter*, 111 Ill. 2d 386 at 405 (1986).

43. Anthony Porter's story and those of others exonerated by Protess and his students can be found on the Web site of the Center on Wrongful Convictions., http:// www.law.northwestern.edu/depts/clinic/wrongful/exonerations/Porter.htm (accessed August 10, 2006).

44. Douglas Holt and Steve Mills, "Double Murder Case Unravels; Once 2 Days Away From Execution, Inmate May Go Free After Another Man Implicates Himself in 2 Murders," *Chicago Tribune* February 4, 1999, 1.

45. A search of the LexisNexis database under the News, All (English) file with the search string "Anthony Porter and death penalty and Illinois" yielded 785 documents as of August 3, 2005.

46. Ken Armstrong and Steve Mills, "Death Row Justice Derailed: Bias, Errors and Incompetence in Capital Cases Have Turned Illinois' Harshest Punishment Into Its Least Credible," *Chicago Tribune* Nov. 14, 1999, C1 (first of a 5-part series, "The Failure of the Death Penalty in Illinois").

47. Ibid.

48. Death Penalty Information Center, http://www.deathpenaltyinfo.org.

49. *House v. Bell*, 125 S. Ct. 2991 (June 28, 2005) (petition for writ of certiorari granted).

50. Ibid., at 2068.

51. Michael L. Radelet and Hugo Adam Bedau, "ABA's Proposed Moratorium on the Death Penalty: The Execution of the Innocent," *Law and Contemporary Problems*, vol. 61 (1998): 105.

52. Clarke, Lambert, and Whitt, "Debating the Death Penalty," 117.

53. This research is available in the following articles: Clarke, Lambert, and Whitt, "Executing the Innocent"; Lambert and Clarke, "The Impact of Information"; Laurie A. Whitt, Alan W. Clarke, and Eric Lambert, "Innocence Matters: How Innocence Re-

casts the Death Penalty Debate," *Criminal Law Bulletin*, vol. 38 (2002): 670; Clarke, Lambert, and Whitt, "Debating the Death Penalty."

54. Clarke, Lambert, and Whitt, "Executing the Innocent."

55. Clarke, Lambert, and Whitt, "Executing the Innocent," 335–336.

56. Gross and Ellsworth, "Second Thoughts," 14.

57. Ibid., 15.

58. Ibid., 14–15.

59. Unnever and Cullen, "Executing the Innocent."

60. Ibid., 19.

61. Steven E. Barkan and Steven F. Cohn, "On Reducing White Support for the Death Penalty: A Pessimistic Appraisal," *Criminology and Public Policy*, vol. 4 (2005): 39–44.

62. Unnever and Cullen, "Executing the Innocent," 20.

63. Ibid.

64. Austin Sarat, "Innocence, Error, and the 'New Abolitionism': A Commentary," *Criminology and Public Policy*, vol. 4, no. 1 (2005): 45.

65. Ibid., 51.

66. Unnever and Cullen, "Executing the Innocent," 29.

67. Gross and Ellsworth, "Second Thoughts," 18.

7. Executing the Innocent (pp. 113–33)

1. Anne Gearan, "As two justices sound alarms, Supreme Court may be ready to set new limits on capital punishment," Associated Press State and Local Wire, August 2, 2001).

2. For an excellent account of this history, see Bruce P. Smith, "The History of Wrongful Execution," *Hastings Law Journal*, vol. 56 (2005): 1185–1233.

3. Ibid., 1193.

4. Ibid., 1192.

5. Roger Pearson, *Voltaire Almighty* (London: Bloomsbury, 2005): 285–86.

6. François-Marie Voltaire, *A Treatise on Toleration and Other Essays*, trans. Joseph McCabe (Amherst, Mass.: Prometheus Books, 1994): 145.

7. Hugo Adam Bedau and Michael Radelet, "Miscarriages of Justice in Potentially Capital Cases," *Stanford Law Review*, vol. 40 (1987): 21, 22.

8. Stuart Banner, *The Death Penalty: An American History* (Cambridge, Mass.: Harvard University Press, 2002): 122.

9. Ibid.

10. Ibid.

11. Ibid.

12. Eugene G. Wanger, "Historical Reflections on Michigan's Abolition of the Death Penalty," *Thomas M. Cooley Law Review*, vol. 13 (1996): 755, 766.

13. Bedau and Radelet, "Miscarriages of Justice," 77–78.

14. See: Alan W. Clarke, "Procedural Labyrinths and the Injustice of Death: A Critique of Death Penalty Habeas Corpus," pt. 2, *University of Richmond Law Review*, vol. 30 (1996): 303, 338–431; discussing innocence and the death penalty.

15. Bedau and Radelet, "Miscarriages of Justice."

16. Stephen J. Markman and Paul G. Cassell, "Protecting the Innocent: A Response to the Bedau-Radelet Study," *Stanford Law Review*, vol. 41 (1988): 121.

17. Michael L. Radelet, Hugo Adam Bedau, and Constance E. Putnam, *In Spite of Innocence: Erroneous Convictions in Capital Cases* (Lebanon, N.H.: Northeastern University Press, 1992).

18. Markman and Cassell, "Protecting the Innocent," 151.

19. Ibid., 150.

20. Figures are taken from Death Penalty Information Center, http://www.death penaltyinfo.org (accessed November 22, 2006).

21. Letter from Margaret Vandiver to authors, September 27, 2006, on file with the authors.

22. Bruce Shapiro, "Wrongful Deaths," *The Nation*, December 14, 1998, 6.

23. Samuel R. Gross, "The Risks of Death: Why Erroneous Convictions Are Common in Capital Cases," *Buffalo Law Review*, vol. 44 (1996): 469.

24. Ibid., 472.

25. Ibid., 475.

26. Ibid. (citations omitted).

27. *Washington v. Commonwealth*, 323 S.E.2d 577 (Va. 1984), cert. denied, 471 U.S. 1111 (1985).

28. At the time of Washington's conviction, Rule 1:1 of the Rules of the Supreme Court of Virginia provided that final judgments remained under the trial court's jurisdiction for only twenty-one days and could be modified, vacated, or suspended only during that narrow period.

29. Jerry Markon, "Wrongfully Jailed Man Wins Suit; Va. Officer Falsified Confession, Jury Rules," *Washington Post*, May 6, 2006: B1.

30. Ibid.

31. See: Kathryn Roe Eldridge and Mathew L. Engle, "Case Notes: Code of Virginia: Va. Code Ann. § 19.2–270.4:1, *Capital Defense Journal*, vol. 14 (2001): 217.

32. As Bryan Stevenson points out:
But innocent or wrongly convicted people who can be exonerated through DNA are not the only innocent people in prison. The death penalty exonerations have established that DNA identifies only a small subset of people who never should have been convicted of any crime or sentenced to death. But a mere 12% of the 123 death penalty exonerations identified by the Death Penalty Information Center were based on DNA evidence.

Stevensen, "Confronting Mass Imprisonment and Restoring Fairness to Collateral Review of Criminal Cases," *Harvard Civil Rights and Civil Liberties Review*, vol. 41 (2006): 339, 346.

33. This account is taken from an account given by Gary Gaugher at the Annual Death Penalty Symposium at Utah Valley State College in September 2005. This talk was videotaped and is available through the Integrated Studies Program at Utah Valley State College, Orem, Utah.

34. Markon, "Wrongfully Jailed Man."

35. Richard Cohen, "One Fatal Mistake Not Made," *Washington Post*, editorial, February 15, 2001, A23.

36. Associated Press, "DNA can exonerate convicts, implicate system: Resistance: Some Judges are reluctant to allow testing, but evidence often upholds convictions," (Dubuque, Iowa) *Telegraph-Herald*, October 8, 2000, A6.

37. Ken Armstrong and Maurice Possley, "Verdict Dishonor," *Chicago Tribune*, January 10, 1999: zone C, p. 1 (first of a 5-part series, "Trial and Error: How Prosecutors Sacrifice Justice to Win").

38. Bryan Stevenson is also professor of clinical law at New York University. According to the EJI Web site, he has "secured relief for dozens of condemned prisoners." Equal Justice Initiative of Alabama, http://www.eji.org/index.html (accessed November 22, 2006).

39. This account is taken from Bryan Stevenson's keynote address to the National Lawyer's Guild annual convention in Birmingham, Alabama (October 2004).

40. Clarke, "Procedural Labyrinths," (1996), 254, n. 280.

41. Bedau and Radalet, "Miscarriages of Justice," 70.

42. James S. Liebman, Jeffrey Fagan, Valerie West, and Jonathan Lloyd, "Capital Attrition: Error Rates in Capital Cases, 1973–1995," *Texas Law Review*, vol. 78 (2000): 1839, 1850.

43. Ibid., 1852.

44. Ibid., 1850.

45. According to the Death Penalty Information Center, there were 1,029 executions as of June 28, 2006. http://www.deathpenaltyinfo.org/executions.php.

46. Richard Lempert, "Desert and Deterrence: An Assessment of the Moral Bases of the Case for Capital Punishment," *University of Michigan Law Review*, vol. 79 (1981): 1177, 1226–27.

47. Laurie Anne Whitt, Alan W. Clarke, and Eric Lambert, "Innocence Matters: How Innocence Recasts the Death Penalty Debate," *Criminal Law Bulletin*, vol. 38 (2002): 670–735. The authors identify ten cases in which scholars have assessed the cases of executed persons and found a likelihood of innocence. Larry Griffin's case, which is the strongest claim of innocence by far, makes eleven. Ruben Cantu, also a very strong case of innocence, makes it an even dozen, that of Cameron Todd Will-

ingham makes thirteen. However, since Roger Coleman was at the time thought to have been possibly innocent, and since DNA evidence now confirms guilt, his case must be dropped; leaving a dozen identified cases of probable innocence.

48. Gross, "The Risks of Death."

49. Ibid., 475.

50. Samuel Gross points out that while the evidence on this is not conclusive, it suggests that perjured testimony is much greater in murder cases than in cases of other kinds of crimes. Moreover, he points out,

The absence of eyewitness evidence in many homicides drives the police to rely on evidence from other sources: accomplices; jail-house snitches and other underworld figures; and confessions from the defendants themselves. Not surprisingly, perjury by a prosecution witness is the leading cause of error in erroneous capital convictions, and false confessions are the third most common cause.

Ibid., 481; citing Bedau and Radelet, "Miscarriages of Justice," 57.

51. Gross, "The Risks of Death," 483.

52. Ibid.

53. Ibid., 485.

54. Ibid., 499–500.

55. These four points are drawn from Alan W. Clarke, Procedural Labyrinths and the Injustice of Death: A Critique of Death Penalty Habeas Corpus," pt. 1, *University of Richmond Law Review*, vol. 29 (1995): 1327–1328.

56. The scope of these exceptions is complex and beyond the scope of this text. For a fuller explanation of how these rules work, see: Clarke, "Procedural Labyrinths" (1996).

57. *Butler v. McKellar*, 494 U.S. 407 at 423 (1990) (Justice Brennan, joined by Justices Marshall and Stevens in dissent). State courts, in effect, are told today that, save for outright "illogical" defiance of a binding precedent precisely on point, their interpretations of federal constitutional guarantees—no matter how cramped and unfaithful to the principles underlying existing precedent—will no longer be subject to oversight through the federal habeas system.

58. Pub. L. No. 104–132, 110 Stat. 1214 (1999), 28 U.S.C.A. §§ 2261–2266 (1996) effective April 24, 1996.

59. Deborah L. Stahlkopf, "A Dark Day for Habeas Corpus: Successive Petitions under the Anti-Terrorism and Effective Death Penalty Act of 1996," *Arizona Law Review*, vol. 40 (1998): 1115–36.

60. For a general overview of procedural default, see: Clarke, "Procedural Labyrinths" (1996, 328–74. These rules were originally judicial creations of the Rehnquist Court, but were ultimately codified by the *Antiterrorism and Effective Death Penalty Act of 1996* (AEDPA). The AEDPA modifies 28 U.S.C. §§ 2254–2255 and adds §§ 2261–2266.

61. *House v. Bell*, 126 S. Ct. 2064; 165 L. Ed. 2d 1; 2006 LEXIS 4675 Part IV (2006).

62. *Herrera v. Collins*, 506 U.S. 390, 113 S. Ct. 853 (1993).

63. Ibid., at 417.

64. Death Penalty Information Center, executions in the United States, 1993, http://www.deathpenaltyinfo.org/dpicexec93.html (accessed November 22, 2006).

65. Ibid.

66. *Ohio v. Byrd*, 145 Ohio App. 3d 318 (2001); the Sixth Circuit Court of Appeals, however, entered a stay on October 9, 2001, to "remand this matter for the development of a factual record . . . relating to the issue of innocence." *In Re: Byrd*, 269 F.3d 585 (2001). John Byrd, Jr., was executed by Ohio on February 19, 2002.

67. *Herrera v. Collins*, at 417.

68. Clarke, "Procedural Labyrinths" (1995), 1327, 1339, n. 43.

69. *Herrera v. Collins*.

70. The NAACP Legal Defense and Educational Fund report on Larry Griffin, http://www.stltoday.com/stltoday/news/special/srlinks.nsf/story/9270DD9B2=C367FB862=703B007B8C70?OpenDocument (visited August 9, 2006).

71. *State v. Griffin*, 662 S.W.2d 854 (Mo. 1983) at 860.

72. Bob Herbert, "Convicted, Executed, Not Guilty," *New York Times*, July 14, 2005: op-ed.

73. Ruben Cantu's case was first investigated by the NAACP Legal Defense Fund and its account of the case, along with links to relevant court documents, police records, and other related documents, is available at http://www.naacpldf.org/landing.aspx?sub=67 (accessed November 29, 2006). Eventually, the LDF turned their findings over to journalists at the *Houston Chronicle*. Their award-winning investigation, from which this book's account draws, can be found at http://www.chron.com/disp/story.mpl/metropolitan/3472872.html (accessed November 29, 2006): "Did Texas Execute an Innocent Man," (July 24, 2006), "Wounded Officer's Words Key in Sentencing" (Nov. 21, 2005), "Executed Man's Co-Defendant Says Years of Guilt Have Led Him to Try to Clear his Friend's Name" (Nov. 21, 2005), and "Man Says His Testimony May Have Saved Cantu" (Nove. 21, 2005). See also "Lawyers Call for Outside Review of Cantu Case" (July 25, 2006).

74. Ibid.

75. Barbara E. Bergman, "Reflections on the Death Penalty," *Champion*, vol. 30 (2006): 4.

76. Lise Olsen and Maro Robbins, "Tapes hint minds are made up on Cantu," *San Antonio Express News*, July 23, 2006, 1A.

77. Ibid.

78. Ibid.

79. Ibid.

80. Ibid.

81. Statement by Theodore M. Shaw, director-counsel and president, NAACP Legal Defense and Educational Fund, July 24, 2006, http://www.naacpldf.org/landing.aspx?sub567 (accessed August 10, 2006).

82. Theodore M. Shaw, "Wrong on Wrongful Executions," *Washington Post*, July 2, 2006, B4; http://www.naacpldf.org/content.aspx?article5936 (accessed November 22, 2006).

83. Andrew Gumbel, "Guilty until Proven Innocent; Capital Punishment in the US is under the microscope and lawyers using the latest forensic scientific techniques have found justice wanting: The Innocence Project," (*London*) *Independent*, May 4, 2006; 32, available at LexisNexis Academic.

84. Maurice Possley and Steve Mills, "Evidence suggests that Texas executed wrong man," *Chicago Tribune*, condensed by the *Star-Tribune*, November 21, 2005.

85. Maurice Possley and Steve Mills, "Did one man die for another man's crime?" *Chicago Tribune*, June 27, 2006, State and Regional News, http://www.chicagotribune.com/news/nationworld/chi-0606270137jun27,1,4210367.story (accessed November 23, 2006).

86. Ibid.

8. The Moral Potency of the Innocence Argument (pp. 134–52)

1. Robert Jay Lifton and Greg Mitchell, "The Death Penalty's Days Are Numbered," *Los Angeles Times*, January 3, 2001, http://www.commondreams.org/views01/0103-03.htm (accessed November 27, 2006).

2. *United States of America v. Burns*, 1 S.C.R. 283, 2001 SCC 7 (2001).

3. *Herrera v. Collins*, 506 U.S. 390 (1993).

4. George Ryan, quoted in "Excerpts from Governor's Speech on Commutations," *New York Times*, January 12, 2003, sect. 1, p. 22; see also: Maurice Possley and Steve Mills, "Clemency for All," *Chicago Tribune*, January 12, 2003, http://www.chicagotribune.com/news/nationworld/chi-030112clem,1,5129094.story, (accessed November 22, 2006).

5. While reference is commonly made, in the literature addressed in this chapter, to utilitarian and retributivist theories of punishment, we are plainly concerned with their respective justifications of punishment, and specifically of capital punishment. Leo Zaibert has recently stressed the importance of distinguishing theories and justifications of punishment. The former tell us what punishment is; the latter tell us when we may justifiably inflict punishment. See: Zaibert, *Punishment and Retribution* (Aldershot, United Kingdom: Ashgate Publishing, 2006): 7.

6. David Dolinko, "Retributivism, Consequentialism, and the Intrinsic Goodness of Punishment," *Law and Philosophy*, vol. 16 (1997): 507, 507.

7. Mirko Bagaric, "Sentencing: The Road to Nowhere," *Sydney Law Review*, vol. 21 (1999): 597, 602.

8. *Spaziano v. Florida*, 468 U.S. 447 (1984).

9. Mirko Bagaric and Kumar Amarsekara, "The Errors of Retributivism," *Melbourne University Law Review*, vol. 24 (2000): 124, 143.

10. Ibid., 143.

11. See, for example, John Rawls's consideration of the practice of telishment—an institutionalized system of framing the innocent with the aim of enhancing deterrence. Rawls contends that telishment would be self-defeating were it publicly known, and the price of keeping it secret would be repression. "Two Concepts of Rules," *Philosophical Review*, vol. 44, no.3 (1955): 12–13.

12. Otherwise, the act-utilitarian calculation of consequences would not yield the proper "moral" of execution that the critic of act-utilitarianism seeks. If too many members of the public are concerned that a similar fate might well befall them, more bad consequences than good will be generated over the long run.

13. Bagaric and Amarasekara, "The Errors of Retributivism," 143. Those who do not condone the actions taken in the war cases presented will reach the opposite conclusion.

14. R. A. Duff, *Trials and Punishment* (Cambridge, Eng.: Cambridge University Press, 1986): 160.

15. What the retentionist ultimately wants to justify, after all, is a current social policy, not some merely theoretical position on the death penalty. While considering hypothetical situations can have some real value in clarifying our thinking about moral issues, it can also produce distorted, if not crippling, consequences for moral appraisal and decision making. The need to return moral reasoning to the actual world, and to its empirical constraints, is imperative. In his discussion of deterrence and the death penalty, Stephen Nathanson, *An Eye for an Eye? The Morality of Punishing by Death* (Totowa, N.J.: Rowman & Littlefield, 1987), makes this point well:

> Philosophers are especially fond of "what if?" questions. Such questions allow us to alter factual contingencies and are sometimes helpful in revealing the principles that underlie our judgments . . . Suppose for example that every execution of a person for murder saved 10,000 lives . . . What does this show? One might think that it shows that the death penalty is theoretically justifiable and hence that it offends no deep principles. If the world were a little different and the death penalty were more clearly a superior deterrent, then it would be morally permissible. I think this conclusion is mistaken. In this instance, the "what if?" questions and the imaginary case of saving thousands by killing one are not helpful. They distort our thinking about the death penalty rather than helping to clarify it . . . [T]he fact that we can imagine the death penalty having extreme life protecting powers does not show that it is not deeply defective in our world . . . In this instance, stretching our imaginations may have the effect of breaking down our ability to make a moral assessment . . . Such examples are in

the end totally irrelevant to our reflections about the death penalty. In our world, the system of law and punishment does not operate that way. (128–129)

16. Among the many important issues we reluctantly set aside in this book are the critiques of punishment that have been proliferating of late, particularly among advocates of restorative justice and of justice as healing. For some sense of these, see: http://www.restorativejustice.org; http://www.livingjusticepress.org/; eds. Elizabeth Elliott and Robert M. Gordon, eds., *New Directions in Restorative Justice* (Devon, Eng.: Willan Publishing, 2005); Dennis Sullivan, *The Handbook of Restorative Justice* (New York: Routledge, 2006); Howard Zehr and Barb Toews, eds., *Critical Issues in Restorative Justice* (Devon, Eng.: Criminal Justice Press, 2004); Wanda D. McCaslin, ed., *Justice as Healing* (St. Paul, Minn.: Living Justice Press, 2005); and Rupert Ross, *Returning to the Teachings* (Toronto, Can.: Penguin Books, 1996).

17. George Schedler, "Can Retributivists Support Legal Punishment?" *Monist*, vol. 63, no. 2 (1980): 51, 61.

18. Some have identified a "minimalist" retributivism, which contends no more than that "no one should be punished *unless* he is guilty of a crime and culpable"; Martin Golding, *Philosophy of Law* (Englewood Cliffs, N.J.: Prentice Hall, 1975): 85. Anthony Quinton, for example, regards retributivism's "fundamental thesis" to be the claim that "only the guilty are to be punished, that guilt is a necessary condition of punishment"; Quinton, "On Punishment," *Analysis*, vol. 14 (1954): 136. However, as David Dolinko has pointed out, one does not need to be a retributivist to accept such a claim. Dolinko, "Some Thoughts about Retributivism," *Ethics* (April 1991): 537, 539.

19. A "pure retributive theory" is "a purported justification of the distribution of punishment for which consequences are totally irrelevant." Douglas N. Husak, "Why Punish the Deserving?" *NOÛS*, vol. 26, no. 1 (1992): 447, and 463, n.1. Kantian theory is the classic instance of pure (retentionist) retributivism. Not all forms of retributivism are retentionist. Robert Pugsley, for example, also embraces pure retributivism, but uses it to argue that capital punishment is morally unjustifiable. Robert A. Pugsley, "Retributivism: A Just Basis for Criminal Sentences," *Hofstra Law Review*, vol. 7 (1979): 379; Pugsley, "A Retributivist Argument against Capital Punishment," *Hofstra Law Review*, vol. 9 (1981): 1501.

20. Husak, "Why Punish the Deserving?" 452. We assume here, for the sake of argument, that mixed retributivism is a coherent theory, though there are ample reasons for doubting this. See: Dolinko, "Some Thoughts about Retributivism," 537. Husak observes that consequentialist considerations are usually invoked to justify the aim of the institution of punishment, playing no further role once the concept of desert is invoked. The mixed retributivism described here introduces consequentialism at the latter stage as well. If infrequently defended as a theory, it is a position not uncommonly held, especially by members of the public who regard themselves as retentionists. Because of this, it merits consideration.

21. Cesare Beccaria, *On Crimes and Punishments*, trans. David Young, (orig. pub. 1764; Philadelphia: Nicklin Publishing, 1986), chap. 25, 43. For a brief discussion of Hart and Beccaria, see: Russell L. Christopher, "Deterring Retributivism: The Injustice of 'Just' Punishment," *Northwestern University Law Review*, vol. 96 (2002): 843, 868–69, and n. 125.

22. H. L. A. Hart, *Punishment and Responsibility* (New York: Oxford University Press, 1968), 4, 9.

23. Don Scheid, "Kant's Retributivism," *Ethics*, vol. 93 (1983): 262, 263.

24. Hugo A. Bedau, "Interpreting the Eighth Amendment: Principled vs. Populist Strategies," *Cooley Law Review*, vol. 13 (1996): 789, 803.

25. Richard O. Lempert, "Desert and Deterrence: An Assessment of the Moral Bases of Punishment," *Michigan Law Review*, vol. 79 (1981): 1177, 1182.

26. Ibid., 1183.

27. Ibid., 1227.

28. Indeed, while Bedau and Radelet argue that "any attempt to calculate the odds of executing the innocent . . . is doomed to fail" for various reasons which they indicate, "it is certain that there are and will be such cases." Hugo Adam Bedau and Michael Radelet, "Miscarriages of Justice in Potentially Capital Cases," *Stanford Law Review*, vol. 40 (1987) 21, 79. Their article documents such cases in the United States during the twentieth century.

29. Stephen Nathanson, "Does It Matter If the Death Penalty Is Arbitrarily Administered?" in *Punishment and the Death Penalty: The Current Debate*, edited by Robert M. Baird and Stuart E. Rosenbaum (New York: Prometheus Books, 1995): 170.

30. Guido Calabresi, *Ideals, Beliefs, Attitudes, and the Law: Private Law Perspectives on a Public Law Problem* (Syracuse, N.Y.: Syracuse University Press, 1985): 6.

31. Ibid.

32. This is especially true in a society that is in such acute, protracted denial over the continued presence of race and class discrimination, and their role in the death penalty. See: Anthony Amsterdam and Jerome Bruner's discussion of Justice Powell's opinion concerning the *McCleskey v. Kemp* decision. Amsterdam and Bruner, *Minding the Law* (Cambridge, Mass.: Harvard University Press, 2001): 194–217. See also the ACLU's analysis of the U.S. Justice Department Report of Federal Death Penalty, (June 6, 2001), "Federal Death Row: Is It Really Color-Blind?" American Civil Liberties Union, June 14, 2001, http://www.aclu.org/capital/federal/10=92pub20010614.html (accessed December 3, 2006). We should stress here that the innocence argument gives added bite to these critiques of the death penalty. Since those on death row are overwhelmingly poor and nonwhite, so too are those who are being executed despite their innocence.

33. Patricia Williams, "No Vengeance, No Justice," *Nation* (July 2, 2001): 9.

34. Ibid.

35. Despite the disturbing passage, in the United States, of the controversial Military Commissions Act dealing with the interrogation and prosecution of foreign terror suspects, most Americans continue to oppose any use of torture, according to a October 19, 2006, poll conducted for the BBC World Service. See: BBC World Service, http://www.bbc.co.uk/pressoffice/pressreleases/stories/2006/10_october/19/poll.shtml (accessed November 29, 2006).

36. Nathanson, *An Eye for an Eye?*, 12.

37. Christopher Hitchens, "Covenant With Death," *Nation* (May 14, 2001): 9.

38. Rawls, "Two Concepts of Rules," 3. Rawls makes this distinction en route to proposing a reconciliation between retributive and utilitarian justifications of punishment. Utilitarian arguments, he claims, address questions about practices, while retributive arguments address the application of particular rules to particular cases.

> [T]hese views apply to different persons holding different offices with different duties, and situated differently with respect to the system of rules that make up the criminal law . . . The justification of what the judge does, qua judge, sounds like the retributive view; the justification of what the (ideal) legislator does, qua legislator, sounds like the utilitarian view. (6)

In doing so, Rawls denies that retributivism need be concerned with justifying the institution of punishment: "Does the person who advocates the retributive view necessarily advocate, as an institution, legal machinery whose essential purpose is to set up and preserve a correspondence between moral turpitude and suffering? Surely not." (7)

Whether or not they are requisite, retributivist justifications of the institution of punishment certainly are commonplace. Similarly, many retentionists have offered retributivist justifications of the practice of capital punishment. J. Angelo Corlett contends that Rawls misconstrues the intent of retributivism: "But retributivists are indeed concerned with the justification of punishment as an institution . . . the overall plausibility of retributivism is contingent on it! Of what value is it to the retributivist to assert that punishments should be meted out in proportion to the suffering caused to the victim if the institution of punishment is itself morally unjustifiable?" Corlett, "Making Sense of Retributivism," *Philosophy Today*, vol. 82, no. 76 (2001): 77.

39. Cases like this are the rare exception to the rule. Moreover, McVeigh's case reveals how deeply entrenched the errors and problems within the justice system are. In a case with the highest profile of any in U.S. history, widely followed by the public and well reported by the media, thousands of pages of evidence were withheld from defense lawyers. What does this suggest for the conduct of "ordinary" cases? As Jack Greenberg observes, in "Against the American System of Capital Punishment," *Harvard Law Review*, vol. 99 (1986):

> Death penalty proponents have assumed a system of capital punishment that simply does not exist: a system in which the penalty is inflicted on the most rep-

rehensible criminals and meted out frequently enough both to deter and to perform the moral and utilitarian functions ascribed to retribution. Explicitly or implicitly, they assume a system in which certainly the worst criminals, Charles Manson or a putative killer of one's parent or child, for example, are executed in an even-handed manner. But this idealized system is not the American system of capital punishment . . .

[T]he reality of American capital punishment is quite to the contrary. Since at least 1967, the death penalty has been inflicted only rarely, erratically, and often upon the least odious killers, while many of the most heinous criminals have escaped execution. Moreover, it has been employed almost exclusively in a few formerly slaveholding states, and there it has been used almost exclusively against killers of whites, not blacks, and never against white killers of blacks. This is the American system of capital punishment. It is this system, not some idealized one, that must be defended in any national debate on the death penalty. I submit that this system is deeply incompatible with the proclaimed objectives of death penalty proponents. (1670)

40. Samuel R. Gross, "ABA's Proposed Moratorium: Lost Lives: Miscarriages of Justice in Capital Cases," *Law and Contemporary Problems*, vol. 61 (1998): 125, 140–41.

41. See, for example: James S. Liebman, "The Overproduction of Death," *Columbia Law Review*, vol. 100 (2000): 2030, n. 149, listing dozens of cases where jailhouse informants lied in death penalty cases.

42. See: Alan W. Clarke, "Procedural Labyrinths and the Injustice of Death: A Critique of Death Penalty Habeas Corpus," pt. 1, *University of Richmond Law Review*, vol. 29 (1995): 1327, 1363–75.

43. David C. Baldus, George Woodworth, David Zuckerman, Neil Alan Weiner, and Barbara Broffitt, "Racial Discrimination and the Death Penalty in the Post-*Furman* Era: An Empirical and Legal Overview, with Recent Findings from Philadelphia," *Cornell Law Review*, vol. 83 (1998): 1638, discussing the most recent empirical findings on racial discrimination and the death penalty.

44. See: Alan W. Clarke, "Procedural Labyrinths and the Injustice of Death: A Critique of Death Penalty Habeas Corpus," pt. 2, *University of Richmond Law Review*, vol. 30 (1996): 303.

45. This untenable result is only enhanced by the fact that the retributivist must also make the case that some alternative to state execution, such as life imprisonment, is not adequate to meet the demands of retributive justice.

46. Dolinko, "Some Thoughts about Retributivism," 540.

47. R. George Wright, "The Death Penalty and the Way We Think Now," *Loyola of Los Angeles Law Review*, vol. 33 (2000): 533, 568.

48. Burton M. Leiser, *Liberty, Justice, and Morals: Contemporary Value Conflicts*, 3rd ed. (New York: Macmillan, 1986): 263.

49. Stephen Nathanson puts the trade-off into perspective:

If we knew that in showing respect for the victims, the state would inevitably kill some innocent person, then the state ought not to carry out executions. The protection of some innocent human lives is a primary function of the state, while engaging in symbolic acts of respect is at most a desirable but not central governmental function.

Nathanson, An Eye for An Eye?, 13.

50. Igor Primoratz, *Justifying Legal Punishment* (Atlantic Highlands, N.J.: Humanities Press International, 1989): 165.

51. Leiser, *Liberty, Justice, and Morals*, 263.

52. Richard Wasserstrom, "On the Morality of War: A Preliminary Inquiry," *Stanford Law Review*, vol. 21 (1969): 1627, 1653. Wasserstrom is not discussing the morality of state execution, but of killing in war.

53. This example was suggested by members of the Philosophy Department at the University of Guelph, especially Andrew Bailey and David Castle, who offered feedback on an earlier version of this chapter in March 2003.

54. For a comparable point in a different context, see: Wasserstrom, "On the Morality of War," 1627.

55. Bedau makes this point in a comparable debate with Ernest van den Haag. See: Hugo A. Bedau, *The Death Penalty in America: An Anthology* (Chicago: Aldine, 1967): 464.

56. See: Christopher, "Deterring Retributivism," especially part 6.

57. The principle, or doctrine, of double effect has a long history, one generally regarded as rooted in the work of Thomas Aquinas. The literature it has generated in applied ethics is extensive, often turning on the proper formulation of the principle itself. For a brief introduction, see: William David Solomon, "Double Effect," in *The Encyclopedia of Ethics*, edited by Lawrence C. Becker and Charlotte B. Becker (New York: Routledge, 2001). Richard Lempert discusses it in connection with the death penalty, in Lempert, "Desert and Deterrence," 1228–31.

58. Michael Moore, *Placing Blame: A Theory of Criminal Law* (Oxford, Eng.: Clarendon Press, 1997): 158.

59. Ibid.

60. For a number of the arguments that follow, the authors are greatly indebted to Alison McIntyre, "Doing Away with Double Effect," *Ethics*, vol. 111, no. 2 (2001): 219–355. While her work is motivated by a desire "to do justice to the various intuitions that lead people to accept" double effect, she concludes that most of the examples thought to support or illustrate it in fact undermine it, and constitute "a gallery of miscellaneous objections to simple forms of consequentialism." (255) She concludes that we should do away with double effect. Although we are less concerned here with the status of the doctrine per se than with its use by retributivists to defend the death penalty, her discussion has been invaluable.

61. Mark Vorobej, "Double Effect and the Killing of Innocents," in *Just War, Non-violence and Nuclear Deterrence*, edited by Duane L. Day and Richard Werner (Wakefield, N.H.: Longwood Academic, 1991): 32.

62. Nicholas Barlow, "Military Necessity and the Doctrine of the Double Effect," Forskarseminarium i filosofi, Filosofiska institutionen, Abo Akademi, vol. 3, http://www.abo.fi/fak/hf/filosofi/Fsemi/Papers/00_0=_08.html (accessed November 23, 2006).

63. Nancy Gibbs, "Botching the Big Case," *Time* (May 21, 2001): 30.

64. Glanville Williams, *The Sanctity of Life and the Criminal Law* (New York: Alfred A. Knopf, 1957): 286.

65. McIntyre, "Doing Away with Double Effect," 224.

66. These are adapted from Lempert, "Desert and Deterrence," 1177, 1227–31. Although we have introduced various alterations in Lempert's original discussion in the appendix of his article, we are much indebted to his work there.

67. Compared to the current state of affairs, and given the error rate and exonerations-to-execution rate discussed in chapter 7, this example is likely conservative.

68. McIntyre, "Doing Away with Double Effect," 219, 238–39.

69. Ibid., 238.

70. The Innocence Project was established by Barry C. Scheck and Peter J. Neufield in 1992, at the Benjamin Cardozo School of Law. There is now a substantial and growing network of such projects across the United States. See: http://www.innocence project.org/ (accessed November 22, 2006).

71. See: Robert M. Bohm, "Retribution and Capital Punishment: Toward a Better Understanding of Death Penalty Opinion," *Journal of Criminal Justice*, vol. 20 (1992): 227.

72. Terry Davis, "Statement of the Council of Europe on the Occasion of the World Day Against the Death Penalty," October 10, 2005, http://www.coe.int/NewsSearch/Default.asp?p=nwz&id=7183&lmLangue=1 (accessed November 22, 2006).

73. *United States v. Burns*, at ¶ 103.

74. Ibid., at ¶ 96.

9. The Imperfectability of the System (pp. 153–72)

1. Justice Jed S. Rakoff, *United States v. Quinones*, 196 F. Supp. 2d 416 (S.D.N.Y. 2002) at 416, 420.

2. George Ryan, quoted in Bruce Shapiro, "A Talk With Governor George Ryan," *Nation* (January 8, 2001): 12.

3. George Ryan, quoted in Robert J. Lifton and Greg Mitchell, *Who Owns Death? Capital Punishment, The American Conscience, and the End of Executions* (New York: Morrow, 2000): 242.

4. George Ryan, "An Address on the Death Penalty," Pew Forum on Religion and Public Life, Held at the University Of Chicago Divinity School June 3, 2002, http://pewforum.org/events/index.php?EventID=28 (accessed December 3, 2006).

5. Gov. George Ryan's commutation announcement, January 11, 2003, http://www.law.northwestern.edu/news/spring03/ryanspeech.html (accessed December 3, 2006).

6. Massachusetts "Governor's Council on Capital Punishment: Final Report," (May 2004): 1, http://72.14.209.104/search?q=cache:abtiXhWasboJ:www.lawlib.state.ma.us/docs/5-3-04Governorsreportcaptialpunishment.pdf1%22Governor%27s1Council1on1Capital1Punishment%221Romney&hl=en&ct=clnk&cd5=11&gl=us (accessed 23 February 2007).

7. "Massachusetts Governor's Council on Capital Punishment," 20.

8. Scott S. Greenberger, "Panel offers death penalty plan," *Boston Globe*, May 3, 2004, A1; Available at: http://www.boston.com/news/local/articles/2004/05/03/panel_offers_death_penalty_plan/ (accessed November 23, 2006).

9. Steve LeBlanc, "Romney Prepares to File 'Scientific' Death Penalty Bill," Associated Press State and Local Wire, December 28, 2004.

10. Jeff Flock, "'Blanket commutation' empties Illinois death row," January 13, 2003, http://www.cnn.com/2003/LAW/01/11/illinois.death.row/ (accessed November 23, 2006).

11. Greenberger, "Panel offers death penalty plan," A1.

12. Jim O'Sullivan, "Romney, Detractors Square Off Over 'Gold Standard' Death Bill," July 7, 2005, http://www.massnews.com/2005_editions/7_july/71505_romney_squares_off_on_death_penatly.htm (accessed November 23, 2006).

13. Pam Belluck, "Massachusetts Governor Urges Death Penalty," *New York Times*, April 29, 2005, A16.

14. Erik Arvidson, "Romney: Innocent will not be executed," *Berkshire (Mass.) Eagle*, July 15, 2005.

15. Report of the Commission on Capital Punishment (April 15, 2002), 207, http://www.idoc.state.il.us/ccp/ (accessed November 23, 2006).

16. Massachusetts Governor's Council on Capital Punishment, 5.

17. *Massachusetts Lawyers Weekly* staff, "Commentary: A Case Against the Death Penalty," *Massachusetts Lawyers Weekly* (November 14, 2005).

18. Belluck, "Massachusetts Governor Urges Death Penalty," A16.

19. David S. Bernstein, "The sudden death of Romney's dream," *Boston Phoenix* (July 22–28, 2005), http://www.bostonphoenix.com/boston/news_features/other_stories/multi-page/documents/04838552.asp (accessed November 23, 2006).

20. Ibid.

21. Ibid.

22. Ibid.

23. Arvidson, "Romney," 1.

24. Jennifer Fenn, "Romney files death penalty bill requiring strict burden of proof," *Berkshire (Mass.) Eagle*, April 29, 2005.

25. Betty Layne DesPortes, "DNA and Doubt: Flawed System Yields Flawed Results," *Richmond Times Dispatch*, May 18, 2005.

26. Sheila Jasanoff, "Just Evidence: The Limits of Science in the Legal Process," *Journal of Law, Medicine and Ethics*, vol. 34, no. 2 (2006): 328.

27. Ibid., 333–35.

28. Ibid., 334.

29. As the legislative counsel for the Massachusetts ACLU observed:

There's something surreal about the idea that everything will be done scientifically, as if humans aren't running the data, gathering the data, comparing the footprints. It's as if humans aren't under the robe, as if humans weren't in the jury box.

Drake Bennett, "Reasonable Doubt Governor Romney Wants to Create a Foolproof 'Scientific' Death Penalty," *Boston Globe*, May 8, 2005, K1.

30. Jasonoff, "Just Evidence," 339.

31. Carol Smart, *Feminism and the Power of the Law* (New York: Routledge, 1989): 11.

32. Jasonoff, "Just Evidence," 330. For more discussion of the alleged value-neutrality of science, see: Robert N. Proctor, *Value-Free Science? Purity and Power in Modern Knowledge* (Cambridge, Mass.: Harvard University Press, 1991)

33. The Innocence Project, http://www.innocenceproject.org/about/index.php (accessed November 23, 2006).

34. Arvidson, "Romney," 1.

35. Jasonoff, "Just Evidence," 328.

36. Ibid., 337.

37. James Dao, "Lab's Errors in '82 Killing Force Review of Virginia DNA Cases," *New York Times*, May 7, 2005, A1.

38. ASCLD/LAB, "Limited Scope Interim Inspection Report." (April 9, 2005): 17, http://www.dfs.virginia.gov/services/forensicBiology/externalReviews.cfm (accessed November 27, 2006).

39. Maurice Possley, Steve Mills, and Flynn McRoberts, "Scandal Touches Even Elite Labs," *Chicago Tribune*, October 21, 2004. This article provides a useful survey of flawed work and resistance to scrutiny in crime labs across the United States.

40. Jonathan Finer, "Mass. Considers Death Penalty," *Washington Post*, May 3, 2004, A2; also available at http://www.washingtonpost.com/ac2/wp-dyn/A61418–2004May2?language=printer (accessed November 27, 2006).

41. James Podgers, "Time Out for Executions: ABA Action at Midyear Meeting Is Expected to Stir Renewed Debate on the Death Penalty," *ABA Journal*, vol. 83 (April 1997): 26.

42. Austin Sarat, "Innocence, Error and the 'New Abolitionism': A Commentary," *Criminology and Public Policy*, vol. 4, no. 1 (2005): 45, 48.

43. Margaret Graham Tebo, "Closing Argument: Barnett Supports Bills Seeking Death-Penalty Equity," *American Bar Association Journal*, vol. 87 (October 2001): 86.

44. Martha W. Barnett, "Call to Action on Executions," *American Bar Association Journal*, vol. 86 (October 2000): 8.

45. Henry Weinstein, "Death Penalty Moratorium Attracting Unlikely Adherents; Movement Gains Steam and Spans Party Lines as Awareness of Wrongful Convictions Grows," *Los Angeles Times*, Oct. 17, 2000; A5.

46. Ronald J. Tabak, "Finality without Fairness: Why We Are Moving towards Moratoria on Executions, and the Potential Abolition of Capital Punishment," *Connecticut Law Review*, vol. 33 (2001): 733, 743–44, summarizing the pending federal legislation.

47. For details on these developments, see: James Liebman and Lawrence Marshall, "The Jurisprudence of Justice Stevens," *Fordham Law Review*, vol. 74 (2005): 1607, esp. 1653–59.

48. Thomas Healy, "Death Penalty Support Drops as Debate Shifts; Foes Turning Focus from Moral Issues to Flaws in the System," *Baltimore Sun*, July 25, 2001, A1.

49. Equal Justice USA, a project of the Quixote Center, http:www.quixote.org/ej (accessed November 27, 2006).

50. Gary Langer, "Death Penalty Ambivalence Poll Points to Support for Execution Moratorium in U.S.," *abcNews.com*, http://abcnews.go.com/sections/us/DailyNews/poll010=04_deathpenalty.html (accessed November 27, 2006).

51. Roper Center, University of Connecticut Public Online Opinion (May 25, 2001).

52. ABC News Poll Death Penalty Information Center, available at http://www.deathpenaltyinfo.org/article.php?did=2163 (accessed February 23, 2007).

53. James Gill, "Moratorium on Death Penalty Gains Steam," *(New Orleans) Times-Picayune*, April 29, 2001, metro sect., p. 7.

54. In Louisiana, the state senate rejected a proposed moratorium. Subsequent polls show 81 percent of Louisianans supporting a moratorium. Ibid.

55. Charles J. Ogletree, Jr., "Black Man's Burden and the Death Penalty in America," *Oregon Law Review*, vol. 81, no. 15 (2002): 36.

56. As John B. Wefing contends, "DNA evidence will in fact lead to greater support for the death penalty in the long run . . . While many people in this country currently may be concerned by the potential for mistakes in determining the guilt of a defendant, once they are convinced that there is little likelihood of mistake, the majority will continue to support the death penalty." Wefing, "Wishful Thinking by Ronald J. Tabak: Why DNA Evidence Will Not Lead to the Abolition of the Death Penalty," *Connecticut Law Review*, vol. 33, no. 861 (2001): 861–62.

To undermine such a development, and to address abolitionist concerns about the strategic advisability of the moratorium movement, Jeffrey L. Kirchmeier advises that the innocence arguments be strengthened to "clarify that the innocence problems are part of systemic problems that cannot be cured by technology." Kirchmeier, "Another Place Beyond Here: The Death Penalty Moratorium Movement in the United States,"

University of Colorado Law Review, vol. 73, no. 1 (2002): 106. This has been part of our goal in this book. The establishment of such moratoria, moreover, may well bring with it the additional time that will be needed for Americans to become aware of the nature and force of the international consensus (discussed in part 1, above) that state execution is an egregious violation of human rights and an unconscionable abuse of state power.

57. Igor Primoratz, eds. *Justifying Legal Punishment*, (Atlantic Highlands, N.J.: Humanities Press International, 1989): 165.

58. Indeed, it does double duty, reappearing when the issue is not innocence, but fairness:

> In practice, critics argue, the death penalty is imposed unfairly. More poor and minority people receive the death penalty than do middle- and upper-class white people. The death penalty should be abolished, in this view, because it is unfairly applied. Defenders of the death penalty reply that this problem is not specific to the death penalty, but endemic to the entire criminal justice system. The remedy, they suggest, is to make the whole criminal justice system more impartial, not to remove the death penalty.

Michael D. Bayles and Kenneth Henley, eds., *Right Conduct: Theories and Applications*, 2nd ed., (New York: Random House, 1989): 206.

59. Primoratz, *Justifying Legal Punishment*, 165.

60. Ibid.

61. Ibid.

62. Ibid.

63. Ibid., 165–166. And what of the knowing execution of that one innocent person "over decades"? This passage puts one in mind of the following: "When Pilate saw that he could prevail nothing, but that rather a tumult was made, he took water, and washed his hands before the multitude, saying, I am innocent of the blood of this just person: see ye to it." (Matthew 27:24)

64. However, as Richard Lempert has recently noted about this period in the death penalty debate, "[W]e collectively misled ourselves about error rates in capital sentencing, even strong opponents of the death penalty like me thought convictions of the innocent would be far less common than it turned out they were." (Personal correspondence, October 4, 2006; on file with authors.).

65. Richard Lempert, "Desert and Deterrence: An Assessment of the Moral Bases of the Case for Capital Punishment," *Michigan Law Review*, vol. 79 (1981): 1177, 1188.

66. R. A. Duff, *Trials and Punishments* (Cambridge, Eng.: Cambridge University Press, 1986), 195.

67. As Jeffrey Reiman notes, "[I]n situations in which we have reason to expect that a policy will be administered with substantial injustice, then that policy will likely be unjust in practice, and in situations in which there is no reason to believe that all alternative policies will be worse, it would be wrong to adopt a policy that is likely to be

unjust in *practice* even if it was just in *principle*" (Emphasis in original). Louis P. Pojman and Jeffrey Reiman, *The Death Penalty: For and Against* (Lanham, Md.: Rowman & Little-field, 1998): 120. While appeal to the in-principle/in-practice distinction is usually made in support of retentionism, Reiman is an exception to this. An abolitionist, Reiman contends (68) that "though the death penalty is *in principle* a just penalty for murder, it is unjust *in practice* in America because it is applied in arbitrary and discriminatory ways." Since "this is likely to continue into the foreseeable future," he argues that the death penalty be abolished.

68. This history is recounted in Alan W. Clarke, "Procedural Labyrinths and the Injustice of Death: A Critique of Death Penalty Habeas Corpus," pt. 1, *University of Richmond Law Review*, vol. 29 (1995): 1327; and Clarke, "Procedural Labyrinths and the Injustice of Death: A Critique of Death Penalty Habeas Corpus," pt. 2, *University of Richmond Law Review*, vol. 30 (1996): 303.

69. In 2001, Virginia modified this rule slightly, to allow biological (DNA) evidence to come in at any time. The rule otherwise, however, remains twenty-one days.

70. Donald L. Beschle, "What's Guilt (or Deterrence) Got to Do with It? The Death Penalty, Ritual, and Mimetic Violence," *William and Mary Law Review*, vol. 38 (1997): 487, 531.

71. Ibid., 531.

72. Ibid., 532.

73. *Callins v. Collins*, 510 U.S. 1127 (1994) at 1130. (Blackmun, J., dissenting from denial of certiorari).

74. Beschle, "What's Guilt (or Deterrence) Got to Do with It?" 528.

75. Ibid., at 529.

76. Justice Scalia's rebuke to Justice Blackmun in *Callins v. Collins* makes a similar point. First he takes Blackmun to task for pointing to the inconsistent administration of the death penalty as a basis for abolishing it. Scalia thinks this argues in the opposite direction—that some of the post-*Furman* procedural protections should be jettisoned to make the procedure more consistent. He then goes on to say, "Convictions in opposition to the death penalty are often passionate and deeply held. That would be no excuse for reading them into a Constitution that does not contain them." *Callins v. Collins*, at 1129 (Scalia, J., concurring in denial of certiorari). Plainly, Scalia does not think that an approach that attacks the death penalty as administered can provide a principled basis for judicial abolition.

77. Whether retributivist theories of punishment themselves fail because of the ineliminable risk of punishing the innocent is another issue, which we will not attempt to address here. See: Richard Burgh, "Do The Guilty Deserve Punishment?" *Journal of Philosophy*, vol. 79, no. 4, 193 (1982): 193 for an approach to this problem.

78. See: Samuel R. Gross, "The Risks of Death: Why Erroneous Convictions Are Common in Capital Cases," *Buffalo Law Review*, vol. 44, (1996): 469.

79. Beschle, "What's Guilt (or Deterrence) Got to Do with It?" 528.

80. The view that the terms used in science are either observational or theoretical is associated with logical positivist philosophy of science. Positivism itself, an intellectual tradition that is both sprawling and lingering, has undergone numerous transformations. Although the legacy of positivism remains with us today, Popper claimed credit for having "killed" it in its manifestation as logical positivism. Karl Popper, *Unended Quest* (La Salle, Ill.: Routledge, 1976): 87–90. Thomas Kuhn has, more appropriately, been awarded this singular distinction. See: Proctor, *Value-Free Science?*, 209–10; for more on the observational/theoretical distinction and its role in philosophy of science, see: W. H. Newton Smith, *The Rationality of Science* (New York: Routledge & Kegan Paul, 1981): 19–43.

81. See: Larry Laudan, *Progress and Its Problems* (Berkeley: University of California Press, 1977), where an analogous argument is made with respect to scientific theories.

82. It is a mantra that makes some obvious assumptions about the effectiveness of non-innocence-based arguments against the death penalty. Our focus on innocence here is intended to add to the substantial array of arguments against capital punishment, not to displace them.

83. Ryan, commutation announcement. (2003).

84. Mistakes-are-fatal arguments "purport to show that a particular action (or type of action) ought not to be performed because mistakes of a certain kind made in performing it (or tokens of it) run a significant risk of resulting in the death of an innocent human being." Douglas Blount, "Euthanasia, Capital Punishment and Mistakes-Are-Fatal Arguments," *Public Affairs Quarterly*, vol. 10 (1996): 279.

85. Ibid., 280.

86. Ibid., 285.

87. Ibid., 287.

88. Constitutional Rights of the Committee on the Judiciary, "Innocence and the Death Penalty: Assessing the Danger of Mistaken Executions," 103rd Congress, 2nd sess. U.S. Government Printing Office (November 1994) 1.

89. Stephen Nathanson, *An Eye for an Eye?: The Morality of Punishing by Death* (New York: Pantheon Books, 1987): 123.

90. Curiously, life without parole has been regarded as inadequate by an abolitionist, while the death penalty has been held to be inadequate by a retentionist. Stephen Kershnar has offered a startling, and chilling, argument for torture. He contends that for those guilty of especially serious crimes, the principle of proportionality requires more than the death penalty. Stephen Kershnar, "An Argument for the Use of Torture as Punishment," *Hamline Journal of Public Law and Policy*, vol. 19 (1998): 497, 516. Nothing is ruled out; the torture administered "should take the form of prolonged sensory deprivation, bodily invasion, beatings, electric shock, or something else, [that] might be determined in part on the basis of the displeasure

the torture is likely to produce on those who have committed the most serious culpable wrongdoings." (518)

Meanwhile, David McCord—who characterizes his abolitionist position as fighting retribution with retribution rather than with mercy—has attempted to devise "a constitutionally permissible non-death sentence of sufficient harshness that it can justifiably be considered as of the same order of magnitude as death itself—in essence, a 'living death' alternative." McCord, "Imagining a Retributivist Alternative to Capital Punishment," Florida Law Review, vol. 50 (1998): 1, 5. He advocates sensory deprivation imprisonment such as that administered in some supermax prisons, for highest condemnation offenders, commenting that, from a retributivist standpoint,

> if the culprit is experiencing irrational anger, confused thought processes, emotional flatness, mood/emotional swings, chronic depression, suicidal thoughts (as long as they are not carried out), overall deterioration, and social withdrawal, GOOD! That is exactly the suffering we want him to be experiencing as a consequence of his heinous acts. (108)

The innocence argument we mount can be adapted to respond to these extreme retributivist positions, though we will not attempt to do so here.

91. And how many is that? To paraphrase Bedau: how many guilty lives is one innocent life worth?

92. For discussion of the ethics of social experimentation, see: Larry L. Orr, "Social Experimentation: Evaluating Public Programs with Experimental Methods," Office of the Assistant Secretary for Planning and Evaluation, U.S. Department of Health and Human Services, (1997): http://aspe.os.dhhs.gov/hsp/qeval/tilepage.htm (accessed November 27, 2006).

93. James D. Unnever and Frances T. Cullen, "Executing the Innocent and Support for Capital Punishment: Implications for Public Policy," Criminology and Public Policy, vol. 4, no.1 (2005): 2–37, 31.

94. Bruce Shapiro, "Dead Reckoning," Nation, (August 6, 2001): 15.

95. See: "Assembly requires Japan and USA to abolish death penalty before January 2003." Council of Europe, June 25, 2001. Available at http://www.coe.int/News Search/Default.asp?p=nwz&id5509&lmLangue=1. While the United States and Japan have yet to lose their observer status, the Council of Europe has continued to keep the pressure on. In 2003, Renate Wohlwend, special rapporteur on the death penalty to the Parliamentary Assembly of the Council of Europe, marked the World Day against the Death Penalty by declaring, "One by one, countries joining the council have ended the death penalty . . . Now we must persuade our observer states, Japan and the United States to join us." See: "The world should follow Europe's lead on ending the death penalty," Council of Europe, October 10, 2003, http://www.coe.int/ NewsSearch/Default.asp?p=nwz&id531=6&lmLangue=1 (accessed November 27, 2006).

96. Renate Wohlwend, quoted in "The world should follow."

97. Mohamed and Another v. President of the Republic of South Africa and Others, 2001 (7) BCLR 685 (CC), at ¶ 7–10.

98. The Agreement on Mutual Legal Assistance between the European Union and the United States of America, however, came into effect on June 25, 2003. Article 8 of the agreement, "Mutual legal assistance to administrative authorities," makes no explicit provision for denying transmission of evidence in capital cases from one country to another. See http://europa.eu.int/eur-lex/pri/en/oj/dat/2003/l_181/l_18120030719en00340042.pdf.

99. Shapiro, "Dead Reckoning," 17.

100. Walter Schwimmer, "Death Penalty in U.S. Must Be Rethought," *International Herald Tribune*, January 25, 2001, opinion, p. 9, also available at http://www.iht.com/articles/2001/01/25/edwalt.t.php (accessed November 27, 2006).

10. Conclusion (pp. 173–78)

1. "Council of Europe Chief says War Must End for Armenia to Become a Democracy," *BBC Monitoring International Reports*, June 24, 2002.

2. Clarence Darrow, "The Futility of the Death Penalty," in *Verdicts Out of Court*, edited by Arthur Weinberg and Lila Weinberg, (Chicago: Ivan R. Dee, 1989): 225, 232.

3. Walter Schwimmer, "Death Penalty in U.S. Must Be Rethought," *International Herald Tribune*, January 25, 2001, opinion, p. 9; also available at http://www.iht.com/articles/2001/01/25/edwalt.t.php.

4. Callins v. Collins, 510 U.S. 1141 (1994) at 1145 (Blackmun, J., dissenting).

5. Bryan Stevenson, "Close to Death," in *Debating the Death Penalty*, edited by Hugo Adam Bedau and Paul G. Cassell (New York: Oxford University Press, 2004): 78.

6. According to Justice Rehnquist, writing for the majority, this is "because of the very disruptive effect that entertaining claims of actual innocence would have on the need for finality in capital cases, and the enormous burden that having to retry cases based on often stale evidence would place on the States." Herrera v. Collins, 506 U.S. 390 (1993) at 417.

7. U.N. Special Rapporteur Bacre Waly Ndiaye mentioned this ruling in the case of Joseph Roger O'Dell, who, he reported to the U.N. Commission on Human Rights, "has reportedly extraordinary proof of innocence which could not be considered because the law of the State of Virginia does not allow new evidence into court 21 days after conviction." "Extrajudicial, Summary or Arbitrary Executions, Report of the Special Rapporteur," U.N. Document E/CN.4/1997/60/Add.l (December 23, 1996): 128. As noted in the previous chapter, this rule was changed in 2000 to allow DNA evidence, but only that, to come in after the three-week period has expired.

8. William A. Schabas, "The Abolition of Capital Punishment from an International Law Perspective," Paper presented at *International Society for the Reform of Criminal Law 17th International Conference*, (2003): 1–26, 20, http://www.isrcl.org/Papers/Schabas.pdf (accessed November 27, 2006).

9. Ibid., 20.

10. John M. Goshko, "Helms Calls Death Row Probe 'Absurd U.N. Charade,'" *Washington Post*, October 1, 1997, A7.

11. "The Question of the Death Penalty," Resolution adopted by the U.N. Commission on Human Rights, U.N. Document E/CN.4/RES/2000/65 (April 27, 2000), http://documents.un.org.

12. Ibid., 4.

13. Ibid., 3.

14. Ibid., 2.

15. "U.N. Human Rights Committee Urges U.S. to Place Moratorium on Death Penalty," *Washington Post*, July 28, 2006, http://www.deathpenaltyinfo.org/article.php?did51860&scid564 (accessed November 27, 2006).

16. *Atkins v. Virginia*, 536 U.S. 304, 122 S. Ct. 2242 (2002) at 2247 (citing *Trop v. Dulles*, 356 U.S. 86, 101 (1958).

17. Franklin E. Zimring, *The Contradictions of American Capital Punishment* (New York: Oxford University Press, 2003).

18. Schwimmer, "Death Penalty in U.S."

19. The "death belt" comprises Texas, Florida, Louisiana, Georgia, Virginia, Alabama, Mississippi, North Carolina, and South Carolina. See: Charles J. Ogletree, Jr. "Black Man's Burden and the Death Penalty in America," *Oregon Law Review*, vol. 81 (2002): 15, 19.

20. On December 26, 1862, during the wars between the Dakota and the United States, 303 Dakota men were condemned to die. President Lincoln commuted the sentences of all but 38, who were executed in Mankato, Minnesota. Buried in a mass grave, their bodies were dug up later that evening for use in medical research. Their "trials" had been "hastily arranged and perfunctorily performed . . . unimpeded by rules of evidence, defense lawyers, or any definable standard of guilt." Carol Chomsky, "The United States-Dakota War Trials: A Study in Military Injustice," *Stanford Law Review*, vol. 43 (1990): 13. An innocent man, Chaska, who had saved the life of a white settler and her children, was confused with one whose execution Lincoln authorized, and was executed along with the rest. See: John D. Bessler, *Legacy of Violence: Lynch Mobs and Executions in Minnesota* (Minneapolis: University of Minnesota Press, 2003): 25–66; see also: Steven Z. Kaplan, "Why Death is Different: Minnesota's Experiment with Capital Punishment," *William Mitchell Law Review*, vol. 30 (2004): 1113, 1117, and fn. 15.

21. Schabas, "The Abolition of Capital Punishment," 20.

22. Jeffrey L. Kirchmeier, "Another Place beyond Here: The Death Penalty Moratorium Movement in the United States," *University of Colorado Law Review*, vol. 73 (2002): 1, 94.

23. W. Fitzhugh Brundage, *Lynching in the New South: Georgia and Virginia, 1880–*

1930 (Urbana and Chicago: University of Illinois Press, 1993): 259. However, Brundage also observes that executions "should not be interpreted as the continuation of lynching under another guise" since there were substantive differences between "violence by state authorities . . . [and] most earlier lynchings." (255) While one cannot infer with certainty that a causal connection exists between lynchings and executions from data that establishes only that executions rose as lynchings fell, this arugment for a causal nexus is strengthened by recent research employing multiple logistic regression analysis. See: David Jacobs, Stephanie L. Kent, and Jason T. Carmichael. "Vigilantism, Current Racial Threat, and Death Sentences," *American Sociological Review*, vol. 70 (2005): 656–77.

24. Zimring, *Contradictions*, 89.

25. John F. Galliher, Gregory Ray, and Brent Cook, "Criminology: Abolition and Reinstatement of Capital Punishment during the Progressive Era and Early Twentieth Century," *Journal of Criminal Law and Criminology*, vol. 83 (fall 1992): 538, 574–75.

26. Ogletree, "Black Man's Burden," 34.

Index

Blount, Douglas, 167, 227n
Bohm, Robert, 102, 207n
Borrel, Josep, 30
Bowers, William J., 84
Brandley, Clarence, 88, 203n
Breard, Angel, 54–57, 66–67
Brennan, William J., 91, 126, 164
Brewer, Victoria, 85
Brooks, Charlie, 206n
Brundage, W. Fitzhugh, 230n
Bruner, Jerome, 217n
brutalization, 79–80, 84–85, 96, 100
Bryer, Stephen, 55
Bunck, Julie, 179n, 181n, 186n
Bundy, Ted, 85, 142, 143
Burgh, Richard 226n
Burns, 41, 43, 134, 151, 190n
Bush, George W. (Bush Administration), 25, 31, 45, 50, 53–54, 63–64, 70, 75, 177, 182n
Bustillo, Mario, 66, 68–69
Butler v. McKellar, 126

Calabresi, Guido, 141
Calas, Jean, 113
California, 66, 82, 92, 94, 97, 106, 204n
Callins v. Collins, 164, 226n
Cambodia, 47
Canada, 4, 38, 40–43, 45, 47, 50, 55, 78, 82–83, 91, 114, 134–35, 151, 152, 171–72, 187n; Canadian Charter of Rights and Fundamental Freedoms, 41; Canadian Supreme Court 41, 151
Cantu, Ruben, 124, 130–31, 211n, 213n
Capital Jury Project, 92
Caribbean, 46–47, 172
Carmichael, Jason T., 231n
Cassell, Paul G., 115–16
Castro, Fidel, 172
CAT. See Convention Against Torture and Other Forms of Cruel, Inhuman

or Degrading Treatment or Punishment
Catholic Church, 48
Central Intelligence Agency, 38
Chamblin, Mitchell B., 85
Cheatwood, Derral, 79
Chicago Tribune, 105,120, 131
China, 25, 29, 42, 47, 49, 180n
Chomsky, Carol, 230n
CIA. See Central Intelligence Agency
Clarke, Alan, 108, 211n
Clarke, Joel, 85
class, 90, 97–98, 100, 110–11, 124, 134–35, 138, 143, 158, 175, 217n
clemency, 60, 63, 65, 71, 118, 128–29
Cochran, John K., 85
Coffey, Wallace, 19
Coleman, Roger, 212n
colonialism, 180n
Columbia, 45–46
comity, 198n
confessions, 118, 125, 126, 143, 212n
Congo, 42
Connolly, William, 11
consular assistance, chapter 5 passim., 175
Contras, 184n
Convention Against Torture and Other Forms of Cruel, Inhuman or Degrading Treatment or Punishment (CAT), 37
Convention for the Protection of Human Rights and Fundamental Freedoms. See European Convention for the Protection of Human Rights and Fundamental Freedoms
Convention on the Elimination of All Forms of Discrimination Against Women, 182n
Convention on the Rights of the Child, 24, 183n

Cook, Phillip J., 94

Copenhagen criteria, 17; Copenhagen European Council, 182n

Corlett, J. Angelo, 218n

Corriere della Sera, 192n

Costa Rica, 45–46

cost of death penalty, 94–95, 100, 109, 112, 133–34, 138, 155, 168, 174

Council of Europe, 7, 12, 29, 42, 151, 171–73, 189n, 228n; Resolution 1271, 40

Coyne, Randal, 195n

Cullen, Francis T., 110–12, 170

Cuomo, Mario, 97

Dallas, 92

Dar es Salaam, 171

Darrow, Clarence, 173

death is different, 95, 151

Death Penalty Information Center, 106, 118, 203n, 210n

death row phenomenon, 2, 36–37, 42, 190n

DeLuna, Carlos, 124, 132

deportation 38–39, 44–45

deterrence, 75–86, 96, 100–101, 108–9, 111, 133–34, 137–39, 168, 170, 174, 215n, 219n

Detroit Free Press, 50

Dicker, Richard, 26

discrimination, 89, 91, 93, 100, 110, 135, 158, 180n, 217n, 225–26n

DNA, 104, 106, 117–18, 120, 155–59, 161, 194n, 210n, 212n, 224n, 226n. *See also* science

Dolinko, David, 136, 216n

Dominica, 47

Dominican Republic, 46

Donohoe, John J., 82–83

Double Effect, Principle of, 140, 146–48, 150, 220n

due process, 42, 58, 128, 140, 164, 168, 175

Duff, R. A., 138

Dukakis, Michael, 97

Duke University. *See* Terry Sanford Institute of Duke University

econometric studies, 80–84

Ecuador, 46

efficiency, 55, 69, 94, 145, 162, 175

Eighth Amendment, 24, 86, 184n

Eleventh Amendment, 58

Ellsworth, Phoebe, 99, 109, 112

Erlich, Issac, 80

error rate, 123, 143, 149, 150, 225n

Europe, 37–40, 49, 91, 135, 172, 228n

European Convention for the Protection of Human Rights and Fundamental Freedoms, 36, 39, 47; Protocol 6, 7

European Court of Human Rights, 36–37

European Union (E.U.), 12, 17–18, 23, 28–30, 39–40, 43, 48, 172, 173, 182n, 192n

Evans, Timothy John, 114

exclusionary rule, 67

exculpatory evidence 68, 119

exoneration, 42, 106, 116–24, 132, 158, 169, 210n

extradition, 2, 4, 26, 28, 30, chapter 3 *passim.*, 172–73, 187n

extraordinary rendition, 38

eyewitness identification, 127, 129

Fagan, Jeffrey, 81, 122

false confessions, 118, 212n

Ferencz, Benjamin, 27

Fifth Amendment, 67

finality, 41, 55, 69, 117, 146, 149, 160, 164, 166, 168, 171, 175. *See also* irreversible; irrevocable